The County Books Series
GENERAL EDITOR : BRIAN VESEY-FITZGERALD

DORSET

THE COUNTY BOOKS SERIES

A Series comprising 57 Volumes. It covers every county in England and there will be five books on Scotland, two on Ireland, two on the Hebrides, and one each on Orkney, Shetland, Wales, the Isle of Man and the Channel Islands.

PLEASE WRITE TO THE PUBLISHERS
FOR FULL DESCRIPTIVE PROSPECTUS

DORSET

by

ERIC BENFIELD

Illustrated and with a Map

London
Robert Hale Limited
18 Bedford Square W.C.1

First Edition 1950

PRINTED IN GREAT BRITAIN
BY WESTERN PRINTING SERVICES LTD, BRISTOL

FOREWORD

IN planning to write a book on the county of Dorset it is surprising to find how much has been written on and about the subject. But perhaps other people have found the same about other counties even if those do not start off with the position in literature that Dorset has.

Of course I am biased but I do believe Dorset has a special place. We Dorset men have imagination which we are not embarrassed to express. We know too, as soon as we begin to speak, when the spark has been felt by a person, and I have seen many come under the spell as soon as they visit the county.

I have not written a genuine guide book but have tried to give a feeling of the county and what it means to me, and I have made use of other books written on Dorset things. It will be seen that I do not always see eye to eye with these others, but I hope that readers will be given an edge to the desire to read them. All of them are well worth it to those who would like to get more of the Dorset touch.

Such books are *Macaulay's Complete Works*, Vol. II, *England* II.—Edmund Blunden who writes with affection and great respect on that Dorset genius *Thomas Hardy*.—Sir Edward Parry who has been fair to the monster Jeffreys and his *The Bloody Assize*.—Marjorie M. Firth and Arthur W. Hopkinson who write with feeling on *The Tolpuddle Martyrs* —and that Dorset lover for whom I have a special place, Sir Frederick Treves's *Highways and Byways in Dorset*.—*The Short History of the Dorsetshire Regiment* which ought to be available not only to recruits of that Primus regiment. Also the Colonel of the Regiment, Major-General Sir Hubert Huddleston, had good material to work on in an article in *Our Empire* for November 1949. Beyond general reading there are the *Reports of the Research Committee of the Society of Antiquaries of London*, No. XII, *Maiden Castle,*

Dorset, by R. E. M. Wheeler, which are an unending interest to those who want to know of our early culture, and which makes the Celts come alive on the chalk hills.

If I can add this book to those I shall feel that it has been worthwhile, and there is my own Dorset which has some of that quality known as the Dorset mentality sticking to it. In fact I can see it running through and through like the weave of tiny spider webs on an autumn morning.

ERIC BENFIELD

CONTENTS

ILLUSTRATIONS

ILLUSTRATIONS

ACKNOWLEDGMENTS

The illustrations above, numbered 2, 3, 4, 5, 10, 13, 14, 16, 18, 20, 26, 28, 34, 39, 40, 45, 46, 47, 48 are reproduced from photographs by Mr Will F. Taylor of Reigate; 1, 7, 15, 24, 25, 27 by Mr A. K. Rittener, F.R.P.S., of Teddington. The remaining twenty-four illustrations are reproduced from photographs supplied by Mr T. Edmondson of Folkestone.

CHAPTER I

THE LIE OF THE LAND

IT would be possible for a man to write a book on his county from the point of view "My county right or wrong," or from the other extreme, producing a cold semi-scientific, analytical description of his own particular part of England.

The county of Dorset would lend itself more to the first for me, giving the picture some hard bright colours varnished over by a not very level finish composed mostly of sentimentality. That would be easy for me as there is nothing in me that is not truly and completely formed by the idea of Dorset first and last, although I am not maintaining that only a native son of the county can produce the best picture of it, but in my case it should be a true picture.

Some humans have the ability to adopt the place where they go to live until they have more real understanding of it than the majority of native people, but that also means that they have in them the ability to love and be loved in return by their adopted place. It is in loving that a man belongs to a place or a people, a love that can be given many points of view, but it must exist before he is accepted. The cynical may say at once that love is blind anyway, but that in itself needs more than constant repeating to make it a proved truth. So many of these age-old sayings have achieved an importance which they do not deserve. They can often be applied to a common experience of life with a semblance of wisdom, and people like to appear clever even at such secondhand lengths.

Love of any sort is not so likely to be blind as forgiving and understanding, not producing complete wisdom perhaps but going to great lengths to forbear. Who would deny that it is one of the greatest human powers for good or bad in the world?

For those who wish to see it, the good can be seen to an amazing extent in everyday life. There is a terrific amount of selfishness in the world which is seen and remarked because it so often hurts others, whereas all the selflessness gets accepted without comment merely because it is expected. Even war, which is one of the greatest evils of human behaviour, can grow out of man's conviction that he must fight and destroy to protect what he loves.

Nationalism can be love of one's own people and the place where one lives, and that brings me to this kind of regional nationalism which makes me want to turn the light on the county of Dorset. Is it a good thing from the angle of a nation as a whole? Yet even those who would say "no" must remember that if they want men to feel any kind of nationalism for their country, those same men must be allowed to develop a kind of regional nationalism first. It seems to be accepted that the good family man is the most likely to be a good citizen, because in his family life he has learnt to forbear with others and take their view into consideration. Just as the future mathematician starts on the elementary two and two are four, the good citizen develops with his experience until in time he should become a better man on a national scale.

I can never feel sure about those people who glibly disdain any ties between family and environment. Sometimes they scorn anything like village or street connections, citizenship or county feeling. Airily they say, "Have a wider view; don't be parochial." Yet some of those people, who would not like to be thought unaware of family duties, are in a very strange position. Untaught, they pretend to have jumped from two twos right up into higher mathematics. It doesn't seem possible to me, but I myself have never relinquished my hold on anything, even when I have reached out into wider ideas.

And that brings me to a second point I must make before this gets too far. This writing has caused me to make more starts than anything else that I have undertaken. A book on Dorset does not seem to go slap off into some hard or glowing or provocative sentence, and I tried to get away in the third person because it seemed that a county should not have the impress of the writer on it too much. Some people can successfully transmit their views by forcing the reader to share in putting such views forward. We, they say, the writer

2

and the reader, need not take this or that into consideration, whereas sometimes perhaps the reader had thought it necessary before. Or the writer will keep on referring to himself as the author who does consider this or that, just as if the author was some poor thing in the background who could be called forward to take any knocks that the reader feels are due.

That is not how I can approach a subject. If my Dorset is wanted, I shall have to crop up sometimes. If a certain amount of truculence shows here and there, it is Dorset truculence. When hardheaded world-dwellers think they can detect any of our alleged softheadedness or leaning towards magic or even love of the idea of madness, they can console themselves that they at least are up-to-date in the nineteen-forties of a thoroughly modern scientific world that is the latest thing in everything, except in humanity.

Put Dorset under the test of statistics, with a range of values based on an oft-times shocking idea of what is really worthwhile, and the county would lag behind many others. The raw material of great industries? None. The seats of learning, or what has mostly become the effort to obtain degrees? Minor. Even the great, giddy, tawdry amusement centres which are the modern holiday resorts where over-worked people seek relaxation are strangely almost lacking.

It is a county that does not boom in any sense of the word, no industrial baron seeks his glory there, the real go-getter who intends to leave a few millions in his will does not include it in his plans. Yet for many things which have been highly valued for very many generations and still have a more real value than an industrial baron and a few million pounds, Dorset has all its own share, and perhaps more because some other places have wantonly thrown such values away.

It seems strange that some who may read this will have to ask where Dorset lies in the scheme of Great Britain, somewhere south and with a coast. So to help them I will say that if the south coast of England is halved Dorset starts just west of that line. Naturally it is lumped under those counties called the south-west, where according to the stage yokels all people talk alike and have big feet. Everything south and west of London is considered as south-western; that terms starts very near London regardless of the fact that London is very much in the east of England.

But Dorset is far enough away really to be in the deep south-west. It fortunately does not include the town of Bournemouth which has tried hard to live up to the idea of being the queen of watering places, whatever that term means. That town has now swollen up against the port of Poole on Poole Harbour. Parts of it may be called Branksome and Parkstone and Canford Cliffs or different Chines, but to all intents and purposes it is Hampshire Bournemouth and what that stands for. But somewhere there our county border runs with Hampshire, with even some County Gates which have long ago lost any real meaning.

The coastal boundary of any county is the most important if only that it is permanent, whereas the actual land boundaries can and often have been quarrelled over in past days. And even to-day a desirable edge of any district can be threatened by such things as Borough Charters. But the Dorset coast is not threatened by its neighbours and not seriously by the sea as some coasts are.

A few words on the geological make-up of the coast may help to show why Dorset is not likely to be washed away. There is a good deal of hard stone in practically all the coast from Devonshire to a point south of Swanage, and even where this stone makes only a part of the cliffs enough of it has fallen out of the softer material to form an apron of rocks to impede the strength of the sea. Also, when the rock stratum lies more or less level it tends to counter the sea by a kind of persuasion rather than brute resistance, because wherever the shore is based on more or less unbroken stone ledges the sea is forced to become shallow long before it actually breaks against the cliffs. And while a shallow sea may appear ugly for the very reason that it has been forced to rear up and break, such waves have very little power compared with the sheer compact weight of a wave which has rolled unbroken for a thousand miles to fall direct on land standing in deep water.

In the western half of Dorset where these hard strata are less in evidence the sea has scored out the great Lyme Bay reaching from Prawle Point in Devonshire to Portland Bill in the east. But it has done all the encroaching that we are likely to have to take into consideration, and where it approaches that remarkable geological left-over called the Bill of Portland, we are faced by the still more strange affair of the Chesil Beach, which has exercised the minds of many people and still has no cut and dried theory to fit it.

The Chesil Beach stretches some eighteen miles from Bridport to join up with Portland, and except for this freak of the sea coming into existence it is certain that much more of the land lying behind it would have disappeared a long time ago. In that case the town of Weymouth could never have been built and Portland would have remained a definite island as it once was.

Why and how the sea placed this great barrier of shingle in its own path is a question that no one has yet answered in a satisfactory way. It is water-placed yet it is over forty feet above high-water mark at Portland. Of course shingle beaches exist on many parts of the coast elsewhere, but here it reached out from the mainland to join up with an island out to sea. It is usual for a tide to sweep strongly between an island just off the coast and to widen and deepen the gap rather than fill it up. There is a local legend that it appeared in a night. One day Portland was entirely an island and next day it had a grand causeway.

It is easy to dismiss this idea as just another local legend, except that the sea will place and remove great shingle beaches in one tide as anyone who has been familiar with a stretch of coast over a period of years will know. And such legends have a way of having at least possibility in them. He is a bold man who flatly denies the possibility of Atlantis; the idea exists among so many peoples who might have been in the position to know something of that lost continent. So why should not word of mouth have been passed down about that great storm which first threw up the Chesil Beach? The event need not have been so very far back in the history of man.

The work of one night or the accumulation of ages, the fact remains that the Beach was placed there by the sea itself, and perhaps startling also is the fact that what the sea put into place it may some day remove. A change in the set of the main Channel current, or even a pier or jetty casually placed somewhere west, could cause the sea gradually to remove the shingle instead of adding to it as it does now, or rather it supplies just enough to equal the constant loss which must arise owing to the grinding away in movement.

That the sea may move whatever it has once put into place may not be easy for some people to accept, if they know only the sea of some sheltered holiday resort. But it is perfectly acceptable to those who really know the sea coasts. In one great storm the sea dredged up a monster ship's boiler from the bottom somewhere and threw it ashore high up on some rocks apparently far above reach. In itself that was remarkable because with its open manholes the boiler could not have floated, it could only have been rolled over the sea bottom and ashore to drain between waves or perhaps a tide. And then when empty it was tossed up well out of reach of any known wave. That boiler was a local marvel for a long time and most people said that anyway the sea would never move it again and boys soon filled it up with several tons of stones thrown through the open manholes. The rusty old boiler seemed there for ever. But one fisherman remarked that as the sea had placed it there it could move it one day perhaps, and I agreed, although privately I never expected to see it happen in my lifetime. But one day during a storm a wave did again lift that boiler full of weighty stones and threw it still further up on the rocks. It then appeared to be even more out of reach of any sea, but it is sea-placed and therefore may be moved again.

So if the Chesil Beach disappears in one storm or as the result of gradual erosion, I for one will not say it could not have happened because it was impossible. Just as I do not see any reason against it having appeared there in one night.

But what a disturbance it would make if Portland Harbour were to be breached from the rear and by such a thing as a mere change of current. What great expense of labour would be poured in to prevent Weymouth being nibbled away by the sea rushing through between it and Portland. Of course scientific man of to-day would do his best, but it would be no light task to build and maintain the equivalent of a natural

6

sea wall eighteen miles long and some two hundred yards wide.

East of Weymouth the coast is protected by the result of the Purbeck Squeeze or Thrust Fault, a geological happening which pushed up a lot of hard material that in time acted as a great natural sea wall. It is just as if a great engineer built a stone wall with one or two weak places which have since been breached. Lulworth Cove, which to many people is just another beauty spot, is one of the most serious breaches. There the sea broke through the uptilted stone and was then held up by the chalk hill that lay behind.

Going east the strata become more level and therefore less giving to the sea, until at a point south of Swanage the stone has disappeared and once more the sea has reached in to eat out the bays which face east across to the Isle of Wight. And a still bigger inlet of the sea made Poole Harbour, although at first the harbour as it now appears must have been just an open inlet with a wide mouth. Here again the sea piled up a barrier, but this time of sand, until it had almost closed what is now the harbour mouth. It is not an impossibility to imagine Poole Harbour silting up and being covered with wind-blown sand. Just think what raptures future builders may have in covering all that new space with modern dwellings. And another thing to think about is who would eventually show himself in the light of complete landowner with all the privileges that go with that position?

Climbing ashore just east of Poole Harbour we should be on the border-line with Hampshire. There is not much thrill about a mere county land border to-day; not one person in a hundred knows the exact line even if they live very near it. The day is gone when such lines, with the parish boundaries, were important in many people's way of living. Perhaps such authorities as the police and Poor Law officials have a line of demarcation, but not even a Hampshire policeman would stop chasing me if I was flying to my homeland.

Some day it might be well worth my while to walk around the land borders and see what, if any, effect living on a border has on modern people. Somewhere up north I should run into Wiltshire and bear off left to join up with Somerset, and then a long slant back to the coast again where Devon joins Dorset

7

a mile or so west of Lyme Regis. It would not be a very long walk as walks go to-day, because the county area is a little less than a thousand square miles; so even in mere bulk we do not loom very big in the world.

It may be seen that so far I have never written the name as Dorsetshire, nor shall I here, because although it may have no importance at all, all my life I have belonged to the school of thought which does not consider Dorset as one of the shires. At one time a shire meant a political division administered by a sheriff, and it probably could be proved that Dorset should call itself a shire. But it is a privilege which I am not going to seek out.

Some seventy-five miles of coastline with open cliffs for most of the distance might cause people to expect some rugged scenic effects—incidentally those cliff faces have been called an ideal training ground for geological students because without digging and delving the geological make-up of the land can be studied like a picture on the wall. But rugged is not the term to use for Dorset as a whole, the long wide chalk hills may be bare and open and some of the heath-lands still have enough space to suggest mystery, but chalk is never harsh in outline and the few rivers are not the kind to tear out awesome gorges.

The main chalk of Dorset is as if the great upland plateau of chalk which is Salisbury Plain had pushed a tremendous limb down to the borders of Devonshire, with the sandy forest land of the New Forest also continuing along its south-ern flank to make the heathlands around Poole Harbour and part of the river valley towards Dorchester. On the north the low-lying plains of Somerset give another entirely different country, where at one time swamps and water could offer safety to such lake villages as Glastonbury.

The people that this land has produced is of course as much a mixture as most of England, with a basis of the original Celt. It is unfashionable to suggest that there is still any appreciable amount of that blood which Rome found here, which can quite rightly be lumped under the heading of Celtic, since the many relics found and expertly examined show that whatever different waves brought in the Bronze to oust the Stone, and then the Iron which followed, all of them

8

had the same original root. Their bones prove that they were a quite remarkably pure stock.

Of course Rome brought in a very diverse stream as Romans were gathered from many sources. Even Jews could become Roman citizens, and we can be sure that a representative of every people between the Mediterranean and the English Channel came over to leave his blood in our part of the newly opened colony. But as their brand of civilization imposed hard class distinctions between their soldiers and administrators and the people who had to slave for them, there was still a mainly native stock when Rome ebbed away.

Then when the wild men from over the North Sea took their chance to conquer the country before it had built up any national strength, they did not penetrate much further than east Dorset by sea and were held up in Hampshire on land. The Saxons overran Dorset from the north after going up the Thames valley and turning down away from the sea at the Severn, but there is no doubt that they held on to the land which seemed good to them and fought hard to keep it against others of their kind who followed.

The Jutes held the Isle of Wight, where the people to-day are still so much not Dorset, and the Danes who came to raid and plunder had their part in our make-up. But none of that blood was alien to the first Saxons, and by the time William brought over his new culture we were a Saxon nation with a growing and advancing civilization. The Celt had been subdued but not destroyed by the strong and virile newcomers.

Nor did the Norman blood have anything in it to upset the balance, as William's people had been men from the north too, who had moved down the continental coast instead of taking to their boats. They had come under the strong influence of the Latins but it was more a matter of culture than blood, so the Normans came to rule over their Saxon cousins rather than to impose an alien strain upon them.

So for all the Norman contempt for the Saxon they found here, we remained on the whole that apparently successful fusion of Romanized Celt and Norseman. And it is still there. The Saxon proved his ability to stay and perhaps that ability to stay is one of the things that have made us what we are. It is one of the things that make people say we are stubborn

9

and conservative. We prefer to think we are sturdy and honest men so very determined to stand up for our rights.

I hope to be able to show how Dorset men have stood up for their rights, and how often I have heard that phrase— "Our rights," "My rights," "The rights of the people," "It ain't right"—I was brought up with the word in my ears. And it was not wholly to do with mere advantage : it was the right to do rather than have something.

When the Saxon had been forced into the position of a mere field worker, one of his masters recorded a telling picture of him which is still warming to the heart. He could be imposed upon and of course he could be hoodwinked by the more educated people who had gained the upper hand, for he was not supposed to be very nimble-witted. But in effect, "Beware of him when he comes to a stand in the furrow like his ox with a gleam in his eye and says, 'This is not right.' "

No, the Saxon was dangerous after he had taken his stand and then it took a lot to shift him; his rights were more valuable than his comfort or his life itself. And to-day he is still there, honest and hardworking and friendly too, but the gleam can still come in his eye and it is not wise to push him after he has said, "This is not right."

And although his qualities are so often looked upon as faults and failings, watch a "Saxon" Parish Council or some such body and see how much useful work they do without fuss because they know in their bones that there are still rights to be upheld. They seem to have an instinctive knowledge of how democracy goes about things and would still like to settle everything around the table of their Moot Houses.

Surely nothing is more English than the countryman who knows that he has been a countryman for ever. Once more the Englishman has recently come out of a very bad time, and although the Saxon Englishman does not strike the casual eye as obvious warrior material he has often proved that he is as good as any other. The county regiments have never been glamorized as have some of the British Army, but when they have been plugged into a hole they can be forgotten, for they will still be there when they are remembered for another hole. The Dorsetshire Regiment has been called the Dirty

Dorsets. It is not a term of reproach as some people have suggested. It is because they have so often been called upon to carry out some dirty task where that Saxon quality of staying-power has been badly needed.

The Dorset stock has proved through many centuries that it is pretty good. It has none of the *élan* of the Latins, none of the arrogance of the Teuton, none of the apparent childishness of some of the younger peoples, but it is there to-day to be seen, comparing well with others and not at all the dull, stupid clodhopper of cheap humour. Of the south-west we are, very much so; but there are few more charming people to those who come with a friendly spirit. Nowhere in all England will the stranger meet more really smiling greetings than on a Dorset road well away from towns and all that towns have come to mean. We are not shy unless you make us so and some of our women are as pretty as most of the children are.

CHAPTER II

DORCHESTER, THE COUNTY CAPITAL

To many good Dorset people it may seem unnecessary to point out that when I mention the name of Dorchester I am referring to the capital town of our county. But loath as I am to record it, it is not unknown for people to think that it refers to a small place on the Thames some seven or eight miles south of Oxford.

In fact, I know of at least one man who set out from London to join his friends who had preceded him on a visit to Dorchester, cheerfully he made his way towards Oxford, and then thought that it was a very good story to tell. He did not see it as a reflection on his own ignorance about his national history and geography; a county capital and a river village were all the same to him. And if the two places had the same name, how on earth was he to know the difference, if any? Yes, it was a great joke to him.

So if good Dorset people will bear with me, I hope that they will see how necessary it was to mention that the Dorchester I mean is in Dorset, if only to stop any other smart townsman from wasting his valuable time going to Oxford-shire; the time which he could not spare to make himself acquainted with mere country matters.

But a good Dorset man as I hope to be, I must plead ignorance of any real knowledge about the Thames-side Dorchester. My hazy idea is that it too is a Roman town, and if that is right, the name may have something to do with such a town on a river. There is a vast difference between the Thames even as high as that, and the Frome just after it is joined by the Cerne river. And here a good Dorchester man may point out that the Cerne joins the main stream of the Frome below the town. The several watercourses running north of the town are confusing to an adult mind which comes freshly to them, and the person who spent his or her childhood in and about them must make a little allowance. They certainly were lucky as it must have been a marvellous playground, saturated with history in an atmosphere very sympathetic to local things.

Anyway, there is a sizeable river to give protection to the north side of our Dorchester, and anyone leaning over the parapet of the good, strong, old Grays Bridge might think that such a well-behaved chalk stream could not have been a very great military obstacle. After all, any man could wade across it in ordinary times without very much effort. But that would only be seeing the Frome as the tamed thing of modern days, when, if it dared to break its banks, the county might spend a penny rate or so to teach it not to get out of hand.

But when it was looked upon as a defensive measure we can be sure that it did not run correctly between two banks, and that it was bordered by wide swamps; certainly there would be no man-made bridges to make its crossing easy. The Roman legion which crossed it just about nineteen hundred years ago probably cursed the mud and slime of a long and tiring crossing. Quite likely they had to swim a deep channel as there was a far larger amount of water lying in the valley then than there is to-day. Not necessarily more water flowing down the valley, but any choked drain holds more water than a clear one.

The rivers do not bring any commerce to the town, for they will not float a petrol barge, which often seems to be the chief aim of river traffic. The barge brings the petrol from the coast so that people can use it to get back to the sea, and then that is called efficiency. Dorchester has not yet reached that achievement probably because the Frome will not float a petrol barge. Nor, so far, have they lined their watercourses with dwellings although there is a tendency that way near Grays Bridge; there is already a house calling itself Grays Bridge House, and while it is a smart new small villa, probably with every modern convenience, it does seem rather presumptuous that it should connect itself with the old stone structure whose quiet dignity was there when it was first used and will carry on until the end.

Fortunately the new houses are not yet across the river, but they have lined up there as if they are waiting the word

13

to spread over the bridge. And being provincial, the town has not yet hit on the idea of covering the main river to build over, although there is one small stream which apparently rises in the bowels of some dwellings. Why it was considered necessary to build over that water would be hard to say with all the space around Dorchester to spare, but there at least the broken buckets and bricks, and all the usual things, can be found fouling what should be a happy brook.

Yet considering what humanity can do with its water-courses, Dorchester has been tolerant. Long may it turn its ear against any suggestion of developing its low-lying land further, although that may be too much to hope for. Some day a man may not come down from Charminster or Stinsford and see the churches of the compact town standing across the green valley. At present the new building, which seems to glare rather than fit in, appears like froth at the foot of the older town on the hill. There is not yet a mile of "built-up area" on that side. I do not know where the thirty miles per hour speed limit signs of the regulation lighted areas are placed; they may well be on the town side of the bridge and stay there.

To the man who is interested in such things, whichever way he approaches the town, he will see that Dorchester is definitely of the chalk country. There is nothing foreign to the chalk anywhere near at hand, as can often be seen in some parts of the country where the hilltops may be crowned with that alien, the fir tree. Somehow the fir does not fit in the scheme of chalk, yet so many perfect English hills are crippled with a scalp-lock deliberately placed there to break the line. There is much to be said against thick high hedges running up and across a swell of rounded chalk hill; such hedges break and cut up the whole idea in a way that patches of gorse and bramble do not. But gorse and bramble patches are not good husbandry so we can do without them. Man should hesitate a long time before he plants a fir tree on a chalk skyline. It would have been no loss if it had been found that such trees would not grow there.

But around Dorchester there is little to disturb the feeling of chalk, and the town itself has a friendly air as if the traveller would be sure of finding rest and shelter and that still important thing in life, a friendly face to meet him. When a drenching rain sweeps over the open country the mere hope of shelter may make a man think that the close-packed town will be a harbour against the elements, while a driven snow storm shows that such hills are perfectly streamlined. And having reached the shelter of the streets, any normal person should be warmed by the friendly way he will be met.

Of course such things rest a good deal with the feelings of the newcomer, but some towns have a way of being personally repellent to the stranger, whereas Dorchester has a good honest homely feeling about it. Perhaps this has something to do with the town having a genuine sense and feeling about itself; it is a real country town and county capital, which gives it dignity without having to stand on its dignity. It has a right to be treated in a good and proper manner, and therefore it can treat the stranger in a good and proper way.

Some towns have a servile air about them; Dorchester has none. Some towns are aggressive or merely vulgarly strident. Dorchester neither threatens nor offends you. Nor is it indifferent, too busy, too rich, or too poor; it is merely a human town in good order where people can live a tolerable life. And although it may be somewhat behind in the full modern scheme of things, that is not because it has dug its toes in, but rather because it knows that it has been well run for a very long time.

Dorchester is very proud of its Roman history, so proud that many people think that everything found in the neighbourhood is "Roman remains," forgetting that the town, being established by the Romans, was made a new interloper in an older civilization. But fortunately intelligent people got hold of the local museum. They have made it a model which could be studied with advantage by the people who control similar local museums in districts which have much interesting matter. At Dorchester Museum you will not find cases containing Stone Age, Bronze Age, Iron Age and Roman relics placed together just because they are weapons or ornaments. Nor among the treasures of the old town days, like smocks and the constable's club, will you find a stuffed cock bird and the marvellous egg it laid sixty years ago. Nor, after examining some old charter or deeds concerning local trade, will you glance up and find a hideous crocodile shot by some lieutenant-colonel on the Nile, which had found its way there when the old boy died and his family were glad to throw out the ugly brute.

Of course the splendid finds of Maiden Castle give the museum a good foundation on pre-Roman days, and the well-preserved Roman pavements which you can walk on have not been faked to make them look complete when they are not; the missing parts are boldly filled in with plain cement. In fact there seems to have been little faking attempted and no undue striving for effect, until you come to the Hardy room.

And here a little explanation may be called for, but not this time for Dorchester people. The Hardy room deals with a man, Thomas Hardy, who wrote in the last generation. Local people must bear with me a while because, incredible as it may seem to them, there are living people who are a little hazy about him. Locally, the merest mention of his name floods the hearer's mind and often his tongue, and it is likely to set loose a lot of confused ideas on the world, because locally they have made Hardy a cult.

His sanctuary, shrine, or room, is as well done as many modern chapels set up to some holy saint; there is not displayed a splinter of his thigh bone or a nail paring, but if he had some distressing habit like biting his nails when he built up his verse, you can almost see him do it. You can certainly wander into his garden and stare through his study window, waiting for him to enter the partly open door from the dark passage and seat himself in one of the chairs which he used for various purposes. He seems to have had a special chair to sit in while receiving special guests, and a choice of desks and tables according to the work he was about to do.

A pen for writing *Tess*, and why not another for signing cheques? In fact they have built Thomas Hardy up until it would not spoil the effect if they placed a barker at the door to shout, "Roll up, roll up, and see Tom Hardy write his famous stuff!"

This is going to bring something down on my head, and there will be plenty of people to point out that I am being offensive to Thomas Hardy. But I am not alone in feeling that surely that precious room with its lighting effects is offen-

16

sive to a famous writer. Can anyone really believe that Hardy is pleased to look down and see his personality exposed as that room now shows it? With Napoleon over the door too. The man should live by his work. And he will. He will exist in his pages despite, rather than because, his carefully placed private goods can be seen by paying sixpence.

No, Dorchester has not served Hardy very well by putting that study on show. I can imagine him coming there in the night, when the museum is closed, and peeping in at his own window. His old shadow would be saddened to see that his chair and his violin were the treasured relics instead of the words he put together. But without a doubt Dorchester has made him pay : the logical thing would be to send the act round the seaside resorts with a wax figure complete as a star turn.

Yet it was only to be expected that a town should make the most of what fortune had brought to it. Almost opposite the museum has been preserved the lodging where Judge Jeffreys stayed for his bloody visit; there is something of a theatrical air about the place as could be expected, but it is still possible to imagine him listening to the tone of the street noises below him as he ate.

Again opposite, and only slightly higher up the street, is the Court House where the judge did his dirty work. There is nothing theatrical about that as it stands in all the grimness of its first conception, and in all the human woe that has gathered there in many generations since. Rising straight from the pavement, its plain unbroken stone front might be a solid Portland cliff; it is invincible, indifferent, and above all the poor weaknesses of a man's mind and soul.

The three great doors are flush with the wall line, with not the slightest relaxation by being set back in a hall, or approached by some steps. What those doors hold they hold inexorably; silently they warn that the Court's time is as inescapable as that of the stars. Any man or woman, watching and waiting there to intercede for some other poor wretch, would lose heart long before the stern judge strode from his lodging.

Slowly I walked past those doors on the pavement edge, and thought of all my fellow men who had descended there

C   17

to learn within a few hours their awful fates. Innocent people, like many of Jeffreys's victims. Jeffreys himself, crossing the road on the slant, aware of the doubtful air that must have filled the street when he was abroad, would enter one of those doors conscious all the time of his gall-stones; never, never would he forget them no matter how much blood he shed or how hard he revelled. He had carried his gall-stones across the very stones I stood on.

But many bad men had faced those doors, as well as poor fools and victims of fate. I had personally known a man who had entered there to hear the dread, "May the Lord God have mercy on your soul." And knowing him I am sure that he was very surprised to find himself in his position. I found that my feet dragged and my shoulders bowed and momentarily I had assumed the weight of all their misery and fear. My eyes on the ground, I counted the six or seven hesitating steps across the blue lias paving stones, the grey light playing on my feet. One more step would have taken me into the door and I should have crossed the fatal line of those grim walls. God forbid that I should ever find myself taking those few steps.

But it was not yet : across the street I found a place where for sixpence I could drink a cup of coffee and eat two hot buttered rolls, the "elevenses" of town life and modern days. The experience at the Court doors had shaken me a little because men's thoughts do stay around such places, and was I really so much apart from them? Or was I one of the few who, having experienced them, had escaped into a man's freedom again? To sit there, with the coffee and rolls, would perhaps be the first gesture a man would make to prove to himself that he had escaped. But escaped or not he would never be the same man again, nor would I, after experiencing the thing so many degrees away from the reality.

It was a sobering thought that so many good Dorset spirits had quailed there in that street, and that the step between freedom and a great load of guilt was so small and unexpected. It is that half-unconscious knowledge in men's minds which often makes them gather to catch a glimpse of their unfortunate fellows. There but for the grace of God go any of us.

But if Dorchester has the awful duty of dispensing the law to us, it also has a busy market where all the things of life and freedom can be seen on public view. Good bulls, rams and great savage boars unashamedly represent the fertility of the surrounding country; sad and gentle-eyed cows are the motherhood, and the innocent young of many creatures cry out for help and guidance in a hard world they do not yet know.

Although the livestock is the mainspring of the market it is in the people that the life of the county can be seen on public show for a few hours of the week. Dorset people are not quite as repressed as is sometimes suggested, and to see a farming community on market day is one way to examine mankind in the raw. There will be genuine friendship on men's faces as they meet an old friend from a whole twenty miles away; greed and cunning exposed on the surface while a hard deal is done privately apart from the public sales. You will hear more real laughter than you expected, and quite likely some real, but crude, sympathy expressed to some poor dying man who will not give up his market day for all that death has marked his face.

And far exceeding the few signs of both moral and bodily decay, there will be much that is bounding in health and vigour. Strong active men with a good life before them and not afraid to let the world see it. Sometimes the younger men are remarkably good-looking if good looks can be anything other than what the cinema gives us. They can have the brute strength of their beasts and the skin of children, the eyes of free men and the tread of a horse.

One thing you will know is that you are in a market of the south-west; nine out of ten men are Dorset to the very bone and it seems good to them. The few strangers are there and the inevitable Scotsman who has come south to easier farming, and that somewhat odd creature who openly calls himself a gentleman farmer. But in the market there is a great sense of real equality.

The town has at least one mild boast which may be heard often enough to be well established; they consider that they have a nice clean little town. And certainly the people themselves have a very clean look about them and there is little of that sordid poverty that can sometimes be seen in towns which are in a much greater state of prosperous trading. A local official of some sort went out of his way to point out that they strove hard to keep the corners clean instead of merely hiding them as much as possible. He said, "We have the cleanest little town in the West Country—and these chestnut avenues." He was a local official, and probably at the mercy of the town opinion as those officials are, but he seemed to have the interest of the place very much at heart. He was doing more than holding down a paid job and struck me as being a sort of city father. He spoke as if he, and others of the present day, had personally planted the avenues of trees which are by no means all chestnuts.

It is to be feared that the wide space for those lines of trees is a gift from the days when town property was not looked upon as capital to be spent. And it seems too good to be true that they have not yet been cut down to give motor traffic a little more room to hurry by. Probably the question has been brought up many times for if the room taken up by the trees was flung into the road, a car could dash more quickly down the whole avenue and save one or two seconds.

And it is thrilling to find a Roman amphitheatre right inside the town and scarcely showing any deterioration for all the nineteen hundred years it has stood there. It stands between two sets of railway lines where the land might be thought too valuable to remain "undeveloped." It is not strictly preserved in the sense that no one is allowed to place a foot on it; the town must have learnt respect for it if only because such things are the local industries. Except for the missing gate it is in the condition to put on a show at any time, and every member of the audience would be sure of a clear view. There would be no seat with a blind view nor could the actors be content to put a good front face on what they were doing. Did the Romans put on blood shows there and witness fights to the death? Certainly many deeds have happened there in the years between and it is not hard to imagine strange things yet taking place.

It is a pity that so many local people will direct you to Maiden Castle under the heading of "Roman remains"; but if a town deals in such "remains" it is to be expected that they

should claim Maiden Castle under that heading. But the
place is not difficult to find because there is a road going there
in the straightest possible line. Probably the makers of that
road made it straight, in a country where so few roads run
straight, because they wanted it to appear Roman.

Probably that is the way the Roman legion did approach
the place, and going towards it the newcomer can feel that
he is seeing the place with the new eyes of a soldier bent on
capturing it. But wending our way up through the confusing
defences of the western gateway it is easy to become a Celt
ready to defend it against the surrounding foe, and standing
inside the forty-six acres of walled township one marvels that
so big a town was in running order when Cæsar described us
as naked savages, painted with woad.

I intend to return to the site and deal with it as a town later
on in this book, but the most casual visitor cannot help being
impressed by the height and steepness of the ramparts even
to-day when every loose grain of chalk trickles downward
into the ditches. Alone and unhurried, without an audience
and still more without an active foe above you, parts of that
man-made slope are hard to climb to-day. At any time a man
needed to be in the very best condition to rush those defences
in themselves, and when kept in good order and well manned
it is not difficult to see why the town was a very real stronghold.

Walking around the town site it is a great pleasure to see
that the extensive excavations carried out in the nineteen-
thirties have left no scar. I have stood alone near the centre
of the town without another being in sight, and been able to
see it just as it has remained for many centuries. Fortunately
scientific men to-day are no longer content to dig into a subject like Maiden Castle and then throw the corpse away;
certainly here they have mended the wounds with as much
care and skill as they made them, for without knowing of the
excavations I could have convinced myself that it had
remained untouched.

It is worth making the circuit of the walls if only to feel
how the defenders felt when they patrolled there, and to get
an idea of what they may have seen in the surrounding
country. Much of what they saw is still to be seen as there

has been little distortion. The wireless masts to the north-west are not aggressive, and Dorchester town in the north-east fits naturally into its setting.

The original inhabitants would not be unduly startled for they would again be able to watch the approach of strangers as they watched the Roman legion come across the wide shallow valley from the River Frome. Then the satisfaction of finding the site still in its setting becomes a little uneasy; the straight road leading from the town to the site was made so that the town could get the benefit of it, which is all well and good as far as that goes. But, as could be expected, keen minds have seen that road as another good place to ribbon build, and not only have houses crept some way along it, but there is a hoarding erected to procaim that this is the Maiden Castle Housing Estate. So when you sit on the northern ramparts watching the legion marching inexorably across the wide green space, you can also see the yellow and white and pinkish houses coming too. It will not be long now, with all the boasted speed of modern building, before the outermost ramparts are rearing over somebody's back-garden fence. Yet I suppose we have much to be thankful for in that there was, and is, an authority to take over the site, and it would be too much to expect that its setting should also be considered.

There are many people who do not sit on the ramparts to reconstruct the enclosed town or to visualize the military history of the district, but merely to bask in the sun and air in a high place. And there is much to be said for just doing that, for it is close enough to the sea to be balmy in any good weather. What balmy means beyond what the dictionary gives would be hard to say—healing and soothing, bearing balm; but it would be hard to find a spot better able to heal or soothe if you use the heights of Maiden Castle as just a place to sit in the air.

And just sitting there like that being healed and soothed, he would have to be a very unobservant person who did not presently glance down at the herbage he was sitting on and notice suddenly that it was of a very remarkable kind. Most people know something of the more common plants and can recognize such things as clovers and certain weeds and flowers, and will find it easy to pick out a dozen or so within reach. But instead of plants being the usual size found in fields and meadows they are all very much in miniature, complete clover plants an inch across instead of six or so, grass plants flowering and seeding while taking up less room than a penny; tall waving weeds, which throw up their seed boxes a foot or so in the air when growing in a lush meadow, are to be found there maturing at a quarter of that height. A complete clover plant one inch across and half an inch in height is a fascinating toy, and if they could be grown commercially, in a minute pot to match, some of the London stores might find them a very good line; fortunately a change of environment would cause them to revert to the ordinary everyday plant. But there on the ramparts they grow in teeming millions, and when a group of people may be seen stooping and crawling about they are not necessarily hunting for a Neolithic souvenir but may be taking their first lesson in horticulture and very surprised to find themselves doing it. Tiny, baby editions of anything, animals or plants, have a tremendous attraction for people of any age or condition.

There is one thing which grows there without having to adapt itself to a small size, and that is the thistle which, as children, we used to call donkey thistles and some people called Scotch. These grow there to their usual size and help bear out the theory that it is not only the poorness of the thin film of soil over the chalk which stunts the other plants : these have evolved a way of life in constant battle against the close cropping of sheep for many plant generations, while the prickly thistle escapes that and therefore grows into its usual size.

Any place where sheep graze permanently, the herbage becomes small and close to the ground; it has to in order to survive, so as to complete its life's circle it has to flower and seed quickly. It seems to learn how to hide under its neighbour instead of pushing up towards the sun, and horses will feed behind sheep even when there seems to be nothing left to bite. A countryman will tell you that "horses will gnaw the ground after sheep," but nowhere have I seen it carried to the extreme that can be found at Maiden Castle.

Of course many of the Dorset hills are sheep country pure and simple, and equally of course they have declined to a mere suggestion of what they were fifty years ago. Any question for or against sheep is not for me to venture on, and even if they satisfied the necessary need to "pay" they will not be popular with farmers as dairy cows are. The man who has capital in sheep will get his return several times a year only, at the main sheep-marketing times, whereas the dairy farmer gets his milk cheque regularly every month besides what odd profit he makes by selling beasts as he finishes with them.

But Dorset has a famous breed of sheep of its own. The Dorset Horn is a handsome creature even if it does not have some of the points that make a good all-round animal. Seen in the autumn when it has grown out of its shearing sadness, but before its fleece has become long and dirty with the winter, it is a tall active creature not too far removed from the wild thing that could take to the hills and learn to race fast enough to survive. The poor domestic sheep is somewhat rightly considered a rather silly animal; his wild cousins even in the captivity of Mappin Terrace have not got his air; but the Dorset Horn is not quite so far removed as many breeds. I do not know any Dorset shepherd who is now working at his calling although I have had several such friends. I do not use the term calling in any precious sense of the word. A man should not set out to become a doctor or parson unless he feels a call towards such things, yet he often attempts it, but no one can become a proper shepherd unless he has the right qualities.

The romantic idea, mainly grown out of scriptural teachings, that the good shepherd leads his flock and loves each individual animal, does not have much place in any shepherding that I have seen. I have seen a shepherd lead his flock but only because two well-trained dogs, who could be fierce when needed, were bringing up the rear and watching the signals he gave. And with regard to his having any love for his charges, it was more in evidence that he expressed a considerable hatred at times, but of course the tradition of knowing each individual seems to be borne out. He can pick out at a glance an animal that is ailing in any way; he knows when one maggot has picked on one certain back and next day he will find that particular back to examine it. But that a shepherd would lay down his life for his flock can hardly be expected; he cer-

24

tainly devoted practically the whole of his life to them in the days of real shepherding, living and sleeping with them in times of trouble and developing a strong sense of duty in the process. Yet the same man might risk his life for his horse or his tractor if the occasion called for such a risk, certainly for his fishing boat. So, when shepherds do stay out in a blizzard to save their sheep it is more a call of duty to the job than because they have any unusual affection for their dull smelly creatures.

The dogs are a different matter, but such dogs are by far the most intelligent things that walk on four legs, and despite the apparent cruelty they sometimes receive for all their devotion, they are at least capable and willing to show their love and affection. I have owned a trained sheepdog from off the Dorset hills, bought for twelve and six, which does not hint at much heart-searching in parting with such a valuable asset and friend; for some years it was just a dog, call it a pet dog if necessary, which is supposed to guarantee the spoiling of any working dog. Yet when that dog was returned to the hills and put to work, it became again the complete worker with apparently no other thought in its head. In fact it achieved such a rehabilitation that instead of receiving the length of rope and a stone, or a charge of the farmer's twelve bore, when its working days were over, it was allowed to come inside the house and lie by the fire long after it was blind and footsore. Such behaviour was far from shepherding practice and a real cause of embarrassment to its owner and his other dogs, which were never even allowed to smell the inside of the house; but probably that old dog's years with me as a friend had taught it how to win its way.

There are still some good types of those dogs about but, like the men, they are seldom sheep-tending all the time; twenty-four hours a day for seven days a week made both man and dog one with the flock. But now the sheep are often just one part of the man's work and the dog has many hours to pick up bad habits. The training of a young dog is very simple on the surface—the youngster is tied to an old one that knows the job and woe to him if he loiters or rushes ahead when he should just sit and watch; the old bitch will turn and lash him even if he is bigger and stronger. But there is much more in his training than that and he may fail in one small matter after months of time spent on him. Like the shepherd, the dog has to have a special calling for the work.

It would be interesting to know what some of our visitors from abroad thought of such things when they watched a Dorset sheep dog at work. Did they appreciate that the sense of things in Dorchester was set by the Romans nineteen hundred years ago? That the civic pride and feeling of law there started then and shows no sign of lapsing in the future? The permanent thing the soldiers left will be the odd offspring here and there, but Dorset will breed that out in a few generations and no great harm done at all.

CHAPTER III

WEST DORSET AND MONMOUTH'S LANDING

THE roads in that part of the world do not always decide to set out for the next town and then push boldly in that direction. Where a stream of water runs, the road usually runs beside it, right in the very bottom of the valley. The water always took the line of least resistance, of course, and the first man to make a road had the sense to follow too, and then later, much later, when that great triumph over water and road, the steam railway, came to push up into the north-west to Somerset, it too ran in the very bottom with the river and road.

All three things crowd each other up the valley where the Frome runs above Dorchester, and yet there is little evidence that either of them trod on the toes of the others. There are valleys where the railways have jostled the rivers aside or forced them to run alongside like any tame canal, but the Frome seems to have been allowed to keep its ordered place which it found long before road or rail ventured that way.

Almost at once there is another large earthworks just outside Dorchester. Poundbury is small compared with Maiden Castle but it is evident that it was a real stronghold. There are the multiple defences well planned and still in good order, and, more satisfactory to the tourist, there are many "Roman remains" to meet their demands. But like most of these sites Poundbury was something that the Romans found in existence and made use of.

Probably through the influence of the Frome which is still a considerable stream of water, the valley has the appearance of being well watered, and the presence of water in the ground often shows itself to the most casual glance. More water, more grass, more stock, more farm buildings, more dwellings, more villages, more churches, and all that usually

27

means more trees, until the place assumes that air of what people like to call a smiling English countryside.

I do not intend to overburden this book by calling attention to all the good-sounding names that are to be found in Dorset; in that way it would be possible to fill many pages with just names which are good words in themselves. Often a "set" of names will appear in a district or along a river, like the Winterbournes or the Piddles and Puddles, although the Winterbournes will be found west of Dorchester and then again far away near Blandford. And such names as Whitchurch Canonicorum and Toller Porcorum are well worth writing and reading for their looks and sound. How or why that part of the country achieved such beauty in names would be hard to say. My suggestion is Celtic memories glimpsed through Roman culture, added to by a love of verse brought there by the Norse conquerors of the Dark Ages; and then the influence of the many church establishments in medieval days. In fact all those things can be found on the signposts, and there is still that lack of anything harsh in the Dorset man's make-up. If he inherits a good name he may slur and muffle it when he speaks, but he does not chop it up with his mouth.

The River Frome probably received its name further down where it is a more important stream, and then lent its name to such places as Frome Vanchurch, Chilfrome and Frome St Quintin, all right up in its headwaters in the chalk. And the small River Hooke which joins it at Maiden Newton also has its nameplace up behind the hills.

All that part of the country is undoubtedly farming country and drawing its substance out of the land itself with very little reliance on anything else. Unassuming is what many people call it, without seeing that such a way of living gives a small village dignity, and under the surface there is an independence which will not be found nearer the coast where other things have a share in shaping people's lives.

Going down another river, one is made to wonder why the town which grew on the Brit became Bridport. Was the hard letter turned into something more acceptable to our tongues, or a mere slip of the pen made when so few people could write or cared much about how it was done? Or as some

28

people say, was the town once a bride's gift? Nor is the town now a port after all, being two miles from the sea, and nothing can come inland by water any further than a few hundred yards or so down on the coast, where men have cunningly trapped the sea through a bottleneck which they call West Bay. The real West Bay is the big sweep west of Portland Bill, and Bridport people have confused the issue by taking the name for their little harbour.

And to call the place a port speaks of hard work when any place where a ship could call was important, and although there was a great need of such a place on the dreaded Lyme Bay lee shore, it could never have served except by expending a tremendous amount of energy to make it possible. And to keep it possible to-day is just as great an effort. It is one of the places where man has to continue the fight without the slightest let-up. One period of neglect after the sea has knocked the harbour mouth about and the whole Lyme Bay area would lose its one small shelter all the way from Lyme Regis to around the unspeakable Portland race.

It is a good example of the great tenacity that man is capable of showing in face of great odds. Bridport itself, now two miles from the sea, at one time had a sea trade and there is still something of a seaport in the look and feel of the place. It is obvious that the inlet of the sea and the river was once naturally open. I have seen a very old map which showed a considerable stretch of water there, and although some of those old maps, drawn by the eye and imagination, often stretched the truth and fail to suggest any sense of propor- tion, it is certain that Bridport once had a natural access to the sea between the two high cliffs east and west.

But on a tremendous sweep of unprotected coast like that, nothing is permanent. The Chesil Beach begins at Bridport and, being formed by the sea itself, is capable of being altered by any unexpected set of the tides. Then again geologists point out that at Bridport comes the break where the west–east beach travel becomes an east–west movement towards Lyme Regis. If this is so perhaps the gap between East and West Cliffs was once something like a parting on a man's forehead —material tended to stream in both directions leaving a parting up the valley. Anyway Bridport certainly once had

29

worthwhile harbour facilities and men have striven to keep them open, although there is now little chance of commercial trading. Apart from the fishing boats there is only room for a few small pleasure craft and such trade can hardly pay the great expense of keeping the harbour in going order.

But men never like to give up a fight against the sea even long after it ceases to pay to do so, and Bridport men have gradually forced a concrete bottleneck there where all the unbroken force of the sea can crash on the shore. Even now it it a very ugly place except in the quietest of weather. Every boat that ventures out does so with the knowledge that it must return through those few yards of harbour mouth, no matter how they have changed in a rising sea. There is no question of running for the shelter of some headland and breathing a sigh of relief when you feel its comfort; the whole shore for many miles is exposed to the full force of every-thing, with that one small angry gap to steer for. Bridport sailors need steady nerves.

And everything now has to be done there under the full glare of publicity; there can be no question of pottering about with a boat up a secluded creek or away on a lonely beach. More than half the pleasure and satisfaction of boats and fishing is trying out new things and making mistakes. Tarring a bottom or getting a ducking is not much fun when it is done under too many eyes.

Bridport town has much to recommend it. It has one good wide street and some old roads which are delightful to see; there is still an air of the old sea days and, of course, the net-making industry. And this is one of the industries which add rather than detract anything from the charm of the place. It probably has its labour troubles like everywhere else, but it escapes many of the terrible disadvantages of factory work. How or why that trade established itself there is one of the mysteries of such things, and a foreman who knew it inside and out and how and why it now worked, not only had no idea about its origin, but considered it a distinct waste of time to spend any thought on the matter. They have a flourishing trade with every sign that it will continue, so why on earth bother why it began there behind the hills?

Two miles east of Bridport, at Burton Bradstock, there

30

are men who think that the harbour should have been built there; the idea might have been possible, but only to men with great courage in their convictions. It might be possible to force out a concrete bottleneck in any exposed beach and keep it open with unremitting labour, but it is hardly likely that another such place will ever be attempted in the Chesil Beach.

Inland from Burton Bradstock and overlooking it is a hill crowned by an earthwork; looked at from below it seems almost out of reach to the man on foot, but the Bridport–Dorchester road runs along the top up there. And on the way up, after gaining considerable height, there is a deep dip and the hill begins again, but then there is still another deep drop down, until the earthwork appears almost as far away again, before Shipton Gorge is reached. That earthwork is capable of becoming something of a nightmare, but using some of the perseverance of Bridport men in their harbour, at last its level is reached and on looking back from the Dorchester road it is surprising to be able to actually look down on it. And that road is well worth the climb as for miles it keeps to the highest ridge of the chalk hill. Southward towards the sea, rounded shoulder after rounded shoulder pushes up through the confusing light over the Channel, and on the north side the road looks down on a steepness which hardly suggests a chalk hill.

The steepness of some of those chalk hills is remarkable when it is remembered that for ages every loose grain has dropped downward; yet to stare down at the village of Askerswell is to be reminded of grander scenery than Dorset suggests. And a man should be allowed to wonder just what the name of Askerswell means; a well of water of course, but who came there asking and was it to be had for the asking? And behind Askerswell a road runs away to Eggardon, a road which climbs gradually upward towards the night; in that direction there is evidence of our early history on every slope and it would not be out of place to think that nightfall was always near at hand. The Romans have their east–west road there keeping mostly to the highest ridges, but they marched through a civilization or at least a culture far older than their own.

That part of the country undoubtedly supported a great

31

density of population in our early history, and yet it is not good farming country at a glance, and there is hardly a sign of water; perhaps we have its very poorness to thank for the fact that the generations between have not swept all the evidence away.

From the high Bridport–Dorchester road, not far from Askerswell, there is a splendid chalk coombe that is theatrical in its perfection; the sinking sun fades it out in a way that any stage producer would approve. Why should such things make me turn to the idea of stage effects to describe them? There is no other way even to think of it : the play of light which makes a rounded hill change its shape and advance or recede, the suggestion of depths in a shadowy valley, the greenness of a slope that may be grey or even almost white when you turn to it again. The human mind can only compare with what it has seen; the stage achievement succeeded in awakening imagination and making it work, therefore when the same thing happens under some natural agency the imagination reverses the process.

On those heights everything waits, just as it has waited a very long time; men's work has scarcely been able to groom any part of it out of its natural shape or colour; the next hill pushes its shoulder up and waits, the bare hollows wait unchanged, and it is possible to believe that the villages you can stare down on are waiting until you are gone. There is not the change and promise that trees and ploughland give. If no man walked there for the next hundred or thousand years there is still nothing to grow out of hand and alter its appearance.

So it is startling to come suddenly upon a modern roadhouse with all that such a house means. Yet, for once, that place has a good reason for being there. Many such houses have come into being near some town to catch the town's pleasure seekers, who have an hour to spare, rather than the real road travellers. But there on the highest part of the Bridport–Dorchester road there is every excuse for a road-house even if at first it does not fit in the surroundings.

Yet, even if it has every appearance of being entirely alien there—and no one has made the slightest pretence towards toning it down—that becomes of not the least importance a

few hundred yards away from it; the scene is too big to take it into account, and the chalk still stays there waiting. All is well, so long as the place does not attract all the satellite erections which might go with it.

If we agree that a modern road-house can serve its turn in the scheme of things there, we still have many miles of country almost untouched by any hand since our forefathers threw up their earthworks all along that road. Circles, round barrows and long mounds are on every hand, with another ramparted hill where the road falls away towards Long Bredy and eventually the sea. All the roads on that side dive away as if in a great hurry to float down the valleys.

At the base of that ramparted hill with its hidden history of busy life, a standing stone sticks up in the corner of a ploughed field; the tractor of to-day ploughs to its very side, as it should, and growing crops must brush against it as they sway in the wind, but man still respects it even if he does so without a thought of why the same kind of man first stuck it up there. Surely its meaning was not very far removed from the wheat, barley and oats which grow around it now. There are far more mounds along that road than dwelling-houses to-day, and soon there is another broad stone which probably marks another place of worship, and by then the road is getting down from the treeless heights. But on a bend of the road there is a sudden group of nine standing stones, and it would be a very unimaginative man who did not stay there to admire them.

I like to believe that they are standing there untouched since they were first set up and that this is some kind of cathedral place, while the single stones back along the road were the village churches. Nor is it hard to see why men set up some place and stone to worship at. To-day we have a pile of blessed stones in most places where men have gathered to live, so why should they have been different in setting up their stones? Neither is it too hard to believe that the stone on the right-hand corner of the nine has a personality which it would be well to acknowledge. I at least would not feel it out of place to spill a little food and drink at its foot.

All the way down that road it is easy to understand something of the power which men thought was in the gods they

D   33

set up, and it is like moving through an unwritten page of our early days. The gods, but not the men, have changed, and just after passing through one of the Winterbournes, Abbas this time, there is all the set-up of one of the newest gods.

It was probably a reaction after spending a day with the old gods still watching from their stones, but suddenly, on a rounded hill above, was a scientist's dream come true. We have all seen a cartoonist's picture of such things and been half afraid that it was possible. Well, there it is. There on the hill great pylons carry wires in all directions; and while most of us can usually see some sense and method in such pylons stepping across the country as they carry three or four wires on and on and on, and we presume they are doing something useful, there on the hill wires lead away in every direction, and in trying to make some order out of it, it will be found that perhaps four wires lead to a pylon yet only three go from it. The lay mind cannot grasp what is going on overhead, only that here is a nesting place of the newer god, and as the pedestrian road also climbs the hill we have to pass dangerously near where he may lurk.

And of course we only find it occupied by one of his trusted attendants, although the constant low hum shows that the deity is at work somewhere within instant reach along the uncounted miles which he controls. And the attendant's living place is exactly as would be expected, a new square box set within that vibrant murmur, and we think of him watching and waiting inside, with his system of bells and gongs outside the very window behind which he lies down to rest. The new god would not wait two thousand years without attention if his field of influence had a slight disturbance somewhere in its long reach—and yet still have a personality such as we have seen in the standing stones set up back along the road.

Nor of course is there anything remarkable to the modern mind in just another electrical installation, except that it is unexpected there on an almost hidden chalk hill, and we know that it will not make the slightest difference to the age-less waiting of those rounded shapes. Besides, we were attuned to the older gods who still remain in the district. But having accepted the new god there, we are not surprised to

34

come soon upon another of the same kind, just where the Romans were able to straighten out their east–west road for a few miles in the way they liked. Here, for what seem great spaces, there are the many tall masts of a wireless station, high, slender and fragile. They have no strength in themselves but rely on even more fragile-looking guys and supports. Rearing on both sides of the road where the legions marched, they can turn the stomach of the poor creature who knows that his feet are still dragged by the friction of the earth's surface. They surely belong to the air age of the future, and even there they threaten, for in the ideal air age there will be no such tall obstructions to hinder the shortest line from point to point.

Some day those tall masts will be looked on as an intolerable nuisance, like an old house standing in a busy road. Already we have seen tall trees uprooted because they were a danger overhead, and cathedral spires practically told that they were in the way. It is logical to think that one day this old earth will have to be streamlined so that humanity can sweep round and round it, unhindered, in giddy circles like a swarm of dancing gnats.

But passing under the area of that wireless station is a sobering experience to us of the school who murmur unthinkingly "Isn't nature wonderful?" How often have we stood entranced to gaze on the dew-laden web of a spider slung in a hedge, and on lucky occasions seen the fat horror itself come out to repair a broken mesh. We give the brute many points for intelligence if it comes rushing out when its furthest strand is touched, even when we know that the vibrations set up by our clumsy finger cannot resemble the struggles of a trapped fly. Yet how often do we express the same wonder at the intelligence which sits in control of that wireless station, which knows what every inch of wire web is for and when it needs attention, that figuratively runs over its strands like the spider does and traps things in the shape of words? Nor is it an intelligence which needs to sit in a silken nest and eats its mate at the proper season; more than likely it drinks beer and plays darts yet controls a far more delicate structure than was ever slung between two twigs on a hedge.

On that Bridport–Dorchester road I was not able to find

the stone on a hill overlooking Bridport which is said to mark the spot where Charles turned back in his unsuccessful attempt to escape by sea from that place. It is likely that the spot is no more authentic than many of the Charles's oaks and Elizabeth's beds about the country, but I had been told that it stood up a dirt track off the road and such tracks are hard to find without definite directions.

Talking about having missed this stone on the hill to a man in a hotel lounge caused him to tell the best story I had heard for a long time. He had been younger, but not so very young, when one day he had pushed a bicycle up another long steep hill on the other side of Bridport on the way to Lyme Regis. He described the climb well, with nowhere to rest all the way up and the bicycle heavy laden with enough baggage for a fortnight. He could merely rest draped over the handlebars, and pant. He was out of condition for that sort of thing. Sitting in that lounge with our feet out, beer within casual reach and comparatively well fed—at least full for the time —we could both afford to laugh at his distress then, although, as staid men now, we could appreciate how his heart had thumped and he had gasped for breath. In fact he had arrived at the top of the hill somewhat frightened at what he had done, and there he found a stone seat where he dropped down with the thankful thought that it was very well placed.

As he recovered he naturally began to take more interest in finding he was still alive, and glanced at the back of the seat where he was leaning. There he read that some worthy old clergyman, who had been a genial soul and loved the countryside thereabouts, had dropped down dead on that spot after climbing the hill and the stone seat had been set up as a memorial to him. I saw my friend throw a startled glance over his shoulder, just as he had done when the full import of the message had first reached him, and he told how he had leapt on his bicycle and dashed a mile or so away before continuing his necessary rest. To the silent disapproval of that lounge I laughed until the tears rolled and I was helpless; then I pointed out the great chance he had missed by dashing away. If he had only stayed there and died too, he would have been sure of immortality, as they would certainly have carved his name under that of the genial parson.

He could laugh too, but he assured me that the horror of thinking he might be the second to expire on the exact spot had been very real. That was another inscribed stone in that neighbourhood which I did not see, and neither did I look for it very thoroughly in case the same feeling occurred to me.

But it is impossible to go down in that direction without experiencing some terrific hills; there is no need to go to the top of Golden Cap on the coast, but it is necessary to go down into the bottom of the River Char where it comes down the surprisingly wide Vale of Marshwood. The Char is another of those rivers which are not particular about having open access to the sea and left to itself it would be content to soak away through the shingle beach. But of course men have taken it in hand and try to show it just where they wish it to go. This is getting right down near the border into Devonshire; and Lyme Regis, partially sheltered from the prevailing south-westerly weather, is very near the edge, with its railway station almost a frontier post. But there is nothing of the wide-open frontier town about Lyme, and if I must tell the truth there is nothing at all suspicious about the Devonian who comes down the road from Uplyme. He would be truly shocked if I, having come across Dorset with all my attention riveted on being wholly and entirely of Dorset, should suggest that he really was a foreigner. He would probably explain that his brother lived down by Lyme harbour, and after all what was that to do with me.

Of course the most important thing that ever happened at Lyme Regis was that Monmouth landed there on 11 June 1685, and if his landfall was not an accident on his part it certainly came as a surprise to the townspeople there. They were startled and uneasy to see three foreign ships without any colours flying appear outside their little fishing port; the big *Helderenbergh* was not the kind of ship which ever came near the lee shore of Lyme Bay without some very good reason.

But they soon learnt who had come to visit them when seven boats put about eighty men ashore and their leader fell on his knees to thank God for bringing them safely from Holland and then asked a blessing on the work before him. There was excitement then, and as men ran through the steep narrow alleys which formed the town, they shouted, "A Monmouth, the Protestant religion." For King James II was an intolerant Popish sovereign with plenty of blood on his conscience if not on his hands, since he had practically wiped out the Campbell clan without trial. And Monmouth was a very popular figure whose weaknesses may have gone a long way to endear him to the common people. Certainly his journey through the West Country some five years earlier had proved that he had charm; the Stuarts had something fatal about them—so often wrongheaded, they were weak, strong, good, bad, brave and foolish all at once. The one thing they showed so often to the dismay of their friends was the narrow selfishness they were capable of pursuing to the bitter end.

Monmouth had all the qualities and weaknesses of his family, and his good looks alone might have made him a popular figure to many who saw him. So the people of Lyme Regis showed every sign of welcoming him as a stalwart of the Protestant cause, and they gave him every help in bringing his military stores ashore and into the town hall. They had come out for him, his blue flag was set up in the market square, and the new adventure had started.

Yet the first act of the adventure was perhaps a grave mistake; instead of his first Declaration confining itself to a few straightforward promises of what he would and could do when he had won his fight, it consisted mainly of an inflated attack on King James drawn up with the greatest of bad taste. James had poisoned the late king, burned down London, and Monmouth's sword would not be sheathed until such a traitor had been brought to the punishment he deserved. There were some reasonable points : all Protestant sects should be tolerated and many charters which had been hardly won and then harshly suppressed would be restored; Parliament would no longer be dissolved by any royal caprice; and the militia commanded by the Sheriffs who would be elected by all freeholders.

Then the Declaration faltered, Monmouth undertook to prove that he had been born in lawful wedlock and therefore had the right of blood to be king of England, yet on top of that he would put that claim aside until a free Parliament would judge on it. The thing was inconsistent; he had landed

WEST DORSET AND MONMOUTH'S LANDING

a declared rebel with the intention of driving James off the throne, and yet he seemed to flinch from claiming the prize until somehow it had been made legal. It would have been better to go the whole way at the outset rather than be persuaded as he was later when most of the force was taken out of his claim.

And while the people who would flock to him for reasons of faith, and just because of his own bright eyes, were quite ready to back his claim against the sour James, nothing would make some of them swallow the idea that Charles II had married Lucy Walters, and his statement that he could prove it was likely in any case to recoil on his head. It would always have been a quibble and under the temper of the times was totally unnecessary. What he wanted at Lyme Regis was appeal and strong arms behind him; the legality of the enterprise could have waited and, if he had any real belief in his adventure, would never arise.

On the face of it he did soon have a following on the Dorset coast, but he was intelligent enough to know that the gentry and clergy were not with him. The turn of fortune which had come with James II had favoured them, and even those who disliked his Popery were more inclined to wait for him to die, for he was an elderly man. And his daughter who would succeed him was considered attached to the reformed faith and was married to a Protestant prince. The same result which so many people wanted would come automatically in a few years without the dreaded blood bath of another civil war.

But the country people believed that Monmouth had a good cause, they were too ignorant to weigh things in the balance as the gentry did; they flocked to him until, before he had been on English soil twenty-four hours, he had fifteen hundred men. That was very good, considering that he had come unannounced and hardly a person ashore had been in the secret; but of all that fifteen hundred men there were very few who had any idea of real fighting; they were plain ploughmen and tradesmen with very few arms amongst them.

They could shout for him, but what he wanted was a stiffening of well-armed and trained men, if only to compose something of a threat while he shaped up his willing followers. Practically every man in Dorset set out for Lyme Regis : fishermen from all along the coast to Purbeck, whence the traditional quarrymen sent their quota, small tradesmen from the towns shut up their shops, and he received an earnest of what might wait for him when he moved inland, when forty horsemen came down from Taunton.

But the horses were more often straight out of the plough and shafts or young colts which were not even halter-broke, and his military experience told him that such horses were poor cavalry at best and needed long training to get them to stand under fire. As it was, every time a drum beat or a trumpet was sounded there was something of a stampede, with the riders far too busy trying to stay on to have either hands or wits to fight. Any enemy who had the sense to advance with a blaring band and a few fireworks would have been able to turn his foe's horse, no matter how stout-hearted the riders were.

And nine miles to the east, at Bridport, the Dorset militia were collecting in the town and the Somerset militia would be there next day. Monmouth decided to strike at once and drew up part of his men in some semblance of marching order; they did not look very much like soldiers although their hearts were good, and the best-armed amongst them were the scythe men who had fixed their tools to a staff. This was a reasonably satisfactory weapon when wielded by a strong arm, and was the traditional way of the English peasant to go to revolution, but there were not even enough of these because many of the men were artisans and miners, who were lucky if their trade tools could be turned into offensive weapons. The farm hand with his pitchfork and the woodsman who had brought along his precious axe were much better armed than many who had to cut a stout staff in the hedges.

Just as he was about to march off to Bridport a sudden quarrel took place between his officers. Fletcher, a fiery Scot, considered that he was too poorly horsed, while a good horse there belonged to Thomas Dare who had brought the forty horsemen from Taunton, and Dare was not a gentleman although he had already done a lot of valuable work for the cause. In the high-handed manner of the times, Fletcher took

Pulpit Rock, Portland
Lulworth Cove

the best horse without asking permission and at once was abused by Dare who ventured to shake his switch at the high-born Scot and was shot dead for his insolence. Fletcher was used to such methods in Scotland where no one would have questioned his sudden and violent revenge, but here in Dorset people were not accustomed to seeing a man killed on account of a rude word or gesture. At once there was an outcry against the Scottish foreigner who had murdered an Englishman, and Monmouth could do little to resist the clamour. Fletcher was lucky to get away aboard the *Helderenbergh* and escape to the Continent.

But his spirit and energy were a great loss in a potential army of raw men who started for Bridport with the shadow of the affair over them; yet the Dorset militia which waited for them were not much better except that they were better armed. Both sides were mainly countrymen, officered by county gentlemen and small-town barristers; the fighting was confused and indecisive as could be expected.

At first Monmouth's men drove the militia back until they were made to take a stand, and the sudden stand threw the attackers into confusion which the other side soon turned to advantage. Grey, who had charge of the raw cavalry, did not stop until he had got back to Lyme Regis and so earned the hatred of the foot soldiers, but in Wade Monmouth found a man who was able to rally them and bring them off the field in good order. Monmouth was strongly advised to get rid of Grey and it was believed that he refused because Grey was the only peer on his side, but whatever his reason Grey was to let him down more than once. The recruits still poured in by the hundred and clamoured for arms which were not there, and it was known that the alarm had been spread far and wide.

The Mayor of Lyme Regis was a bitter Tory who had at once sent off news of the landing; he had reached Exeter himself where the Duke of Albemarle was actually holding a muster of militia. At once the latter was able to set out for Lyme Regis with the four thousand men so fortunately gathered together, and he had every reason for thinking that he could nip the rebellion in the bud before it grew out of hand. But by the time he reached Axminster, Monmouth was

41

Lyme Regis, from the Cobb where Monmouth landed
The Cobb, Lyme Regis, with Golden Cap in right background

already there drawn up to meet him with four guns ready to start the battle, and suddenly Albemarle seemed to realize that amongst his own men were many who were merely waiting to go over to the other side. Monmouth was as popular in Devonshire as he was in Dorset.

Rather than fight with that uncertain temper in his ranks, the Duke thought it better to retreat after coming so far with so much assurance, and although he had great superiority in numbers of trained militia, the retreat soon turned into a rout in which Monmouth's men were at last able to fit themselves out with arms and even uniforms if they cared for them. Perhaps Monmouth would have gained more by pressing the retreat right to Exeter but he preferred to go north to Taunton where he arrived in exactly a week after landing.

That was no mean achievement, considering that he had arrived without much preparation being made for him in advance, and it proved that many people were ready to throw out King James and his works. But as Monmouth had already moved out of Dorset this is not the place to follow him in any great detail. It will be useful to take a look at the way it was all received in London and how far the grudging James would go, and we can then go round with Monmouth to the sorry end of his adventure back again in Dorset.

London did the usual thing in ordering that Monmouth's Declaration should be publicly burned by the hand of the hangman, and at once brought in an Act of Attainder to deal with him, promising a reward of five thousand pounds for his capture. London and James were not bothering much about any legal quibbles, because the Act attainting Monmouth was carried through on evidence of treason which at the time was merely hearsay. Even such a corrupt judge as Jeffreys could not have hanged a dog on anything that had reached London when both Houses rushed the Act through.

But James was taking no more chances if he could help it, and he had every excuse : he could remember how Monmouth had confessed to being mixed up with the Rye House plot and escaped the consequence by promising allegiance to the Duke of York if and when the Duke came to the throne. The young man was not to be trusted in any way and James certainly had reason to put an end to his adventuring. But

apart from that, the triumphant tour Monmouth had made
through the south-west country in 1680 showed what a dangerous popularity he had in that quarter, and he had also
been militarily successful, and much loved by his men, when
he won a victory at Bothwell Bridge.

While London was making every preparation against him,
Taunton was giving him a reception capable of upsetting a
stronger character than his. And in those days such towns in
the south were comparatively more important than they are
to-day, because the northern industrial towns scarcely existed.
Taunton occupied a prosperous place in the woollen industry
and was a very important town to have on his side.

Everywhere the people flocked to him, but he soon
realized that it was still only the people; no peer, baronet or
knight, not even one member of the House of Commons, had
sided with him. Yet he had been told that the Whigs were
eager to take up arms for him, and he was then advised that
they held back because he had not proclaimed himself king.
For some reason it was said that such men would not fight
for anyone unless he came out openly for the throne. So he
went all the way, and proclaimed himself King Monmouth at
Taunton, and next day he too put a price on the head of his
rival. But all this made no difference to the Whig gentlemen
who could now point out that he was a man whose word did
not last a week, because a week earlier at Lyme Regis he had
bound himself not to accept the throne until a free Parliament
had accepted him.

From Taunton he marched up to Bridgwater and even
then some of those who saw him remarked that there was a
gloom on his face. He himself was not an unqualified adver-
tisement for his desperate cause, but still men joined up with
him and still there was a shortage of scythes, while many men
who came to march with him had to be turned away because
of the lack of arms of any sort.

But the King's forces were beginning to gather around and
James was exerting another power which was not so immedi-
ately apparent on the field but which played an equally
important part. In London and the whole country no Whig
was safe from arrest, hundreds of eminent men were shut up
where they could work no harm, and the most prudent Puri-

tan might at any moment find himself flung in a dungeon however careful he had been.

Then Monmouth went across to Glastonbury and up to Wells and Shepton Mallet, and still he had no plan of military operations unless he was aiming at Bristol, but Bristol was strongly held for the King and could not be lured out to fight a battle in the open field. He seemed at a loss what to do then, unless he were to cross the Severn at Gloucester and raise the border counties; he had his popularity up there as well as in the south-west, but popularity without armed strength was getting him nowhere. As he moved his enemies moved in behind him and harassed his tired men at every opportunity.

And Monmouth's raw troops were tired, too tired even to make the march to Gloucester even had they been spared the hostile cavalry gnawing at them all the way. He therefore decided to move into Wiltshire where he had hopes of getting reinforcements. He summoned Bath to surrender but Bath would have none of him, then south to Norton St Philip where his half-brother the Duke of Grafton caught up with him with five hundred men, but Grafton was on the other side and perhaps wanted to prove that he had no connection with his disloyal schemes. Grafton was driven off but Monmouth could not wait and hurried down to Frome.

And although Frome was as much for him as Taunton and Bridgwater had been, it had little to offer him, as a premature rising there had led to the rout of his potential followers a few days earlier and not even a scythe had been left. Monmouth gave way to his misery and complained of evil counsellors; he showed then what he really was, for he was ready to abandon all who had left their homes and families to follow him. He proposed to escape to the coast before his flight was known and believed he could forget his ambition and shame in the arms of his Lady Wentworth. That was the only plan he could offer his advisers at the moment, and they must have known then that the cause was as good as lost.

Naturally the scheme was turned down, since the others did not want to offer James their necks as a free gift just because their leader had lost his nerve. They would return to Bridgwater where there was no real reason to expect better luck than they had before, and on the way they committed a lot of wanton damage to Wells Cathedral through sheer bad temper.

And at Bridgwater he was trapped where he must fight or escape by sea. He still wavered, but the King's forces were waiting at Sedgemoor, and although in the end he started the attack hoping to gain the advantage of surprise during a foggy night, his plan of battle soon broke down owing to an elementary error in thinking that he only had two ditches to cross when there really were three.

At that third ditch his guns and ammunition wagons could not follow, and the King's forces came up to line the other side. Although his foot soldiers were soon deserted they fought to the last and most of them died there under the horses of King James. Monmouth had long ago galloped away hoping to reach the south coast. France and Lady Wentworth lay in that direction, and to face them as a failure was better than looking into the cold eyes of his uncle James. But there were plenty of dangers on the way and back in Dorset, in the Cranborne Chase, the horses gave out. It was a miserable candidate for the English throne who soon found himself alone with a few peas to stave off his hunger.

Somewhere he had changed clothes with a shepherd, and a few days' beard showed prematurely grey. But there is no point in dwelling long over the humiliation of his last days; for a young man of such promise his behaviour was scarcely believable except that there are too many witnesses to leave any room for doubt. He certainly must have forgotten that he was a grandson of the first Charles.

True to his character, James allowed himself the bad taste of letting Monmouth plead and grovel and then refusing him the mercy he craved. The adventure which started so gaily in Dorset ended on Tower Hill, and even there the headsman fumbled.

But the aftermath was yet to come and is a black story which even to-day makes King James II a hated name in the south. Judge Jeffreys was the tool he used, but James's was the merciless fear which set him going. The Stuart was still fatal, just as Monmouth had been in a very different way.

CHAPTER IV

JEFFREYS'S TOUR. MILITARY MOVES

BEFORE Jeffreys was let loose on his Bloody Assize, the Royalist Army had already taken ample revenge on the deluded people who had followed Monmouth's weak and untrustworthy leadership. Kirke's Lambs was the ironic name of the most ruthless regiment in the English Army; they had been raised to fight the tribes in North Africa who knew and cared nothing about any rules of war. Such service had resulted in something which scarcely seemed the same thing as the kind of men who made up the bulk of Monmouth's followers.

These were the men who tidied up the countryside after the fighting. They ignored any wounds a prisoner might have and hanged whom they pleased without the semblance of a trial. Kirke and his officers would have men strung up where they could see them while at meals; he used anything as a gallows and might have a man cut down before he was dead so that he could be hanged several times. But even this brute could not satisfy the Government, because for thirty or forty pounds he would write out a safe conduct to pass through his lines.

And a greater revenge was travelling out of London in huge style; Jeffreys and James had decided to open their labours at Winchester in Hampshire although the rebellion had not reached that county. They were determined to bring about the death of Alice Lisle who was known and would continue to be known as My Lady Lisle. Her trial at Winchester has no place in a writing on Dorset, but as it was the opening of Jeffreys's tour it has a great bearing on things.

James had two ends in view when he picked on her to start. Lady Lisle was a frail old woman of blameless life, but she was the widow of John Lisle who had been one of the men

who sent Charles I to the block. And if they were ruthless
enough at Winchester, as they fully intended to be, such a
wave of terror would precede them westward that not only
would the work be easier and more quickly done, but people
would hurry forward to save their skins at all costs.

That her trial was illegal to start with, because neither of
the two men she was charged with harbouring as fugitives
had yet been found guilty, is not important here and now.
Jeffreys was determined to kill her, and he went to every
length that was necessary to do that. Of course, that she had
protected and relieved Cavaliers too when they needed such
help as she had given, and was willing to do any Christian
act regardless of politics, had no weight with Jeffreys; he
sentenced her to be burned alive, which James was gracious
enough to mitigate to plain beheading.

Then Jeffreys went on to Dorchester to start the main
work and at once let it be known that any man who pleaded
not guilty would be executed within a few hours if found
guilty. The only slight chance of any kind of mercy was to
plead guilty, when the victims might be left a few days longer.
In this way his work could be speeded up, and he needed all
the help he could get from both court and prisoners as he had
so many cases to get through.

But whatever the prisoners pleaded the result was the
same in the end; he convicted twenty-nine of the first thirty
put before him, and showed what all the rest had to expect.
He had boasted that any lawyer or parson who came before
him should not escape, and when he found an attorney
amongst those first thirty he made his boast good although
the man was clearly innocent. Matthew Bragge had been surrounded by some of Monmouth's horse when out on a legitimate journey and made to point out the way, while at the
same time they had taken his horse. So the solid attorney took
his gloves and cane and then set out to make the long walk
home. He had a right to feel an aggrieved man. But as he
had contacted the rebels it was perhaps his legal mind which
made him report himself at Dorchester where he found himself before Jeffreys on Saturday and led out to slaughter on
Monday. And a constable named Smith had been forced to
give up some money belonging to the militia; he had certainly

47

been unwilling to have anything to do with the rebellion, but he too went out with the attorney on that Monday morning.

Nor did it make any difference that many men had taken advantage of the Proclamation and surrendered within four days to win grace. Jeffreys overrode everything of that kind as well as flouting every legal rule. No wonder he was able to send a report off to Lord Sunderland that "I this day began with the trial of the rebels at Dorchester, and have dispatched ninety-eight," which was good going even for him.

He made sure of his victims and saved his own time by sending two officers to see a man before he was brought to court to say that the only way to obtain the slightest chance of mercy was to plead guilty. And then if the poor man altered his mind at the court and pleaded not guilty there were the two witnesses to prove that he had already confessed and therefore no time need be wasted on him.

To make sure that Lyme Regis would not welcome another rebel on their shore, he ordered that twelve prominent men should be taken there and executed on the very spot where Monmouth had stepped ashore. One of these was a Colonel Holmes who had been a confidant of Cromwell and therefore must pay for that now; he had lost an arm and a son at Sedgemoor, cutting off the arm himself because there was no medical attention. He must have been a tough old soldier, for he recovered sufficiently to travel to London, where James seemed to offer him his life, since he was not arrested and went back to Dorchester on his own, but that made no difference to Jeffreys, who saw in him a good example to set up at Lyme Regis.

Christopher Battiscomb was another example chosen to serve the same end with even less reason; he had been lying in Dorchester jail at the time of the rebellion and in the disturbance had escaped until found in Devonshire. But he had been out and about in the country when the fugitives from Sedgemoor had also been using the roads and byways; that was more than enough for Jeffreys.

The scaffold to carry twelve victims had been erected on the west shore at Lyme Regis and the carts had brought them from Dorchester while, according to custom, they were to be dragged the last stage on sledges over the sand. Then the

people standing by saw what they hailed as the hand of God stretched out to save them; the horses refused to move ahead. It is likely that those horses were merely strange to the sea-shore and sand under their feet; probably they were the same Dorchester horses which had dragged the carts from the inland town, and no horses had yet refused to take a man to the gallows. But everyone there saw that they refused to drag the sledges over the sand, and although others were fetched these new ones too refused and broke their traces and the sledges.

Of course that was not allowed to delay the hanging for long; the prisoners had to walk instead of ride the last short distance and they were accompanied by a wailing and sobbing crowd, some of whom were Baptists come to see the last of their aged pastor. Jeffreys hated such people. Many of them were the same people who had shouted for Monmouth with joy on that very shore and now they could only mourn at the sorry end, which of course was the idea intended. It was a long-drawn-out scene; there seemed no end to the addresses and prayers offered by, and to, the condemned men, and after they were dead there was still the horrible business of quartering them and dipping the quarters in boiling pitch to preserve them.

The lesson they were intended to teach had to be lasting. The people who saw parts of their friends and relations hung in appropriate places could not even hope that the law of nature would soon allow the grisly relics to moulder away. Fortunately science had not then developed beyond pitch and tar as weather preservatives or perhaps some of Jeffreys's victims would still be hung about the countryside. A chronicler at the time wrote "some places quite depopulated and nothing to be seen in them but forsaken walls, unlucky gibbets and ghostly carkases. The trees were loaden almost as thick with quarters as leaves; the houses and steeples covered as close with heads as at other times with crows and ravens. Nothing could be liker hell than all those parts; nothing so like the devil than he [Jeffreys]. Caldrons hizzing, carkases boyling, pitch and tar sparkling and glowing, blood and limbs boyling and tearing and mangling, and he the great director of all."

E   49

That was a picture of Dorset at the time, and hangings were spread through the length and breadth of the county so that no one should be ignorant of the fact that King James had a long, strong arm. Apart from the unnecessary cruelty and shortsightedness of it, it proved that Jeffreys was capable of good organization : if a house or hamlet had sent a rebel they could be certain of having him, or one of his quarters, brought back there to hang where they could see him, and if not, there were plenty of others to hang and four times as many quarters.

And the cost of it all fell heavily on each district; each had to erect gallows and provide halters to match, "with a sufficient number of faggots to burn the bowels of the traitors and a furnace or caldron to boil their heads and quarters, and salt to boil them with, half a bushel to each traitor, and tar to tar them with and a sufficient number of spears and poles to fix and place their heads and quarters." Besides axes and cleavers to do the work and carts to carry away the finished articles to the proper places, each district had to supply men to guard the foul work and sometimes even a poor wretch who worked his pardon by cutting up and boiling his friends. No wonder half-crazed men spent the rest of their days under the terrible name of Tom Boilman, and, as so often does happen to such creatures, came to a miserable or violent end so that people could point out that some higher power had punished them although Jeffreys had spared them for his own ends.

But sometimes when even Jeffreys could not get a conviction of death for some minor offence, he got his end just the same when he ordered that the victim should be whipped on continuous dates at various places. A man might be whipped every market day all through Dorset, which was merely an extended death sentence, and a fourteen-year-old barber's boy of Weymouth received that sentence at Dorchester because unfortunately he had somehow learnt to read. His crime was that when Monmouth's Declaration had been posted up in his town, people had fetched him to read what they themselves could not.

Even the jailer at Dorchester did not like carrying that out and laid the lash on the boy as lightly as he dared, but the

Rev. Mr Blanchard, a clergyman, threatened to send the jailer before Jeffreys for the dreadful offence of not carrying out the punishment in the proper manner. So next day the whipping was repeated at Dorchester in the proper manner and the boy sent off to Weymouth to get his quota for that place.

Perhaps those who were hanged and quartered were those who escaped lightest because in some cases the sentence might be transportation. And this became a game in which the Tory gentlemen of the county and the Court favourites tried to get the better of each other, while "to the Queen's order one hundred" shows that she herself was willing to benefit by James's revenge.

The value of a convict sent to the West Indies was too good a thing to be missed, but in the scramble for the prizes the Court creatures had the advantage over the Tory gentlemen in Dorset, although the latter might have the excuse that they had suffered damage in the disturbance. Even Jeffreys wrote to James pointing out that there was not much to be gained by handing over so much of the "booty" to Court favourites who had not suffered. Using the term booty to describe the men he had sentenced showed that he and James understood each other and were carrying out a plan.

And although he had his price, a case had to be free of other motives that might arouse his spleen before he would discuss terms. One thing which was fatal to any attempt to buy him was for the victim's relations to approach some other person first. If he knew that even James had been sounded nothing could save the rebel after that. And his price was very high, far too high for many people even to start thinking of the matter, and so many of the rebels who had not been able to get out of the country were very poor men. As always those who had wealth had the best chance to escape or buy their pardons.

Yet economically the loss of those poor men was something which showed up at once, as most of them had been the best and their labour could ill be spared. Skilled craftsmen and labourers are not easy to replace in the countryside, especially when the people of a district have been thoroughly frightened and made resentful. The large numbers of widows and orphans had to be provided for out of the district, and although that was a great burden, it did not cause so much resentment as having to keep hundreds of men in the jails until James and his creatures could sell them abroad.

Dorset had received the first shock of the Bloody Tour, and in the massacre and sending of heads and quarters to hang on almost every tree and signpost it is likely that Jeffreys overplayed his hand in one way. The news spread far and wide as he intended, but many honest and decent men were disgusted and ashamed that they themselves had hunted down or informed on a rebel. Many a fugitive was hidden and got away by people who had had no sympathy with them, and only the worst characters came forward to claim the rewards. Even the Tory gentlemen and the magistrates were sickened and slackened in their work as soon as Jeffreys had moved on.

So Devonshire did not hand over many victims, and Jeffreys made out a list of 342 prisoners he expected to be ready for him when he returned. But in Somerset there was no lack of numbers, and although that part of the story does not really concern Dorset it is necessary to mention one of the crowning infamies he achieved at Taunton. A schoolmistress named Susanah Musgrave had got her children to make colours for Monmouth and for that they were brought up before Jeffreys. One, a child of eight, was set before him and he raved and threatened her in his usual way until she collapsed and died in a few hours. By no stretch of the imagination could such children have been guilty of rebellion against King James II, but they were handed over as booty to the Queen and her maids of honour. And these gentle ladies wrung the utmost penny they could out of them, while such men as the Duke of Somerset were willing to carry out the negotiations for the Court. He advised that £7,000 would be a reasonable sum.

Eventually the deal was carried out for about half that amount, but such business shows how some of the royal and aristocratic fortunes were built up; Jeffreys himself reaped a rich reward for his work, but it is good to know that his end was not much better than some of the poor wretches he harried for James in the south-west.

In time James also had to run for his life, but as is usual with kings he got away safely : when Jeffreys ran he shaved off his eyebrows and put on a seaman's rough clothes, but he got no further than Wapping and later was committed to the Tower where he died in bed.

Much of the rebellion and the Bloody Assize which followed it occurred outside the borders of Dorset, but it all still lives in our county where countless gibbets swung in the wind, and on most of the old churches you can be sure that at least one grisly quarter stained the wall or a drooping-eyed head was spiked over the door.

It is easy for a man of the south-west to hate Jeffreys with a personal hatred. Despite the excuses that have been made for him on the grounds that he suffered from gall-stones, from any angle he was a monster. And James was fear-ridden, perhaps because he was a bigoted Catholic in a nation which had at least learned to fear that creed. But even so it is hard to see why they were so ruthless to the deluded people who flocked round a likely lad who turned out to be a man of straw.

It was not as if the Stuarts had a grudge to work off down in those quarters, for during the Civil War of some forty years earlier the people of Dorchester had been favourable to the King if anything; probably they had just hoped that they were far enough away not to be dragged into it. But certainly it had not been a stronghold for Parliament and it had taken the excesses of the Royalist Lord Goring, with his mainly foreign cutthroats, to bring the south-west eventually into line with the rest of the country.

Of course the Dorset coast has seen some of the military history of Britain, and although the pre-Roman evidence is shadowy, there was an Iron Age migration from east to west even if that was not accompanied by a defeat of the original Neolithic people of the Stone Age. But when we get to the Roman invasion of A.D. 43–70 there is plenty of real evidence. The future Emperor Vespasian campaigned there with the Second Augustan Legion, and was quite likely the man who reduced Maiden Castle.

It was then that the military town of Durovaria (Dor-

53

chester) was founded beside the river, near the old ramparts of Poundbury, and our British history started in the sense that it was recorded, at least was recorded in a way that is satisfactory to those who wish to see it. The four hundred years of Roman occupation became peaceful and progressive as far as Dorset was concerned, and probably built up that sense of the fitness of things which still seems to exist in Dorchester town.

The withdrawal of Rome did indeed bring in some very dark days for which there is little to show, and when the Saxons had arrived they were at first even less able to leave us any sign of culture, nor was Dorset one of their early conquests, as those which came along the south coast were held up and kept out much where our eastern border now is. We were eventually overrun from the north and west by the hordes which had penetrated right up the Thames valley to the Severn and then turned downward to the sea again.

And for a long time these invaders were occupied in holding what they had won against their own kind. Whatever the force which made them leave their own countries across the North Sea, it did nothing to bind them together, nor were they at all interested in the native population they found here. They exterminated what they did not want to use and fought a lot between themselves; also they had the raiding Danes and the settled Jutes of the Isle of Wight as uneasy neighbours and occasional foes.

We can leave out the legends of King Arthur and his Table; they belong to Wessex all right and must have some foundation, but there is no real evidence of that romantic period. There is better evidence of Alfred, no matter where he burned the cakes. We like to think he did battle with the Danes off Swanage and drove them on to the Pevril Ledges. Certainly Danes raided the coast and went up Poole Harbour to burn Roman Wareham several times.

We had little to do with 1066 and all that, but that is hardly a very glorious incident in our history. William had a very efficient fifth column in this country before he started out from Normandy. It seems strange that some people should boast about having come over with him rather than having been here before.

There is one theory which I like to expound : that all the Bowers on and near the coast are descendants of bowmen who once defended the sea there, and when men were forced to take a second name they often chose their trade name. John the Bowyer (Bower) would of course want to be known as such, and it is a good sound name and has been ever since. John Bower will be found in many records of all ages as a well-thought-of man; Alfred, Hubert, Harold, Edgar Bower —don't they all smack of good sound Saxon bowmen?

In Elizabeth's time the coast defence was called out more than once when the drums sounded and the church bells rang out, if only to repel streams of sea mist as they did attempt at least once. And we watched Drake whip the Armada up the Channel although Devon has the glory of that; we only put out to harry the stragglers. Boney was a very real bogy in his day, and my grandfather, born in 1826, used to speak of him as if he had personally shared in the threat, nor did he like to be told that he had picked up the idea at his mother's knee. Sitting in the light of the old man's fire I too shared the bogy within sound of the sea. It would have been easy to start up and say, "Hark, listen, is that he?"

In 1914–18 we remained careful the whole four years, but it was in '39–45 that the bogy nearly did materialize. *His* plans (and *he* might be Philip, Boney or Hitler, they were all the same when you are waiting for them), his plans included a landing on the Dorset coast and a push up towards the back door of London; Dorset would have been in for a lively time if the Few had not won the Battle of Britain.

There are people who think that the bogy did come to them, especially in the shipping attacks and when Portland and Weymouth received attention in the blitz on the ports. But all places thought that they were being picked out for special attention, and Dorset did not get the worst. Particularly unpleasant were the tip and run incidents when a couple of fast, very fast, fighters came out of the haze at sea level and reared up to spit their venom perhaps without coming over the coast at all. Some places have still many newish patches on the roofs where at least a cannon bullet came down out of the smiling sun.

Some of those incidents, dignified as "raids," are reckoned

in seconds, with the enemy back in the haze before that first sickly crackle of flames came from the dust cloud.

One old man told me just how such things happened. "I was out on the hill thatching a rick, and he shot up over the cliff past me before I knew he was about. He hopped over to North Hill, but he didn't know what *I* did. They had a Bofors over there and I think they tickled him up, 'cos' he then jumped up in the air and turned off down to the sea again and he was smoking well then. *He* didn't get back to the other side I think—then I slid down the ladder pretty quick."

Dorset also escaped another bit of unpleasantness planned for them alone, and people slept without knowing that others were sitting over plans concerning them closely. Plans that must have included field paths and narrow lanes and even the walled backyard of the house on the corner. Near the village of Worth a wireless station had been set up, and although it was guessed that it was something out of the ordinary, no local person really knew what it was for; it was just the wireless station with its attendant tall masts and many local people were sent to work in and around it.

But since the end of the war it has been disclosed that it was an important Radar installation and that an enemy plan had been found showing that they knew all about that, and on paper at least they intended to saturate the district with bombs, and then drop a parachute force to destroy the station for all useful purposes. That would have been fatal to my favourite village in which I have a special interest and many friends of my youth would have felt what it was to have the enemy come down on them.

Yet the Intelligence Services, which so often come under the lash of ignorant tongues, appear to have known that such a suicide raid was being considered, for the station was suddenly removed from its dangerous position on the Channel edge and transferred to a place far inland, taking with it many Dorset people to a district they never expected to see. And it looks as if the enemy Intelligence was working too, as the plan was never put into operation.

As far as I know the Home Guard was never called out by the ringing of the church bells as in olden times. I say as far

as I know, because one morning we were told that the bells
had rung out during the night in the next parish to the west.
At the time it seemed so probable and what we expected that
people spoke definitely about those bells ringing. My feeling
at the time was that perhaps I had slept too soundly and not
heard what other people might have heard.

But soon it was apparent that no one had actually heard
the bells and it was always "to the west," and since then I
have traced the alarm from north Hampshire to as far west
as Bridport, and it is still a little bit further to the west that
they really rang out that night. I have at least hoped to meet
someone who was actually wakened by them, if not to find a
man who pulled the bell rope.

And if there was nothing in that scare, as seems likely now,
although I still remain to be corrected, how did such a story[1]
obtain such a sudden start and remain constant down through
the south-west at least? It is a minor Russian-snow-on-the-
boots story and people will tell you about it now with exactly
the same look on their faces as had the first man who told me
at the time when it seemed so very possible. It happened all
right, but always just a little further west, in the next parish
where all the exciting things occur.

Then the time came when the evidence of the great
counter-invasion to come became too big to hide from people
on the spot. Everyone knew that something was preparing,
but surprisingly little of that knowledge seeped many miles
inland. There were still people who pretended to believe that
it was all part of a great bluff because *he* had been over there
on the opposite coast for so long and had grown to loom so
big in their minds. But when there was no longer room to
push in even another jeep on the side roads, and great sleek
guns were actually parked in people's back gardens, and it
was quite impossible to find room to stand up to drink a pint
of beer, then the thing was really afoot and certain person-

[1] On 18 November 1946 the Prime Minister, Mr Attlee, stated that
from captured documents it was revealed that in September 1940 the enemy
had an invasion fleet of barges in readiness for the outcome of the air battle of
Britain. Bodies of German soldiers were washed up along the coast at the rate
of thirty-six a month, probably the result of air bombing of French ports.
The General Headquarters, Home Forces, issued the "invasion imminent"
at 8 p.m., 7th September, by ringing the church bells.

ages came to give them God-speed, and the great armada moved across and up and down the Channel while the whole world waited for news of the early success.

Once more Dorset shared in the sea story of these islands and people looked out on that changeless stage where so much of our destiny has been played out. There is some degree of truth in the idea that Britain became no longer an island when the first plane flew over from the other side, but that water makes all the difference in the world. It will be a good thing if the guidance of this country is always in the hands of men who understand the sea. That is a necessity, yet so easily lost sight of. The people who know the sea cannot realize that there are others who have no idea of it, and so many people only know the sea as something they have dipped into a few times in the height of summer and really did not like it much then.

There is one great scar on our county to which is added the injury that it now no longer seems necessary to keep the healing hand off it. It started during 1914–18 when the War Office took over land round and about Lulworth and Wool, and then unexpectedly hung on to much of it permanently. That was bad enough as the Army does not usually improve the land it uses, but in time it became accepted more or less, and there was the considerable sop that it brought a certain amount of money into the district. Village shops enlarged their turnover or were swamped by others eager to come in; local public houses became more like purely beer-selling machines; and the loss of land may have been partly compensated for to those who saw it in that light.

And of course this time, 1939–45, there was even greater need of training space unencumbered with that apparently half-witted creature who is still a civilian. No one suggests that a yard of land or a cubic foot of housing space was taken without good reason—that is one thing which must be borne in mind; and everyone agreed that it was all for the best possible cause towards the only possible end.

So from East Lulworth up to East Stoke near Wool, almost to Wareham and down to the sea again at Kimmeridge, all this was thrown in with what the War Office already held in that district. About 7,300 acres of farms and smallholdings went out of production at a stroke of the pen, and already 500 of such acres had gone east of Kimmeridge, which left that small secluded village very much out on a limb.

Of course there are historical buildings and good church buildings inside that area, and villages which were quietly flourishing for all that nothing seemed to happen there. In fact several hundred people were living a way of life which they thought was as satisfactory as most of their ancestors had thought it; it certainly was a better way of life than most people's. The archæological value of many ancient sites there was enough to make us hope that the Army has not thoughtlessly swept them away, and every inch of the cliff face has served as the training place where young geologists can study their trade at its best.

It was a big slice to take out of Dorset, but it was only a second and smaller slice compared with that taken on the south side of Poole Harbour. There nearly 12,000 acres had been sterilized and over three hundred people involved, all of whom had to be fitted into a district which had already lost many houses to the enemy, and still carried some evacuees who had gone there with the idea that it was safer in what they thought was the very depths of the country.

From the seashore at Studland back again to near Wareham and going close to Corfe Castle, there is an area set apart, and a glance at the map shows that there is very little of the Isle of Purbeck left free, and to go to Swanage is to run your head into a very dangerous bottleneck. I have played with the idea of living there again, but travelling from Wareham to Corfe Castle I am very conscious that I am entering a trap. On my right I can look up and see Grange Hill and a considerable china clay industry which is lost, on my left there is the solitary dead area of the heath running down to Poole Harbour.

And if there are people who say that that heath always did look solitary and dead, I can point out all the white masts from which the red danger flags are drooping. The heath is now really dead and deserted, where at one time the independent heath-cropper found a living and lived almost as long as he wished to; and in any case 349 people did have to pack their chattels and migrate out of that area. Now not one rogue heifer finds a living there, and has the War Office left one tree of the bitter-sweet apples which once made it worth visiting?

That narrow bottleneck makes the position of Swanage look pretty precarious; another war and its fate is sealed. But supposing some War Office pundit glances at the map and sees how the position lies. At the back of his mind he knows that there are bigger and faster war weapons which are cramped for room; how easy it would be to take that last peninsula of freedom and draw the line at Wareham.

All that was taken as a war emergency measure, and the people who left their homes with a heavy heart—and a countryman's home with all that he has put into the surroundings can be something totally beyond anything a townsman feels about his house—went with the knowledge that it was necessary and it was up to them to put a good face on their uprooting. But they were never told that it was anything more than a war emergency, and as it was explained that every care would be taken to avoid intentional damage to buildings, it was natural that they expected to be able to return when it was over, and take up their way of life which could be so much more than just living that life. And now the war is over, the uncounted myriads of armed men are no longer there, and if the war vehicles are not standing there to rust some of them have every appearance of doing so. Anyway they no longer crash and roar over the playground where they learnt the grim lesson of total war. In fact the awful game is over and people want some assurance that they may soon get back to what they consider their real life.

The Wareham and Purbeck Rural District Council, who naturally want to put their house in order and at least know where they stand, have made representations in various quarters to find out what the War Office has in mind. So far, in late 1945 they have received what is mildly termed "somewhat negative results." The Army looks as if it is going to hold on.

The National Trust and many other such bodies and societies are backing the Rural District Council who have produced what they call their Isle of Purbeck Representations from which I am drawing most of my information. We know that it is pathetic that old people are not allowed to go back and tend the graves of their loved ones, but that sort of thing has so little weight.

So much insistence is being brought to bear on the idea that Purbeck was the perfect beauty spot and natural national park, that although people can be momentarily touched by a sentimental appeal, they are likely to come to think that it is only some trees and sea views that are at stake. Perhaps it would be better to keep forward the fact that much of it was the very best farm land with many good buildings on it. Add up all the value of the things that used to be produced there, the milk, the meat, the corn, the china clay and bricks and stones, then the really heartless and fickle public might take more notice instead of thinking that only the living of those who serve the holiday-makers is at stake.

And although the Representations try to insist on the natural beauties of Purbeck and the efforts to preserve the amenities, in the next paragraph they use a passage which I am tempted to lift bodily : "the traffic census taken by the Dorset County Council. Between the 15th and 21st August 1938, and between the hours of 8 a.m. and 8 p.m., there passed the census point of Norden on the road A351 between Wareham and Corfe Castle 1,042 motor-cycles, 20,336 motor-cars, 502 motor-buses and 2,338 pedal-cycles. Pedestrians were not recorded. It is believed that this is the biggest census of traffic recorded in the County of Dorset and this is only one of the roads by which the Isle of Purbeck can be entered—traffic and visitors continued to increase very largely between 1936 and 1940."

Perhaps I could leave that without comment, but knowing how bare figures like that make no impress on some people's minds, I will say that I know that road well, and I don't like to imagine those thousand motor-cycles roaring by, the twenty thousand cars and the five hundred buses all thundering their way into the natural beauty spot of Purbeck. It is to be hoped that the vehicles enjoy the trip into the good sea air. Could the Army do much worse if they would only allow people to live along the roads they keep closed?

I have already filled more pages with this matter than I expected, but we want our acres back to plough and to sow, and our own roads to rush up and down ourselves, and if you like, our own family graves to lie in. Perhaps too the whole of Purbeck will soon become far too small to serve as a training school. The Rural District Council do not presume to offer any comments on that matter, and if as a private individual I suggest that there are other wider and wilder spaces inside these islands where less than one-tenth of the people would have to be moved off good farm land, the poor people in those wider and wilder spaces may be after my blood.

There are two other things which may influence this affair. How unpopular would it be from the Army's point of view to move away to one of those further sites where it would not be possible to run a car "up to Town for the night"? Considerably unpopular from what I have heard from men who think that even Purbeck is at the very back of beyond.

The other matter is that, although most of the stress has been concerned with the cottagers, the smallholder and the farmer, and the beauty spot—the things it is easy to get sentimental about but whose welfare is seldom allowed to influence big things—so far the powerful road and ferry people who sunk so much money in the private road from Studland to Poole Harbour and put the chain ferry into operation there have remained very quiet as far as I can gather, which is strange when it is remembered how much they spent on the undertaking and the lengths they went to obtain every advantage they could wring from it. Perhaps if and when they throw their weight into the fight we shall see the wealthy road and ferry company lined up with the lowly heath-cropper, and that would be something like the lion and the lamb.

CHAPTER V

THE CERNE GOD AND THE
TOLPUDDLE MARTYRS

A DORSET man can be on terms with God or the gods which
most men cannot or will not accept, and the usual reaction is
to think the Dorset man is a bit off his head simply because
the other man is made uneasy. Mankind as a whole feels that
there are powers which are not predictable and although
propitiation has been conventionalized into a few almost
automatic thoughts and observances for most of us, there is
still an uneasiness and shyness about dealing with God or a
god.

But, in literature at least, the idea of any kind of god is
not quite so strange when it occurs in Dorset. Anyone who
has read Hardy or the Powys brothers becomes aware that
the thought of such things can be in men's heads as they go
about their daily business; there is always the possibility that
a man might meet a god and even walk along and talk with
him.

And as writers can only reflect what they feel is around
them, the idea of personal contact with a god must exist. We
can leave out the possibility if we like, but that still does not
alter the thing a man has in his soul. Nor is it any use a man
saying that he has no room for such things in any form, or
convincing himself that he has found the one and only real
god. And even if that tiny doubt that touches a man occasionally is merely a relic of our early days, before we had
obtained the comparative safety we now have from such
things, the uneasiness still remains there underneath everything, and sometimes it looks out.

That is quite a bit of writing if it is just to introduce you
to the River Cerne and get you to follow it up to its
beginning. And it is not much use rushing up the valley in a
car if you really wish to get the feeling of the place; on your
feet will be best, with your mind as timeless as the hills on

either side, or pushing a bicycle which amounts to much the same thing for most of the way. But don't expect anything if you send your mind ahead to opening time or tea time or the last bus back, and if you think you are bored by the dull sameness of what you see, let your boredom deaden itself in its own ache.

The great thing is to let the valley draw you on and on without any conscious will of your own; such things are possible in the country and are really the only way to experience the full pull of unseen things. It is the difference between the trained countryman and the trained townsman : one lets himself go and accepts because he does not understand everything, and the other resists and often reacts with scorn or abuse for the same reason and because he feels that he might be missing something.

But where the Cerne joins the Frome at Dorchester the valley floor is very much the same until it pinches in above Charminster, and near there is the institution where they take us when the gods have touched us a bit too closely. And once more we find the road and river running actually side by side in the very bottom of the slopes. For miles they never leave one another, as if the men who made the first road there wished to gather comfort from the river.

And gradually that may come to seem wise as there is something grim about the valley. It seems right that men kept to the bottom and have little to do with the steep bare slopes that soar away on either hand. The few villages have an air of being outposts and it is easy to believe that people gather together for the comfort of human contact. It certainly seems to have repelled the villa builder who likes to place his mark conspicuously on country roads.

If there is something grim up that way it seems reflected in the people; they are rather silent and without the friendly feeling that most Dorset people have. You get used to smiling greetings outside the towns but you don't get much of that up through the Cerne valley, and perhaps that is how it should be because we are going up there to meet a god.

You can say you are merely going up to take a look at the Cerne Giant, and that is all you will do if you sweep up there under any power but your own. But I hope you have set out

64

The Frome, Lower Bockhampton

as so many thousands have before you, drawn on and on and gradually preparing yourself to see him face to face where he certainly waits to see you.

The first time that I met him I know that we communed across the space between us. I had waited to see him and I knew he too had waited to look me over. Perhaps he had waited many generations for me to return and there seemed to be approval in what passed between us. A man of whom I am very much a part had once stood there before I did, perhaps not since the day when we lived in hilltop towns like Maiden Castle, but a being with arms and legs and all that the Giant has, had come there to make contact with him as I did. I knew in my bones that I had been there before.

Apart from any idea that he was and still is an old god, he has an amazing look of intelligence and understanding and to me there is nothing at all uncouth about him as so many people claim to see. But we live in an age which has distorted the values of many things; some people can avert their eyes because the Giant is a god of fertility; to them that means sex and sex alone, so they want him made respectable according to their own feelings because such things are not to be seen in the light of day. Yet they can live untroubled in a society which legally practises birth control.

I know people who approve and practise that negative cult of fertility and yet would clothe the Giant in innocent verdure because he is positive. But he will stay there on the hill no matter how dim and grown over he becomes, until one day people will rediscover him and remember that he stands for the good of all mankind.

It is likely that he was the big god of all the people who once lived in that well-populated part of the country and they came to him when they needed the thing he stood for. He seems too gigantic to have been the private god of the people who lived on the hill opposite him although within a very small radius there were many settlements.

And technically it would be very interesting to know how he was actually cut in the turf; one brain must have directed the work and that must have been done from the opposite hill as it is impossible to make any sense when climbing about on him. How did the artist responsible get his directions across

Packhorse bridge, Fifehead Neville

nearly a mile of space? It would be no light undertaking to-day with a telephone between the workers. He must have been able to stop them going too far and to encourage them to give the god's knees a good shape, because he is still a well-shaped giant and full of the virility he stands for. Compare him with the White Horses of modern days and see how we have lost the art of making our hill figures live—because there is no longer any real meaning in putting them there.

After making your peace with him, and sometimes you can remain there undisturbed for hours at a time, you will notice a disused workhouse on the side of the road. Most old work-houses in that part of the world were obviously built from the same model and equally obviously no one ever thought that such places had any part in the rehabilitation of the unfortun-ate people who found themselves in them. So the Cerne Workhouse is a dreary-looking place even now, and it must have defeated the spirit of perhaps thousands of people in its time. What did they think of the fertility god always facing them, and what did he think of them?

To-day it is different and perhaps it is a sign of an awaken-ing. Instead of housing old people to whom the idea of fertility had become a sorry jest the building has been turned into a Youth Hostel. Perhaps the old Giant looks down with approval now, but what about those who claim to have the well-being of our youth at heart?

A mile up the valley from the Giant, opposite the good-sounding name of Minterne Parva, is Up Cerne, which explains itself, with more trees than are really right for that part of the world. And to explain the trees is a manor house which goes a long way to connect the continuous way of life set by the Giant when he was a real awe-full god.

If we accept that the Giant gave importance to the Cerne Valley and we know that Cerne Abbey was very important in its time, the manor connected the Giant and the Abbey and has survived in pretty good order until to-day. Undoubtedly a manor has stood there since manors were carved out of our way of life, and the present house has absorbed much of the history it has seen as some houses do.

I know someone who once had great hopes of living there, not only because it would be a marvellous place to live, but

66

because she felt that the house accepted her as one of the family who have owned it for a long time. She could stand by a fireplace with a fire burning and feel that she had lived there in a past life; some houses and fireplaces are like that with those people who have the right tone of the place, and as no one knows all the complete details of their ancestors perhaps she was returning to her own home.

Anyway when the prosaic business deal fell through she shed tears in the night because it was so like being torn from her home in the real sense, and while in some cases these could have been the tears of a woman who could not have a particular house, I prefer to think that one more person had come under the influence of Dorset and that she did once live there.

The Cerne and the road go up together to still another of those places with such a good-sounding name which is just as delightful to see written, Minterne Magna, but soon after that the water you may see will be flowing north, eventually to enter Somerset where the River Yeo marks the county boundary. That water makes a long journey across the Somerset plains and ends up in the Bristol Channel; Dorset has reluctantly to give it up as soon as the pull of the Blackmoor Vale is felt.

But instead of descending to the level where men live it is worth leaving the valleys and even roads to wander on the top of that great heap of chalk. It is a different world up there and on a dull day the work of man does not exist; there is an almost complete lack of animals and even birds, and only another shape pushes up a long way across a shrouded space. Again there is that sense of waiting and some people find that frightening, but the next hill is not even watching you because it is indifferent to one other human making his small way about there.

It is surprising to find well-made roads up there as sometimes no one passes along them for hours at a time, but those roads may lead to some startling slopes when they go down to the lower levels. The people who first decided where those roads should be did not do it with an eye to wheeled traffic, and often they swoop directly up or down in the shortest possible line between two places.

And unless the next place on the map is up the same valley it has to be over in the next one; no wonder there are people living there who have never visited the next village over the hill in all a long life. Nor do some of the villages offer much temptation to come down to them from the heights. There they seem to lie miles away and so far below, looking small and huddled and even frightened. The stone they have set up in place of the standing stone is now the church and according to the angle from which you see it the dwellings are either crouched around it or have stood it aside ready to be forgotten.

Like the water, we have to come down in a valley and find a level, and if we find the River Piddle it at once seems a more friendly stream than the Cerne. Yet it comes from the same hills and has to keep to just as confined a course in the bottom. It too has the road keeping to its very bank as there is no other place where a road could be, and when the village of Piddletrenthide begins there is scarcely room for the stream, the road and the houses.

Sometimes all three seem to occupy the same strip and for three miles or more the stream, road and houses dodge each other by inches. Many a house has the water flowing along one of its walls and practically everyone has a bridge either to the front door or to the garden at the back; there is and can only be the one street and as most of the houses open right on to it there is very little that you can do except share your life with all your neighbours.

If you go up the street you are seen and if you go down you are watched, and if you have bad news by a letter the people far down the valley are ready to console you within a few minutes. But you are back amongst friendly people again, perhaps because the hills above are not so lofty as above the Cerne and of course there is no watching god up the valley.

There is nothing to show it, but somewhere the village of Piddletrenthide becomes Piddlehinton, nor perhaps is that important, any more than that by the time the river reaches the next village it has become the Puddle instead of Piddle. It does seem that someone may have been a little too embarrassed and changed the name : there they had a piddling little stream and quite honestly called it a piddle, and so it is, only

68

it is a very delightful little one. Then the nicer-minded people stepped in and called it a puddle which it is not, not even after it has flowed through Puddletown, Tolpuddle, Affpuddle, Bryants Puddle and Turners Puddle, to find its way all across the dark heaths to Wareham and Poole Harbour. Nowhere in all its length should it be insulted as merely a puddle, and it would be interesting to find out why and at what period of time it changed its name, as we do know on which stretch of it the change came.

It is easy to think that nothing very important can have happened all down that small river. It has turned a lot of millstones in its time but seldom has it even given the land near it a well-watered appearance. It was too confined up in the chalk and does not irrigate the heaths, nor is it big enough to open up the country by trade and it has every appearance of being tucked in behind the course of history. Yet an important bit of social history did take place on the banks of that slow river.

The story of the Tolpuddle Martyrs is not something which happened in the dim past nor even during a blood-heated period like that of Jeffreys's Tour in 1685 when at least the country was used to death and treachery in most quarters. 1834 is recent enough for us to think it enlightened, and certainly newspaper reportage should have reached the stage where such a perversion of law was impossible.

For it was no miscarriage of justice but sheer cheating, and although very welcome to the powers of the day it was a very shortsighted gain for them in the end. The six men were martyrs in the fullest sense in that they did not see even the beginning of the light they brought into the world.

That a light was needed in Dorset at the time can be shown in a very few words, and for those who can see below the surface and know something of both sides, it is easy to believe that such things are not so very far beyond the bounds of possibility even to-day. The descendants both of the Martyrs and of their persecutors are still in much the same position in and around many villages like Tolpuddle. I have heard them speak and can assure anyone that the spirit is still there. Fortunately nearly everyone realizes that it is the martyr's spirit which triumphs in the long run.

69

But in 1834 the short-term outlook was allowed to have its way because farmers and squires were blinded by the prosperity they had gained from the Napoleonic wars and their aftermath, and the farm workers were at their lowest ebb where the Enclosures had forced their spirits as well as their bodies. A farm worker no longer had any means of providing any part of a living outside of his weekly wage; he had been driven off the soil in every way except for the hours he had to work for another man. That may be looked on as a blessing by many of those who boast that they forget their work on the instant they put it down, because they will find it lying on the bench or desk next day just as they left it.

But work on the land is not just like that, if only because the job is not lying there idle while the worker is away. It has moved ahead according to the season and weather and needs intelligent and interested planning every minute of the day and night. In fact it needs more than that and it is no romantic idea that men can love their work on the land, even to-day when so much farming is carried on as a heartless big business. The tie between man and earth is a very real thing in spite of generations of social and economic contempt.

Dorset has achieved a reputation of being a very backward county, and many people have come to believe that such an idea fits the countryman in the lanes and on the hills. But the records of 1834 go to prove that the backwardness lay in the ruling classes and certainly not in the workers. Instead of belittling the man ploughing the fields it would be nearer the mark to look into the background of the others.

It has sometimes been loosely claimed that the Tolpuddle Martyrs were pioneers of the trade union movement, even to making them something of revolutionaries; yet they were nothing of the sort and had the equivalent of the Wages Board behind them, in that the general wage for farm workers in the south was ten shillings a week. It was the sheer greed of Dorset farmers, squires and landowners which kept the Dorset wage down to seven shillings with often a rent of one and sixpence for a dwelling in which the animals would not be expected to thrive. Britain had legally wiped out the African slave trade but allowed some of her own most valuable people to be actually starved to death.

Nor were the Martyrs breaking the law in forming their Agricultural Labourers' Friendly Society, and they had already exhausted all other means of approach and been harshly turned down. Nor was George Loveless, or any of the others, a reckless character in any way; four of them were Methodist lay preachers, and while that does not always speak for a man's moral worth, it did make them something of respected public men whom it was not easy to blacken. It was an asset to the other side in that the Church of England was against them and weighted the scales in favour of the cheating.

The law could not touch them for their trade union because the Acts against Combinations of Workmen had been repealed in 1825, but Lord Melbourne, the Home Secretary, suggested that something under the Unlawful Oaths Act of George III might be tried. This was something which had been brought in to deal with the Mutiny of the Nore in 1797 and nothing to do with civilians, but there it was, still *a* law, and it was raked out again as a means to prevent the Dorset farm workers getting more than seven shillings a week.

But even in this it was a very shaky case and could not have succeeded without the pressure of everything that represented money and power. The oath that the Martyrs used was merely a copy of the procedure of such bodies as the Freemasons and the Oddfellows and no one dared suggest that the Freemasons were making themselves liable to transportation. To-day it seems just mumble-jumble that new workers were blindfolded and taken into a dark room to swear that they would not disclose any secrets of a trade union, with a skeleton before them; now such a thing seems ridiculous, but then it was the usual thing.

Yet the charge of administering an illegal oath was brought forward at Dorchester Assize in the same court which Jeffreys had had hung with blood-red hangings. And in one way Jeffreys had been on better ground as his victims had known that to rebel carried with it the risk of severe punishment, but the Tolpuddle men had not attempted anything that was not accepted in other places; they had merely respectfully asked for the wage rate due to them. And even if there was any legal ground for a Proclamation which had been posted up giving four days' grace, this was ignored as they were arrested before they could have taken any steps to disband the union.

The evidence was all rather vague, but Judge Williams, like Jeffreys before him, was out for convictions; it can be said that he was within a law which had been twisted, but he must have known that he was serving the Tory Party with some very dirty methods. He must have known that it was a distortion when he spoke of the cruelty of making each union member pay a penny a week towards the funds. Of course a penny a week was too much out of seven shillings which had to provide everything no matter how big the family, but that crow should not be roosting on the dock. "If these men had been allowed to go on with their wicked plans they would have destroyed property. If you do not find them guilty you will forfeit the goodwill and confidence of the members of the Grand Jury."

Of course the verdict was "guilty" and two days later the Judge showed even more plainly what he was aiming at. "I am not sentencing you for any crime you have committed or that it could be proved that you were about to commit, but as an example to the working classes of this country."

That was justice as understood by the other classes not much more than a hundred years ago, and the sentences were transportation for seven years which was nearly the equivalent of a death sentence in that few men ever came back from it. It scarcely seems possible now that anyone could get away with it, and it makes me wonder if in another hundred years people will look back at our justice with the same feeling of horror and disgust.

What the six men suffered is not entirely a matter for Dorset, and I do not agree that especial sympathy should be worked up because they were decent men thrown amongst the worst. The whole system was rotten and just as degrading to those who used it : it is more worthwhile to know that all six men bore it with dignity as could be expected of them; they went through all that a brutal system could do to them and even then the influences which had gone to such ends inflicted another blow.

At last public opinion obtained a grudging pardon, but

72

Bulbarrow Hill
Hambury Tout

there was no hurry to put that into operation; anyway Australia was a long way away from Tolpuddle in Dorset and it was a long time before any of them got back there. One of them might never have known he was a pardoned man if he had not accidentally come across it in an old newspaper somewhere up country in Australia.

Money and privilege could move against them without a few days' grace and go to every length to obtain the desired end, but when it came to putting the pardon into operation it was quite another matter. It was a long time before any of them got back to go eventually to Canada, and none of them sought the limelight and could hardly have dreamt that one day their names would be history.

It is only incidental and unimportant that on the Memorial Gateway at Tolpuddle we can read :

> Erected in honour of the Faithful
> and brave Men of this village
> Who in 1834 so nobly suffered
> Transportation in the cause of
> Liberty, Justice, and Righteousness,
> and as a Stimulus to our own
> And future Generations.

> GEORGE LOVELESS
> JAMES LOVELESS
> JAMES HAMMETT
> THOMAS STANDFIELD
> JOHN STANDFIELD
> JAMES BRINE

What is important is that once again Dorset men had made a stand against vast odds for the right to live, and it is well that everyone who walks through the village of Tolpuddle, and others like it, should remember that the very people he sees and talks to have the same stuff in them. Martyrs like heroes are everyday people until their quality is called into the open.

As the Piddle-Puddle has brought us down to Poole Harbour, and with the meeting of the Frome and the sea there is plenty of water, it is a good chance to float down and see the

73

Tolpuddle, the Martyrs' village
Studland

port town from which the harbour takes its name. The town of Poole is well worth a book on its own and some day I hope to give it one. From every point of view and in every age, except ours which calls for mere size, Poole must have been the ideal site for a port.

But long before civilization called for such a thing and only odd adventurers came to this outlandish island, the large stretch of sheltered water was perhaps the most inviting place for a strange ship to lie up. And any boat that could cross the Channel must have been comparatively big to those who saw it arrive, big enough for it to be safe from attack while it remained out on the water; its crew could choose their time and place by being able to outwit and outpace any body of people who gathered on the shore to repel them.

There are unlimited places and spaces around Poole Harbour where a newcomer could land unopposed, and it is likely that some of the Celtic people arrived there before some of the ancient "British" earthworks were placed about on the hilltops of Dorset. I certainly like the idea that one of my forerunners looked over the smooth waters around him while he planned on which side he would land.

The Romans used the place as a port and have left their evidence of civilization there, while the Danes knew it well as a landing place where they started their raids. And by the time of comparatively recent history, in the last few hundred years, Poole was well known as a swashbuckling sea-going place whose people knew well how to look after their own ends.

The town grew right out of the water because the inhabitants were always as much creatures of the sea as the land; a boat could put ashore or take off its crew or goods at the very windows, making it easy to carry on business which need not come out in the open street at all. No wonder smuggling and other such things thrived there. The creeks and islands could hide many a quiet arrival and just behind the town was the heath and forest which gave a quiet and hidden road inland.

The Romans must have left adventurous spirits there if only in the casual offspring such occupations leave behind; the Danes committed a lot of shortsighted slaughter and

74

damage but must also have added to the reckless strain; Canute landed there in 1015; and all through the years since then ships have called there. Poole must have an admixture of adventurous blood which outstrips the modern ports like Southampton and Cardiff.

It is not surprising that unusual things have happened there, and perhaps may do still : in my own lifetime I have known of one thing which I thought at least unusual but quite satisfactory to most people concerned. And while I may be accused of romancing in a sordid tale which I am quite unprepared to prove to the hilt, although very young at the time I believe that I came to the right conclusion.

Some foreign seamen quarrelled in the town and one of them was seriously injured, and just another row like that was not very much to talk about, but I believe he was dead before anyone took any steps in the matter. The men were off one of the small sailing ships tied up on the quay and there was a little unobtrusive coming and going with the captain and the police, and presently the injured man was carried aboard by the police. He was carried just as if he was another drunk although he had a serious head injury, and on the next tide the ship moved away on its return to some Scandinavian port. That small slow ship either carried a seriously ill man who needed more skilled attention than he could possibly get aboard her, or a corpse which would be put over the side somewhere on the way. In the latter case a short entry in the ship's log could tell of just another fatal accident at sea with few if any questions asked, and the authorities back at the port were spared another bothersome affair. Quarrels and fighting were so easy to start, manslaughter trials often unsatisfactory, and no one wants a ship to be held up for so long. I may have seen it all in a romantic light it scarcely deserved, but still maintain that my conclusions were to the best end for all concerned, including the unfortunate victim.

To mention such an incident is not through any eagerness to uncover another port scandal, but to show how true to life Poole may still be. Even to-day Poole people have a harder upbringing than most; they have always been known for the way they demand their rights and have so often got them. As long ago as 1248 they obtained a charter from William de Longespee, and at one time the mayor of the town was a very powerful person, his office carrying the rank of admiral with it.

In 1347 they provided Edward III with four vessels and ninety-four men towards the siege of Calais, and of course demanded their proper price. Queen Elizabeth went as far to gain their approval as to make Poole a county on its own apart from Dorset, and Charles II had a good time there in 1665 when the Duke of Monmouth was with him. Twenty years later Monmouth was making for the port when he was picked up in a ditch a few miles north of the town. He must have know that there was every chance of being smuggled out if only he could have reached it.

It was a Poole coal brig which took Charles across to France in 1651 after the battle of Worcester, for which service the captain was paid £60. Nor was that all the reward which fell to the little Poole coal ship, as after the Restoration she was taken round to London and painted up to anchor off Whitehall, and then entered in the Navy as a fifth-rater under the name of *Royal Escape,* with the same master, who received a pension of £100. She served 140 years in the Navy which was good work for a coal ship out of Poole.

It would be interesting to know just how that incident was received in the town, for during the Civil War the place had been a stronghold for the Parliament against the King. The Royalists were not able to take it by storm and the Earl of Crawford thought to succeed by treachery; he spent £140 in gold preparing the way and in the end was admitted in the gate one dark night with 500 men. But it was a trap in which few of them escaped. Poole was not for sale.

The boldest English buccaneer was Harry Page who brought 120 prizes into the port, but he was the known terror of the English Channel and adventured as far down as Spain. On the other side of the Channel he was known as Arripay and carried on until the kings of France and Spain gave up trying to capture him at sea; they fitted out a joint expedition to smoke him out at home and went to the length of landing at Poole where, however, the townspeople got him safely away.

By 1770 the customs amounted to £13,747 which was very

good considering that some of the port business never went through the process, and the port had 230 ships of all sorts with 1,500 men to man them. The place was flourishing, but Poole has always been in the front of new adventures until modern days; it had its share in the slavers between Africa and the West Indies.

Probably it carried on the tradition of sail as long as any other port in this country; a big sailing timber ship from the Baltic might lie against the quay with all the grace and dignity such things have even when their long, sweet-smelling cargo is lowered on to stinking noisy motor-lorries. And next to her might be a little onion boat which merely pops across the Channel, yet the onion boat may have earned a lot of money because few people know all that such boats have carried. Probably such sea traffic has been driven off for ever in this last war and Poole may have to find some other way to carry on, but I am glad that I saw some of it.

The war has found a use for the stretch of smooth water, as flying ships of various kinds have used it. There again is new experimental adventurous work, but such war uses have a way of not being much advantage after the particular job is over. The harbour and even the wild waste shores surrounding it have played their part in the struggle yet it is difficult to see it taking any part in our sea history at all comparable to what has happened there in the past.

Of course Bournemouth, which now adjoins Poole on the east, did not exist when Poole was important, and the resort which now spreads far and wide has tended to look down on such industries as make up a thriving port. Acre for acre Bournemouth has held as many rich people as any other place, but for many years I watched the local Press and saw how those riches made people spurn the very thought of having Poole so near them. It was as if, although they loved money and insisted on the privileges it brought them, they wanted to draw their skirts away.

Yet it is hardly likely that the well-spaced-out resort, with yet its rows of mean dwellings around it, will ever have a history like Poole. Of course the port would have lapsed in modern days with the ever-growing demand for size; its water is shallow, its ships small, its streets congested with two level-crossings to compete with all and every day, and modern Southampton not far away with all its room ashore and deep water. But still Bournemouth must take some of the blame for Poole's decline as men did not want it there detracting the glories from an up-to-date resort.

The town of Wareham might also be said to be on Poole Harbour although now there is a considerable stretch of the River Frome between the two. I had intended to write of Wareham with the Isle of Purbeck even if the supposed boundary of the Isle does not cross the river. But the town is on the north, or mainland bank, and although I had thought that I knew the town rather well, I have learnt a lot from Sir Frederick Treves. He writes of the town as if he had an affection for the place and that often lets a man make his subject come alive.

A glance at the map shows that the two rivers run side by side there, the Frome in the south continuing its easterly course from Dorchester, and not far to the north the Piddle-Puddle has come down from the chalk. They run neck and neck to Poole Harbour and a glance at the spot makes one wonder why they never seemed to have joined up. I say "seemed to have joined" as probably they did in flood conditions across the place where the town now is. But each returned to its own channel and then man came along to tame them.

Probably the Romans were the first to see the military value of the site. They certainly built the high earth walls enclosing the town and there at little cost was a strongly forti-fied town such as they loved. A respectable river defence on two sides with a raised causeway across the low-lying meadowland leading from the north and south gates, and on the seaward side the protection of Poole Harbour which per-haps came up much nearer the walls than it does now. That left only the west approach at all open and there they built the highest wall, while even on that side any attacker had to come on straight with no room to deploy between the two rivers. The Romans had military genius, but the site seems obvious to the eye in any case.

The layout inside the walls is typical Roman work, and how simple it has made life for the townspeople ever since :

North Street, South Street, East Street, West Street, it is all so easy, the smallest child learns the points of compass with its first steps, everything that happens in the town is so nicely fixed in everyone's mind in the right particular quarter of the town. People brought up in Roman towns ought to have a very clear picture of life.

Perhaps Wareham did. It certainly has had a very eventful history, at least after Rome seeped away down the river. The Danes came up to the quay many times with all their fire and slaughter; sometimes they held the place and sometimes the Saxons lined the walls. It was the scene of many battles and much incidental fire and murder; Canute once more burned it down, but by then the townspeople had come to look on another fire as just one of those things which make life a burden. Few towns in England have been defended or taken so many times. Matilda took it and then Stephen snatched it away, Wareham suffering its usual fate every time, burnt to the ground and rising again to await the next occasion. In the Civil War it surrendered to the Royalists but during that troublous period it changed hands more than once; the Parliamentary garrison of Poole made it their week-end outing to go across and beat the place about a bit.

It was then that Wareham had a rector who at least was a very tough man. The Rev. William Wake was for the King when the town was against him and during the reading of a proclamation on the town cross the rector saw fit to interfere. Someone hit him over the head with a pistol butt which damaged him a bit and next day a man shot him in the head so that a bullet lodged in his forehead, and as he lay on the ground he received two large sword cuts on the head too; it makes one wonder what his head was made of because he was still alive a few days later when he was sent to Dorchester jail. When he was set free he promptly joined the King's army as his treatment might well suggest to him, and was taken prisoner at the fall of Sherborne Castle. With others he was stripped naked and sent to Poole where the plague raged amongst the prisoners, and later he somehow managed to be in at the end of Corfe Castle where once more he was made a prisoner. It is good to know that such a gallant rector lived to return to his living at Wareham. He had been taken no less than nineteen times and it just showed what the people of Wareham could put up with.

Many people died on the part of the wall called Bloody Bank, but such things have happened in all places which have a long history; prophets and witches and some of Jeffreys's victims. The town was so used to alarms that once the militia turned out to repel an attack of several thousand men who did not exist. But such affairs do not belong entirely to the past; perhaps the Home Guard manned their posts during the several occasions in recent years when the enemy was more than expected in that quarter. The history of Roman Wareham may not be finished yet.

It was in a little public-house up West Street that I had my first experience of being offered a loving cup. I was quite a youngster and can hardly believe that the profferer was expecting to gain anything by it. As I entered the small bare wooden room, walls, tables and benches all clean plain timber, an old man sitting there pushed his cup across to me and said, "Drink up." What he meant was that I should take a drink from his cup while I waited for mine to be brought to me, the theory being that a newcomer must be so thirsty that he needs a few swallows at the moment. Then when the new drink had been brought in I should hand it over so that the old man could recover the amount I had taken from him. There may have been some point in the procedure in the old days when sometimes it was necessary to wait a long time to be served; such houses were open from early morning until late at night and customers might be few and far between while the people of the house had to get on with their daily life.

I have not been asked to drink from such a loving cup for many years now and do not approve of the idea from a hygienic point of view, and many old men carried on what might be a hospitable gesture because they often gained by it. They sat with the dregs before them until a likely customer came along, and I know from experience that it is not easy to refuse what might be a gracious act, while if the newcomer found it distasteful to drink from the cup offered him, he was also likely to dislike having to offer his own cup in return and

Milton Abbas village

so paid for a whole fresh pint to repay the gift-swallows offered him.

Wareham was always important to Purbeck folk because the Big House was situated there, the House which loomed over so many people's lives. No one wanted to end their days in the workhouse but there were some who frankly took it into consideration. Men have told me, "You want to get a good south window and be able to sit in the sun. There's nothing much wrong with that as they can't make you work like you'd have to outside."

That was a philosophical way to face old age, but it sometimes was a pointer to a man's character; the man who planned to "get a good south window" was likely to be one who had grabbed such advantages as he could all through life. He was ready to push some other old man out of his place in the sun, while the less grabbing did not expect so much and so perhaps took more steps not to have to enter the Big House.

Yet it was never beyond possibility for anyone; old parents were not only put in because they had made no life savings but sometimes because they had done so, if the greedy children could get hold of it while they lived. It is surprising to think of all the old people I have known die there, and it is perhaps proof that there has been social change in my life-time because it is not now looked on as such a terrible disgrace, to either the old people or those who put them there. Workhouses, under any name, should at least be as honourable as any cats' home for decayed ladies.

There was one thing that I know the old people dreaded more than just going to the Big House, and that was that when they died their children would not "bring them home" and put them in their own village churchyards. They did not want a pauper's funeral at Wareham as so many worthy people had had through no fault of their own. Alone, unhonoured and unsung, society had taught them that such things counted and yet could then forget them entirely because they had lived too long.

Of course many people did fetch their old people home and there was one old man at Swanage who had fetched many of them in that direction at night in a donkey cart. He used to

Church Hill, Swanage

tell of how once he stopped at the Half Way House between Wareham and Corfe Castle after dark; there was a wide open space before the house and all kinds of vehicles have drawn up there and a donkey cart was quite in order. He went inside and ordered a drink and told the landlord to take one out to "the man in the cart," and soon there was the sound of a dropped cup and the shaken landlord crept in out of the night. All he could say for a long time was, "He's out there in a box."

Chapter VI

PURBECK

The Isle of Purbeck might easily have become another water-surrounded piece of land like the Isle of Wight some sixteen miles to the east, with perhaps no chance of a geological freak like the Chesil Beach to join it up with the mainland. As it is the Isle still has a good stout land connection and it does not appear likely that it will achieve full islandship without some major upheaval.

But it has always been something of an island in outlook, with the alleged backwardness of islands, yet there is no exact political or administrative boundary to it, and the physical line can be disputed. The generally accepted line is the River Frome at Wareham which puts that town outside it, and a vague line drawn towards the sea somewhere at Arish Mell.

The unbroken line of Purbeck stone forms the southern edge to the sea and Poole Harbour on the north provides the indisputable boundary there. Only Swanage and Studland on the east expose a soft flank to the sea and there the vested interests tied up in the summer resort business would pit their strength against the water if it threatened to nibble them away.

Swanage is the only town, and that boasts some 6,000 or so inhabitants who have now thoroughly learnt how to live on mankind. In peace time it is crowded during the summer with all the kinds of people who like to spend their holidays in the company of others exactly like themselves, and in the winter the local people have learnt to live on their summer fat and taking in each other's washing. Between whiles they bicker amongst themselves as to how far the town should lean towards an exclusive watering place or pander to the holiday resort idea with up-to-date amusement provided chiefly by the penny in the slot.

The dispute has gone on for a great many years with a great victory to the exclusive faction when the town turned down the project of a short breakwater which would make the wide bay a safe harbour, for a safe harbour would attract trade and trade was not wanted there. In fact the non-traders have gone as far as to put on record that Nature herself always had the place in mind as an exclusive holiday resort; but they have forgotten that even in living memory there was a small but healthy sea trade in Purbeck stone which had a good market in the days of sea transport

The town used to live on its stone trade and still could if such trade was not deliberately pushed into the background and hidden up in providing houses for retired people to die in. It appears to have become more exclusive to wait hand and foot on sick and ailing old people who are waiting to die than it was in supporting or even allowing a healthy stone trade which in its day has supplied much valuable building material. Perhaps running a resort is nearer the modern ideal of becoming some kind of blackcoated worker—but what a let-down to men's characters and their belief in themselves.

It looks as if the personal author has cropped up a bit there, but those quarrymen who have dug and shaped the stone from the hillside and cliffs for many centuries are a personal matter. Somehow in the long past they obtained by charter the right to the mineral wealth of Purbeck, and in the face of much opposition have nursed those rights from father to son inside the Company of Purbeck Marblers and Stoneworkers. And those rights included nothing except being allowed to earn a living by one of the most laborious forms of work, but it had resulted in a strangely independent and perhaps proud body of men who had shared in the glory of British architecture when that term meant something.

From one point of view it would be interesting to discover how that company of workmen weathered Cromwell, Monmouth and Jeffreys, the Georges, the various Enclosures and even Victoria, yet have been pushed aside by local authority in the shape of bakers and grocers and an occasional retired admiral or colonel, who prefer the sick and the dying, as long as they can pay for dying there.

Of course it is the same kind of struggle that appears on the surface in many coastal areas which want to reap the rewards of being by the sea. Bournemouth has often pulled its skirts away from industrial Poole, Weymouth has fretted about the naval harbour of Portland, and Brighton and Hove have not always seen eye to eye.

The particular brand of local politics does not greatly matter as, like many other seaside resorts which want to remain exclusive, Swanage is doomed as such because it will go on spreading until there is nothing but town and roads within reach; when that time comes it may discover that like a dried up oil-boom town its chief reason for being a town at all is gone. It will be a pity if the town does link up with the villages of Purbeck lying along the stone belt. The villages were built where they are, each with its public-houses and church, to give the stoneworkers a complete life.

Yet at one time Swanage, or Sandwich as it was then called, was a village coming under the wing of Worth some four miles to the west looking towards St Aldhelm's Head. Worth sent a priest to Swanage to do the church work just as the modern vicar may visit an outlying parish church to-day. But there are stories of church affairs around Worth; there is a Saxon doorway built into the fabric of the Norman church and St Aldhelm built his indestructible chapel out on the rearing headland after seeing his daughter shipwrecked in the tidal race below it.

The ghost of a walled-in nun is said to appear around the foundations of a religious house and a pot of gold and the usual golden coffin are said to be waiting for a finder. A local man has a good story to tell of the finding of that pot of gold. He was a house repairer and in tinkering with an inside wall he broke through into a hidden space that had been built up, and there was the pot. He described that pot and it must have been a delightful thing in itself; tall and of goodly proportions, it was probably an interesting relic of old. It stood in the space all alone as if it had been placed there with care and not just left as forgotten rubbish and the finder said he knew he had found the pot of gold, and the shock was too much, he swayed on his feet and fainted under the stress. When he recovered he opened it up and it was full to the top with old pieces of iron, like old shut-links and things that any countryman might gather in a lifetime. There was no gold and there is a possibility that someone long before had walled it in with a joke in view, a joke which did come off as planned and may have caused the joker's shade to have a nice feeling of well-being.

The old-time value of every bit of arable space is shown by the lynchets running around the steep hills towards the sea at Worth. Such lynchets are fairly common in south England but not often on such steep hills; the amount of labour put in them points to there having been very little other available space or a tremendous density of population. Nor are the hills ideal for growing crops, not only because the soil could never have been very rich, but because the hillsides being exposed to all the bleak sea winds meant that every crop was thoroughly flattened even if it survived the conditions. Certainly only people willing to cut every stalk by hand would ever consider it and probably it is Neolithic work. Worth village is the ideal site of human habitation and feels that it has always been lived in. The spring of water there is in itself enough to keep it always so.

There are people who will debunk all stories of south coast wreckers, but foreign sailors believed in them not so very far back. At one time I knew an old man very well who in his youth had gone down to the sea near St Aldhelm's Head to help a Spanish ship that had come ashore. The ship had been flung well up on the beach and the local men offered to help the crew ashore, but to their surprise they were repelled with naked knives nor could they convince those Spaniards that they were trying to be helpful. The language difficulty looked like holding up the rescue until someone had the bright idea of fetching the parson down from Worth, who as an educated person should know enough Latin to calm the fears of the crew.

It would have been interesting to know just how that old parson got in touch with them with his rusty Latin which had come to him by the overland route with Norman William's followers, and which he had perhaps laboriously picked up in his youth; yet it was acceptable to those Spaniards fresh from Spain, and recognizable enough to tempt them to leave their stranded ship and venture ashore amongst the people they had been afraid of as wreckers. Also it shows how easily such foreign blood used to come ashore along the coast, as at one time there had been no authority to pack those foreign sailors off to Southampton to be shipped home as soon as possible. That would have been nobody's business and some of them might have stayed there if only long enough to leave a descendant.

Quite close to where that ship came ashore the sea did throw up some unknown blood which obtained a hold there, and it is a romantic story well worth putting on record. After a night of storm someone visited the beach near Kimmeridge to see what the sea had brought ashore and there lashed to a spar was a baby still alive; the boy was taken to Smedmore House and in course of time grew up there. Such a thing could not happen to-day because authority with a great capital A would step in and whisk the unknown away into another unknown, and at least fill the poor mite with inoculations against every possible disease. But the boy did grow up at Smedmore House and rightly enough was given the name of Smedmore; in later life he owned a business at Swanage and his son was a well-known character there.

Perhaps there are descendants of the Smedmores still there and they would be strangely lacking in imagination if sometimes they did not think of their totally unknown ancestor, lovingly knotting the rope around that small figure with the ugly sea licking at their doomed ship, and then the test of will needed to cast the spar adrift with a prayer that it would land safely. The chances were more than a thousand to one against the child surviving, but for once fate was kind.

That such castaways did sometimes make a safe landing is more than hinted at in the name Lander in this country; there are many on the Dorset coast and it is believed by some of them that their fathers at one time were thrown ashore and at once were dubbed landers and therefore Landers. It is easy to imagine a stranger coming ashore, and perhaps, unable to speak a word of English, he would insist that he was some unpronounceable name but to the local people he would be just a lander and his descendants still are.

Looking down the valley towards Swanage, and in a prominent position to be seen from a large part of Purbeck, there is a collection of houses called Gallowsgore where at one time the gallows stood in "the crook in the wall." It was there that the victims of Jeffreys's tour through the west suffered after the fiasco of Monmouth, and it was a sentimental spot to us of later generations because our fellows had died there. But some years ago a motorist who had averaged about seventy miles an hour on a considerable journey, crashed there at some incredible speed because, we will believe, he slowed down somewhat in passing through the towns and villages. Then within a very short time the County Council in their wisdom pulled down the wall and destroyed "the crook in the wall" which had nothing to do with the accident at all, the inference being that it was all right to hurtle pointlessly about the country with a lethal weapon like a powerful car and the fault, if any, was at least 300 years old in placing a gallows in a recess.

Gallowsgore on the Purbeck stone belt looks down on a valley of rich farm lands contained by an abrupt range of chalk in the north, and that chalk hill would have cut all that part of Purbeck from any sight of the mainland except that there is a deep gap where Corfe Castle stands in its ruins. Through that gap can be seen a section of heathland running to Poole Harbour and beyond that the hills of Dorset rising shoulder to shoulder into the distance. Seen through the gap the view stands out in detail like a picture on a screen and in the full red light of a summer sunset it is well worth watching.

The village or small town of Corfe Castle used to be a kind of capital of the Isle, which was natural with the mighty and well-planned castle standing there between the hills controlling everything. It has been said that the town lies at the foot of the castle like a faithful hound, or that the castle regards the town as an image might notice an admiring worshipper. I prefer to think that the massive bulk has sat there in the break of the hills for a long time watching how each year on Shrove Tuesday the quarrymen came down out of the Purbeck hills.

When the castle was a proud stronghold well able to defy the whole world, it had little heed for the puny men whose skill had reared it there; the quarrymen held their yearly meeting in the Town Hall under the protection of the castle and perhaps then it did demand something very like adoration. But all through the changing history of England which the castle saw, the quarrymen still came every year to carry out their customs as a right, a right which ignored even the power of those who looked down on them.

Fathers brought their sons to see them entered on the records and the mighty castle was indifferent. In time those sons brought their own sons in their proper turn. Uncounted men died at its feet to return to the dust and still the castle was indifferent. But through the years treachery and rottenness worked its way inside the imperishable stone that put such an unbroken face to the world, until the strong stone was riven and much of it crashed down the steep slope of the hill. It was then that the proud fortress became merely an interesting ruin and children poked their fingers in its joints, while the quarrymen still continued to come on Shrove Tuesday without glancing up unless to pass judgment on how their own forefathers had worked the stone of its making.

One version of the popular story about Edward the Martyr is that he was stabbed to death by his stepmother while drinking a stirrup-cup of wine at the castle gate, but there was no castle there then and the incident occurred outside a hunting lodge on the site. The beautiful Elfrida did remove him in that manner to make room for her own son and it does not spoil the story that it could not have happened on the actual bridge still there.

Nor is it likely that the story would have come down to us in such a romantic guise if the wonders which soon followed had not had so much heavenly light about them. The beautiful widow of a king, the hidden knife, the treacherous goblet which crashes to the ground, have such a position in the high places of our history that they are almost commonplace. Too many thrones have been lost and won by their aid to make Edward a martyr by them alone.

If Elfrida had promptly buried him deeply in the ground his name would scarcely have reached us now and she and her own son Æthelred might have an honoured place in our history. But she allowed him to be taken into a blind woman's cottage nearby and covered over with some mean clothes with the idea of hiding his identity, while the old blind woman would sit up all night to watch by the dead. Before the night was through the room was not only filled by a heavenly light which shone through the wooden window shutters into the road outside, but it even penetrated the old woman's blindness until she could see all the details of her room. In that way she knew that the unknown body in the mean clothes was the king himself. It does not matter if we believe that a heavenly light could touch the royal clay, somehow the legend grew and it was not long delayed for the body was treated as something holy when it was eventually buried at Shaftesbury.

King John also carried out much evil at Corfe Castle and used it as his treasure house as well as a prison; its strength made it very suitable for both purposes. Many people walked up its hill to the dungeons where they never saw the light again, but royalty has always needed the payment of such heavy costs in other people's lives.

Even viewed to-day in its ruinous state it is easy to see why it was never taken by storm and eventually fell to treachery during the Civil War, when Lady Bankes held it against all the improvements in military methods of attack. And without wishing to detract from her gallant defence, "A demy cannon, a culverin, and two sakers" could not have had much effect behind the massive walls. The picture of the kitchen maids pouring hot ashes down the attackers' necks from the towers is more in keeping with military methods of even 1643.

Also that an officer of the garrison sold out in 1645 has an authentic ring about it, and then Cromwell blasted it into the ruins we can now see. To-day the stoneworkers of Purbeck have every right to feel proud of the work of their forefathers. The stone facing of the bastions is worth seeing not only because of the careful smoothing of the outside face to prevent even the slightest grip, but each stone fits so closely to its neighbour that not even a penknife could be driven in the joints to provide spikes for climbing. And it seems that some of the secrets of cement-making have been lost since its building, as some of the towers were blasted out of their position on the hill and rolled down where they can still be found. The shock of explosion might have shaken the stones apart and rolling down the steep slope completed the work, but there they still lie in solid masses just as the builders placed one stone on another while the mortar shows no more sign of crumbling than the stone.

It has been said that the people of Corfe Castle "were prone to idleness," but perhaps that was too hurried a description of them. It may be that they are aware of being so steeped in history that a man as he walks about the town feels that events are moving towards him instead of himself having to seek them out. They had a Court Peculiar, where there was a distinction between being drunk and merely drinky. John Pushman, Anthony Vye, James Turner, John Rawles and George Gover were all haled before it for various reasons, and it is well to know that such men are still there in the neighbourhood to-day even to the same Christian names.

But Corfe Castle not only concerned itself with upholding the moral tone of its citizens; in 1686 it gave two shillings to two seamen who were driven ashore at Chapmans Pool. What tragedy of the sea had occurred at that dangerous place? And their hearts were good when they gave sixpence to a woman whose husband was in slavery and a whole shilling to a one-armed soldier. Two and sixpence to five Dutchmen, and three and six to ten Frenchmen, with a shilling to three Turks and a like sum to one American, show that the authority of Purbeck where shipwrecked seamen were helped was at Corfe Castle. No other suggestion could be given why such various nationals from distant countries should present themselves there at the Town Hall. And that one American received as much as three Turks proves that it was no heartless official bound in red tape who interviewed them.

Of course the whole of the original town was built in Purbeck stone and even to-day there are few intruding materials to upset the harmony of the streets. It is not so very different from when the whole life of the place flowed down the two streets towards the castle. Some of the houses still have their strongrooms where a determined man would have to be smoked out, or a chamber over the doorway so that callers could be examined from a safe distance. Corfe Castle has still much to attract those who can appreciate worthwhile things.

Once through the hill of chalk there is an entirely different country; the stone and all the rich valley is left on the other side and the sandy wastes of the heath come right up to the chalk. Geologically this is part of the New Forest, and at once the force of environment on people can be seen. Gone are the independent Purbeck quarrymen, proud of their traditional skill, also the heavy peasantry of the rich farm lands and the nondescript people who live in towns. The people who live on the heathlands are leaner and it is easy to believe that they are drier and healthier than other people. Sometimes they boast that like their cattle they have to be hardy enough to subsist on furze stalks; the cattle do respond amazingly to better food and there is no doubt that the Purbeck heathcropper would exist in tolerable comfort under conditions which would wipe out most people.

Nor is it surprising that environment can produce a type of human. Environment like the New Forest produced a forest pony that did well there until Queen Victoria mistakenly meddled with the breed. The Forest heifer is still well known in the south as a doer well able to stand up to the disease-ridden conditions of some modern dairies. The heathcroppers' animals have much in common with the Forest types and although there is no actual forest on the heath the man himself would fit in like a native Forester.

The heathcropper does not necessarily live on what he can produce on his own homestead to-day, and it might be possible to find one who journeyed daily on a motor-cycle to work in some town garage, but at home they can never relax their vigilance against the encroaching wind-blown sand which would swamp them after a few years' neglect. Their holdings need constant nursing and in that way they have a harder time than the New Forester, where the trees prevent a lot of sand movement; but the heathcropper seems to have had none of the rights which the Forester so rightly stands up for, nor would any public body or Queen Victoria feel called upon to speak for them.

And there was a small but healthy china clay industry, until the War Office took over the land, which produced a very good pottery material. This as usual has often been overlooked by British potteries although the clay is of such good quality that foreign ships, especially Germans, came up the harbour to tie up at the ancient quay at Arne. But perhaps in the marvellous ramifications of the commercial world small British ships at the same time did creep up winding water channels to pick up German clay, for the ways of the commercial world are very strange sometimes.

The clay industry is also responsible for the "bottomless" Bluepools between Corfe Castle and Wareham. The clay is often found in pockets and the result is a deep hole in the ground which in time fills with water, a few trees planted around and in certain lights produces an unreal blue pool of still water. Given a little time and a certain amount of ignorant talk, plus a few bathing fatalities, and they are believed to be bottomless. Apart from that they are still worth seeing because such unreal colouring is so unexpected in this country.

On the heath towards Studland, near the harbour mouth, there is a great rock which has caused a lot of speculation. Like a great anvil it rests on its mound of sand with no other rock near it; of course there is the usual legend which, however, in this case cannot be so very old. The Devil flung it at Salisbury Cathedral and it fell short. It is interesting that it fell short, as that shows that the Devil was somewhere in France and not so very long ago it was well known that he would be quite at home there. So the legend in that form is moderately new as such things go, and in any case Salisbury Cathedral was not built until 1220–74; it is strange too that the legend makers must have forgotten that the culture which built the cathedral there had come directly from that part of France where the Devil must have stood to make his faulty effort.

So the legend is pretty poor stuff compared with some which have been handed down. Also the rock itself is easily explained. There is no other such rock near but it is a sandstone of the type found on the heath, and although it now stands on a mound of sand, that is because the sand around is always being blown away by the winds which cannot move the rock.

It is easy to leave the Isle of Purbeck from the heath because it is a very short distance across the mouth of Poole Harbour, although there do not appear to be any local stories of hardy people swimming across to save the ferry toll. There is the new and modern private motor road from Studland which in truth does save a few miles of trundling all around the harbour, although why, with the alleged speed and cheapness of motor transport, it should have been necessary to spend untold wealth in making a road and installing a big chain ferry to save so few miles, is hard to say. On balance the saved miles seem very poor exchange for all the trouble and effort needed to put the road and ferry in action; the time factor does not come into it because in many cases it is quicker to travel all around the harbour than it is to queue up to get on the ferry.

And in the name of progress the new ferry had to wipe out the ferrymen of long standing, although it was not done without a great deal of effort. A family had run a ferry there for generations and although there was no road across the heath there were enough passengers who walked or cycled along the hard sand of the beach when the tide was out. It was a livelihood and those ferrymen hung on ferrying after the new chain ferry was in action, nor could the new ferry company stop them in law at first because they had the right of long custom, in fact perhaps they have the right now, but in time the company got them by preventing them from landing passengers on a private shore.

There must be good stories of odd and mysterious people taken across to the Purbeck side and put down on the windswept tongue of sand three miles from anywhere, and how often did a fugitive suddenly appear there on that same tongue of sand and wonder if the creeping boat or the hunt would reach him first.

One Purbeck man who had soldiered in his youth was on his way home but delayed to spend his substance in the urban delights of Poole. Penniless, he stepped into the ferry and allowed the ferryman to take him over, and being a young active fellow he leapt ashore and then had the decency to stop and make his offer. "I haven't got any money, so if you want to take it out of my hide you can—but you'll have to run as far as Studland before you'll catch me."

CHAPTER VII

DORSET WRITING

THERE is one thing about Dorset which has already given me considerable mental exercise before attempting to put it into writing. It would be so much easier to leave it to those who know and accept, without necessarily understanding, that there is a Dorset mentality. Those who will not accept such a thing so often then maintain that therefore it cannot exist. What does not fit into the well-worn grooves of their own minds and habits can have no meaning for anyone else.

Yet the same people will openly declare for such things as the north countryman's belief in, and affection for, "brass," the idea that a Scotsman is "near" and that somehow a Jew. is very clever in money matters, and there are very few people who do not recognize the charm of the Irish or that the Welsh can sing together in a way that no other Britishers can. But write or mention anything which suggests that a Dorset man may see, and even more feel, things that are not open to everyone, and at once there is a torrent of disbelief or ridicule from the stupid and perhaps an alleged tolerance from the better behaved.

To take the things mentioned above about other Britishers; they can be proved true or untrue and no one would be rash enough to say they always worked out, but they are accepted on the whole. I myself have been more surprised in how true they are, but I am well aware that I often approach a subject at a different angle from most people; I certainly have the Dorset mentality. But I have lived amongst north country people in their own environment and soon realized that a tremendous amount of their thinking really was governed by the money substance; they made no pretence that it was otherwise and although they would claim that that was more honest and open, few southerners would envy them the apparently hard realistic outlook which colours practically every

95

contact they have with their fellows. It is a real cult which they have carried too far until they are very proud of it. If they only knew how limiting it was both to themselves and others!

The Scotsman often encourages the idea that his nation is "near," and in many cases that tendency is the result of excessive and deliberate caution in money matters rather than any meanness of character; but careful habits have a way of growing out of control until what started as a "good" habit becomes at least a mild form of vice. It is so seldom that anything to do with money has any improving value on a person and that is one of the things which cause feeling against the Jew. He does seem more clever in the gathering of it and then seldom resists the temptation to show that he knows how to use the power it gives.

The charm of the Irish is too obvious to need any more said about it; how many people can resist a blarneying Irishman? And although more people than will admit it are unmoved by Welsh singing, there is no denying that the Welsh have something in them that most of us have not. And all that just gets me back to the Dorset mentality which some people do not accept. I do not say understand, because there is no need to understand it any more than some of the other tendencies, and they are not all of the kind that result in a stocking full of money which most people will accept as a worthwhile aim.

Perhaps I must do a bit more accepting and believe that only such tendencies are worth acknowledging; a heavy thick woollen stocking full of hoarded wealth has a more real substance than the feeling a man can get when sitting tightly on the ground and just being part of the earth. That is what people will not have; they are either jealous or frightened when some men can commune with the things that make up the earth. Those same people will admit what they call the forces of nature although they like to use a capital letter as if they have formulated a new religion, but they do not like to read or hear that someone can, and does, give and receive a love in the mere act of being in contact with those forces.

A reviewer once wrote a few worthwhile things about one of my books, but he also wrote, "this is another of the dotty

Dorset school of writing," and whatever his intentions were it pleased me, for I was in very good company as any real book lover will know. Another reviewer of the same book also had a few good things to say but she "thanked God that she herself was a hardheaded Yorkshire woman." And whatever else she meant she was enjoying the idea that her head was "hard," her thinking was hard and she liked being that way; her mental arteries had been conditioned by her northern culture until she could no longer accept the warm pulsing force of the earth through her being. She was like so many people who no longer feel the forcing beat of any unexplainable urge and therefore they deny such things ever exist, they limit themselves to what they can see and feel, or as they would prefer to express it, to what their mental achievements will allow them to accept.

Perhaps they forget that in this alleged rational thinking they are pushing aside a great deal of real literature which has been accepted over a long term of years and a great part of the world's surface. Thomas Hardy's novels are literature in the best sense and yet at the time they first came out they caused a not always favourable excitement. These two things by no means necessarily go together, as much of the writing which is exciting to look forward to, and exciting then to read and discuss, does not last very long outside its own circle as Hardy's always did.

Of course the times were different. With all the so-called efficiency of modern publicity there is little sign that the ordinary reading public ever gets prepared for a book in the way it used to. It is not that the writing giants no longer exist or that the readers are less voracious, but most reading is much less leisured and there are so many easier ways of getting the same emotions tickled. Also readers as a whole have far more knowledge of what does happen in the world and, even more, they have learnt that nothing is really surprising. Victorian society could at least be shocked and aroused in a way that is impossible now and in many ways it was less developed.

I know very well what that may bring down on my head, but to maintain otherwise is to deny that education has made any advancement in the meanwhile, and I mean education in the popular sense which is admittedly more in the field of

H   97

Stone quarry, Portland

knowledge than anything to do with the word culture. The
ordinary reading public has picked up very little in the way
of the virtues of mankind, but it does accept in its everyday
thinking many subjects which were either banned by a
warped moral idea or were unknown in a public way.

It is difficult now to understand why anything Hardy wrote
was censured in any way; the trouble must certainly have been
in the mind of the readers and not in the writer's. I read many
of the novels as a small child with a very raw and tender
conscience because I had been brought up in a backwash of
Victorian morality which may have been worse for being at
best secondhand and out of date, but I do not remember
experiencing the slightest shock or the budding sensual excitement that a small male child can have.

But I do remember the excitement of getting hold of
another Hardy book, and my reading was not governed by
any such thing as that because I liked reading him it was just
automatic that all his books could be obtained. A Hardy was
an unexpected treat to me every time and never failed, and
some local feeling may have entered into it as would be
natural to a Dorset boy who was more than interested to have
a live Dorset writer writing about live Dorset people. For
they were still living people to me although the books were
anything around a quarter of a century old when I got hold
of them and Hardy had written a good deal of the past.

But his people walked along roads and looked down from
hills that I might have known, and spoke and acted exactly
as people I did actually know. Any of his people might have
lived next-door to me and he wrote of them in a way I would
have known the neighbours. He could not surprise or shock
me as I knew what he wrote was true in every way. He had
the Dorset mentality, his people had it and I had it, and in
all his readers he could not have had a more perfect connection, for he wrote of me.

I was the Mayor, I was Tess, regardless of sex, age or
social standing; it made no difference that I was a youngster
in the process of being brought up in poor circumstances, his
writing was like the unfolding of my experience, imagined
and yet to be, entirely possible and probable. In fact some of
what he wrote has been just as much my experience as the

money I have earned and the women I have loved; and it was not entirely experience at second hand because Hardy was the perfect link between those experiences and a boy child walking on the same earth with the same thoughts and ideals.

That is what partly makes up the Dorset mentality, something that is not afraid to accept; it can be called soft-headedness as against the hard-headedness of the north or the smartness of sophisticated town life, or just the dotty Dorset school. It is not as if anything that Hardy wrote could be specially picked out as dotty or that his career as a writer was not just as firmly established as that of any other man : from all that I have read of his life I have found no evidence that there was anything muddled about his business methods, his working and home life or his married state. It would be hard to pick on something he did or created to show that there was anything abnormal in him except that he knew that there were deep, strong forces abroad in the world which he felt and could hand on to those who shared the same level of experience. I say level of experience rather than state of mind, and the experience has nothing to do with worldly experience as understood by most people. Nor does it matter whether the level is higher or lower or advanced or retarded in time; naturally many people prefer the easy assumption that it is retarded, forgetting that Hardy was more than able to hold his own as a man of the world.

There may be cause for saying that Hardy was a pessimist, but why such a thing should have been brought forward almost as a charge against him is hard to understand. He did not have that effect on many of his readers and it hardly concerned the outside world if in himself he did not show great zest for life.

He belonged to that intermediate stratum which so often does not grasp life in the full and there is evidence that he was weak enough to "feel his position." It may cause a snort of rage if I suggest that beyond being a master of the written word he had very little of the great man in him; so many people will be able to say that they saw this or that in him when they had personal contact with him whereas I did not even set eyes on him as far as I know.

99

But they were seeing him as the famous novelist or poet and in such circumstances it is so easy to read a lot into a few words or a knowing glance. Would anyone have sensed any power in him if they had interviewed him across an architect's desk while dealing with the repair work of a small-town church, or bothered to make the obvious effort needed to engage him in conversation at some gatherings if they had met him as some unknown?

He had many of the drawbacks that go with an upbringing in a small business world. His father was a stoneworker with evidently much of the natural assurance that so often goes with that dignified calling, but the young Thomas was placed at school in a way which points to the conclusion that his parents had ideas of setting him up in the world beyond hammering stone. Apparently a profession was to be aimed at and it is not surprising that the studious youth landed in an architect's office.

If he had remained there and eventually become a shining light in a small-town society he would have been looked on as a success in life; it is no small thing for the son of an artisan to make his way into a profession and Hardy would be well aware of the fact. Yet when he had reached a position which left a small-town professional man a long way behind he still seemed troubled that he did not possess the correct "standing" to go everywhere. That is where that artisan-professional-business outlook fails a man; he starts off on such a frail rickety foundation, being just a shade above what we can call the real peasants, and yet has to discover that he really has no start at all.

Whereas the real peasant starts from the firmest foundation of all and although he is usually a man of a thousand inhibitions, the social inhibition often does not exist for him at all. He may be totally ignorant of the enormity of social offence but the very fact that he does not think along those lines often relieves other people from the limiting influence such things have. What is surprising is that Hardy as an artist did not always have enough assurance in himself to stand on his own as he was well able to.

It has been suggested that his great interest in Napoleon was because he himself had the makings of a man of action in him; but any man less likely to take action would be hard to imagine. And to me it seems quite unnecessary to wish that idea on him; he was a creator of people who lived for his readers and such a creator does not need to possess the same qualities himself.

There is one thing that I might have taken up with him if we could have met on anything like equal terms, in spite of the pleasure it would have given me to speak to the connecting link between his people and myself. He repeatedly brought forward the theory that some of the good faces full of character which he saw and met about the country were the result of loose-living squires of the previous century.

As a writer I know that he would like to play with it as an idea. It was the basis of Tess and she was important to him, but it puts the stamp on his own artisan-business-professional upbringing more than it puts the squire's stamp on the country. Of course squires and many other men have sown offspring in places where they should not, and always will, with perhaps no real harm done on the whole, but a good-looking face is usually the result more of an inner assurance than any superior blood given and received in some underhand manner.

He might have come to reject that idea if he had lived long enough to see the better-looking children of to-day when there is so much less of that squirearchy business, and few of even the poorest of children have the first important years of their life blasted by all the fears that were encouraged until very modern days. Many of them are as free and open in their outlook on life as any roving squire, with the better food and living conditions, and it shows itself in better looks and the more important personality being allowed to shine out without the veil of fear.

Or even if he had got to know the stoneworkers of the Isle of Purbeck, where for many generations a squire has caused less excitement than a louse in a shirt, amongst them he would have found no faces which belonged to the galleries of the Big House, but he might have found steady eyes in keen faces which would have stared down at the small student of mankind. And he was impressed by the stoneworkers of Portland who had a similar outlook to the Purbeck men. His *The*

Well-beloved deals with the way in which three generations pursued an ideal woman, and he could not have carried round the idea that those three generations of men wore faces which were the outcome of some squire's indiscretions.

If his theories were anything more than the musings of an author on a subject he had enjoyed using, they were just as far-fetched as mine may be that he himself showed that as a man he was neither fish nor fowl nor good red herring. Because so often a small business man's son who has had some success in another sphere has resulted in just another such person as Hardy appears to be in portraits and is revealed in what has been written about him.

I have nothing to say about him as a poet although there is plenty of reason to believe that he himself wished to be known as such as opposed to his deserved fame as a novelist. The lack of ability to appreciate his poetry is entirely in myself.

The Dynasts should be a great thing to me, but it does not come off at all, and even in some of Hardy's simple little things like,

> "The lamps, just lit, begin to outloom
> Like dandelion-globes in the gloom . . ."

or

> "And the wind flapped the moon in its float on the pool
> And stretched it to oval form;
> Then corkscrewed it like a wriggling worm;
> Then wanned it weariful."

Such things do at least make me see the dandelion globes losing themselves in the night as it creeps across the grass and make it very important to wonder if they will be there when the light looks over the eastern edge to see if it can find them again. And I know that the moon struggles in countless ponds every clear night when the wind stirs down the grassy banks or across the slimy mud to press on the face of the water. But that is not getting the value of poetry, as poetry, nor finding the pleasure that many people get from the play of words in themselves.

It is never safe for one person to assume that another is or is not a happy man, but the world of his day seems to have quite decided that Hardy was not one, and some of the things he wrote go a long way to bear out the idea. But from what I know of his old age I should say that it was the most delightful period that any man could achieve. Obviously he was not one of those men whose old age is little more than a reminder of all the things they can no longer do or even want to do. Men can become soured by success simply because it comes too late for them to use the advantage they imagined would go with it, whereas with him there was little of what he thought worth doing well which could not be done at eighty as at thirty.

There is one thing which according to my reading of him would count quite a lot in his later life. He had long reached the stage when any shortcoming in his social standing could be ignored by other people. He was accepted and honoured by everyone who mattered, not only as a famous writer who had produced good work but also as a man who must be taken into account.

He was working up to the end of nearly ninety years of life and not just squeezing out the tail end of what had once been a good man, as so many people do after it would be a mercy to their reputations if they confined themselves to the equivalent of pottering about the garden. It would be impossible to detect the hand of age in any of his last work. Even his handwriting did not fail. Any writing man will envy him his last years of life, full sight, hearing and spirit, apparently no vain regrets to fret him, serenity which was the growth of a lovable character and not merely the weakness of flagging powers. Complete mental health and the sort of quiet physical health that might have let him live on in comfort for another decade.

And Dorset was his; it had grown to love him in return for the love he had for the actual soil and rocks, the friends who tended it and encouraged it to fructify and even the dead lying thickly around the churches. Certainly he himself would not mind lying in the ground he loved so well and instead of wandering abroad to watch how life progressed he could wait there while the force of living things came to him. He would never be far away and I for one cannot feel that he ever went out of touch.

It is a great pity that his humorous old bones were not allowed to rest at ease lying near a quiet old church, where other old people could wander by and perhaps face their own passing with no more fuss than he did. Other Tesses might have wondered if he looked on at them with approval and they could be sure of his understanding, and virile young men might occasionally feel his eye following them down the road and swagger a bit, which would harm no one.

Certainly the peace of trees standing by and the smell of the earth should have been his, and the hushed faces of children staring down. The hiss of rain and the scalding sun should have fallen on the earth covering him, to be followed by the biting black frost of winter and every few years a covering of snow. The gentle brilliance of flowers should have pushed through the sod above him and wilted to lie silently across him with the quiet reverent leaves in their time. All these should have been his for ever as he had earned them by giving so much to all who valued such things; and what did the world give him with all the pomp of best intentions? It took his body, which was already on the way back to the good earth, and twisted it in the force of fierce flames until it had obtained the necessary handful of sanitary ashes which it could then accept in its own dusty Poets' Corner. To be thus honoured by the nation is a rare event, but who can believe that he likes the curious eyes of idle people who, many of them, do not even faintly know the man Hardy?

Of course Thomas Hardy was the highlight of Dorset letters, whom the rest of the world has been glad to share. But he was by no means the only one. He himself once said something to the effect that the county had perhaps been backward in some of the industrial development which he had seen ramping about, but he believed that it had given its share of men who had advanced the thought of people.

I wrote that last sentence by putting into my own words what I could recall; at least that was what had registered with with me a long time ago. Then feeling dutiful I hunted it up, as his own words must have been so much more gracious. He had said that the province had not been commonly considered remarkable "for the energy and resourcefulness of its natives" but "ventured to say that in the arts

and sciences which soften manners and tend to make life tolerable the people of South-Western England had certainly not been behind those of other countries."

I think that I am right in assuming that he meant what I had registered, that Dorset had a place in some of the good work of mankind. He believed that the work of his old clergyman friend, William Barnes, was worthy of much more attention than seemed to be given it; there is no doubt that Barnes had been a great help to the young Hardy who had ideas not altogether connected with becoming an architect.

Of course such a boy would soon figuratively be sitting at the feet of our county scholar who lived almost next-door. Barnes has sometimes been dismissed as a dialect poet, but he was just the man to excite the mental appetite of a young Hardy. In many ways Thomas Hardy, with an Abbey funeral at the end of his life, never surpassed his old friend and master. Hardy's own words when he saw Barnes carried to his grave and the sun flashed a farewell on the polished wood, give an immortal touch to the old man which may be more lasting than a small plaque in a dusty corner.

The words were Hardy's, but the flash was from Barnes. Those who will say that the immortal touch was supplied by the genius of Hardy must remember that he *and* Barnes had built up the contact from which the flash came.

Again I must refrain from saying anything about a poet's work, as although I can find delight in the pictures that Barnes's verses give me, that is only part of what can be found in them. And once more will not be too often to give Hardy's own picture of his friend, when in a memoir he wrote, "Until within the last year or two there were few figures more familiar to the eye in the county town of Dorset on a market day than an aged clergyman, quaintly attired in caped cloak, knee-breeches and buckled shoes, with leather satchel slung over his shoulders, and a stout staff in his hand. He seemed usually to prefer the middle of the street to the pavement, and to be thinking of matters which had nothing to do with the scene before him. He plodded along with a broad, firm tread, notwithstanding the slight stoop occasioned by his years. Every Saturday morning he might have been seen thus trudging up the narrow South Street, his shoes coated with mud or dust according to the state of the roads between his rural home and Dorchester, and a little grey dog at his heels, till he reached the four cross-ways in the centre of the town. Halting there, opposite the public clock, he would pull his old-fashioned watch from its deep fob, and set it with great precision to London time. This, the invariable first act of his market visit, having been completed to his satisfaction, he turned round and methodically proceeded about his other business."

In that we can see the old man far more fully than did many of the people who actually saluted him on those market days. There may be a hint that such an old clergyman might have been just a bit of a trial to those who were not altogether sympathetic. We see the dust or the mud of roads when a rural home really meant coming in contact with such things, and the hand of Rome is suggested in the background by Barnes trudging up South Street to the four cross-ways. It would be far from Hardy's intentions, but he has firmly placed his old friend in a position where it would be an easy step to come to think of him as a rather tiresome old man. Those publicly regular habits can be achieved by people of little mental development when they discover that the world has learnt to expect them.

That the sons of a Welsh clergyman, put down by the law of chance in a Dorset parish, should write Dorset literature as distinct from writing about Dorset, is something which could be taken to support the idea of a Dorset "school" in the way there has often been a painting school which is said to follow a style laid down by some master. But apart from the novels written by the Powys brothers, they have so often written about Dorset people who are definitely moving along through life with the Dorset mentality, that their genius must have recognized something that seemed good to them.

These Welshmen accepted the county and the people and were able to feel it in the same way as the Dorset-born Hardy with his line of ancestors behind him. It exists in their written words and can hardly be a trick they have picked up. Like him they would not be surprised to fall in with a god walking over some hill, not necessarily a young virile god after the style of Pan, who might burn the grass with his cloven feet as he rushed off to rape some female, but perhaps a middle-aged god who could discuss the speed of modern transport.

There again it may be said that "the dotty Dorset school" has shown up in my writing once more. How could there be a god of any sort abroad on the land at the same time as modern transport? At least, such things belong to the mid-night hours and only disclose themselves with burning bushes or the smell of brimstone.

But can anyone believe that Hardy would have been startled to discover such a being sitting waiting for him in his study at Max Gate, or rushed into print with a sensational story which would bring so much misery about his ears? And would either of the Powys brothers embarrass an acquaintance by bringing the public eye on their next meeting? No, the gods move abroad sometimes with no idea that they are no longer believed in, and their rare meeting with mankind is none of their seeking. When they sit down or stand at a man's elbow as he ponders, it is because in a weak moment they have drawn near another who has tuned in with them.

The only god or power that the world will accept to-day is one with rules and regulations like any registered society; a committee of some sort will alter and argue over these rules and observances and bring them up to date at various times to suit the particular outlook of the moment. But how many people will accept the fact that a god without rules and regulations may be walking past the house at any moment or that the world itself is a big female goddess stirring in her sleep?

Theodore Francis Powys once called himself a priest, and he loved the broken things of the world because a god was likely to sit down beside them. And even God with a capital G would be more likely to sit on a broken field roller which had been worn out in its long life in caressing the seed to give its best out of the soil. Surely God is to be found there more often than near the brassy altar in a church building.

But if a few men feel it in their bones that a god may have just crossed the road and may be still looking over the bridge around the corner, those men are said to be soft-headed when they talk or write of it as some people do about making money, or doing good or harm to other people. But such gods do walk round in Dorset and a few men know that they pass.

CHAPTER VIII

THE CHURCH AS A STANDING
STONE

IF I ask you to come along another Roman road it is not because I have a Roman complex, but if you live down in our part of the world the nineteen-hundred-year-old fact of Rome strikes you wherever you turn. How satisfied some of those administrators, who are lying about there in their stone coffins, would be if they knew that the plans they drew up and must have put on paper are still working to-day and working well.

Somewhere in their Office of Works in the new town of Durnovaria, they had a plan which showed a road to the sea in the south. To-day that road still stretches four miles as straight as a gun barrel, and providing you go along it at a reasonable pace you will be seeing just what they saw. There is still little that shows the years between you and some portly official going about his business; Maiden Castle on the right, unchanged since it no longer gave the official a headache; stubble fields, or growing corn according to the season; grass on the hillsides neither shorter nor longer than he saw it; and still the road going straight ahead until it reaches the heights overlooking Weymouth.

There the official would see a change; his road used to drop straight over the hill like a curtain and now makes the street of Upwey at the headwaters of the River Wey. I am going to call it Upwey instead of the Upway now used. Surely it means the upper part of the river and if we have the Weymouth we ought to have the Upwey. Upwey is a very pleasant place and that steep roadway which is their street is interesting to examine. You will find that for many genera-tions that terrific hill was the main road between Weymouth and Dorchester. Remember, all through the many long years when road traffic was horse- or oxen-drawn, everything had to take the shortest way up the hill; there was no nonsense about that road and when I say that it went straight up, it did go soaring above the horses' heads.

There are people living there who will tell you about certain horses and what they would take up that hill, and we must agree that even the people who walked had to be in good order. Then when the new internal combustion engine came to take all the hard work out of road traffic, the iron monster whose parts were tireless and which carried the boasted power of ten or twenty horses in a small box, then thoughtful men said they must have an easier road and so it now sweeps out in a great curve and comes back to the Roman straight line at the top.

And the official who may have stopped his chariot on the brow of the hill to fill his eye with the great expanse of sea in the distance, would receive a shock when he saw that all the land below him was apparently covered with buildings. Upwey has become one with Broadwey and achieved the dignity of a Lighted Area and Weymouth is not far away. The poor official would be all the more startled because the four miles behind him had offered so little to surprise him, and if he did attempt to drive down the new curving road his nerve might be shaken to read a great notice at every few yards saying "Slow."

All the way down those warning words stare the driver in the face, and they are needed because few roads can so suggest that to get out of control would mean taking a leap into space and landing far out in the open. But the Roman official would have the last triumph for, just where the old and the new roads meet, he would be startled to see a railway train pop out of the hillside. They planned well because modern railway engineers could do no better than follow their original line.

When we come to Weymouth I find that I am not very good at writing-up seaside resorts, and they do rather speak for themselves. But Weymouth has much that can or should be looked for in the business of providing for holidays. Popularized by George III, who startled people by putting his royal person in the cold wet sea water, it has a splendid beach and the sun can shine there. Nor is the rising moon, reaching its reflection all down the length of the Channel, a thing that anyone could easily turn his back on unless he is engaged in one of those mild flirtations that spring up in holiday places.

But it can rain there in no gentle manner when a gale pounds over the Chesil Beach at the back, and if fate is unkind and sends an east wind to whip the sea front, the place can be anything but a health resort. And of course, as so many of mankind must spend their holidays where people know how it all should be done, Weymouth has a place in the front rank and the crowd on the sea edge and the beach are quite thick enough not to let the individual holiday-maker feel he is being left out of anything. He can have his boats, his bathes, his swings, his beer and his cockles, and go home from there as poor and sunburned as from any other place.

And Weymouth has one very real attraction that many resorts would or perhaps would not give a lot to have. The Royal Navy is there at Portland Harbour and sailors have a great way with them. A sailor may come from the chalk ridges inland or the grim streets of a mining centre; he may be a Kensington man or a north country farm hand, but when he is a navy man he becomes a sailor in the best sense of the word. We used to sing that all the nice girls love a sailor, and it seems a well-known fact that a sailor has a wife in every port, and "Jack's ashore" means something in the places which know him, while they themselves like to make the lay mind think that every sailor is irresistible to the ladies. Also they will drink a town dry and then perhaps playfully take it to pieces, and being the Silent Service does not mean that they are mute in the midnight street.

But with all that or because of it, the sailor is the Britisher at his best and long may he remain so and look on the land as his playground. Treat him fair and he is the easiest man to get along with without the least thing ugly in anything he may do, and even his voice raised in song is less untuneful than any other group of the British race, leaving the Welshman aside for the moment.

With all the man-made sea works and sea defences around Weymouth and Portland, there is still nothing to compare with the mathematical perfection of the Chesil Beach which is really all that makes the peninsula possible and perhaps urged man on to compete. And there are many local opinions about the long narrow stretch of water held behind it; East and West Fleet are often considered very dreary places to go, but they have every right to be considered one of the marvels of the world.

By any ordinary reasoning the sea should be beating on the low-lying inland shore of the Fleets, and how long would the land last if a few great gales got to work on it? Yet the waters held there are as smooth and quiet as an artificial lake, just the setting for the proud swans at the west end at Abbotsbury. It is said to be sea water entering at the Portland end, but the rise and fall of the tides outside do not seem to affect it and it certainly is not so salt as the sea itself, because I have tasted both.

Abbotsbury brings the high land back near the coast again, where the chalk presses down against the Purbeck and Portland beds; for a long way back towards Upwey there is an upflung stone ridge where it would seem natural to come across caves pierced by our ancestors in our cave-dwelling days, but that cold hard Portland bed was too resisting for them.

Back inland behind Portisham where he was born, there is a monument on Black Down to Admiral Hardy in whose arms Nelson is said to have died; anyway Nelson's "Kiss me, Hardy" has a place in things, for all that Bernard Shaw does not like it. Poor Admiral Hardy, or Captain Hardy as Nelson knew him, has not had a very fair deal. Hardy was and still is a good old Dorset name and another came into the public eye in a way the gallant Admiral never achieved. A writer, named Thomas, became the Hardy who jumped to people's mind when they used the name, and while he still lived and still wrote words in the peace of his study near Dorchester, people went out to Black Down to pay respect to his memory. For such is the kingdom of the public's affection. If another Dorset man of that name succeeds in capturing the people's regard, he will sometimes be given credit for Thomas's work and from that have them paying homage at the Admiral's monument. For the mind of the public works very dimly at times when it works at all.[1]

[1] On 7th November 1949 even the Ministry of Town and Country Planning explained that the site is "one of the most prominent hills in the western part of the Dorset downs, and is crowned by the monument to Thomas Hardy."

Along this bit of coastal area is that undefinable line where soccer and rugby football meet and mingle, Portland being definitely a soccer stronghold, while at Bridport rugby has assumed the ascendancy, and as you go on into Devonshire they know no other ball but the oval. It is not always a good policy to get on to that usually so safe subject of football in the villages hereabouts; you may find yourself suddenly very much in disgrace as the game is taken much more seriously than their politics. With the very best intentions you may be made to feel the most outer of outers, so it is well to glance at their local field before you open your mouth from one village to the next.

All through this writing I have never said anything about turning aside to look at the churches of the county, and I am very interested in the church as a building and have looked at hundreds with, I believe, a seeing eye. Also the real Dorset man revels in that church feeling which stays around the place where so much of man's life has its being. I have all that feeling and have sat for hours in or around one trying to live again all the hopes and sorrows which have filled the grand places.

But churches have been written about so many times, and local guide books can usually give particulars, especially about the restorations of the last century which upset the balance of so many and gave the rich persons who supplied the money a cheap way to get their names recorded. But as every village and even group of houses is accompanied by its own church, the power of the Church as an establishment is proved down every valley and on every hillside.

And if I say that I see these erections in the same light as I see the ancient Standing Stones now alone in their silences, I am attacked as an unbeliever, whereas it is my very belief that makes me see the small church tower standing up in the distance as another standing stone, to be respected as the other man's right to believe in the power of the unseen.

It must be remembered that most of these old churches which many of us love, even if for different reasons, were set up where they are when the people did go to them and bow down to a graven image. That has died down now to the merest nod to the altar, although I have seen older women

bend the knee in a complete curtsy as they pass it on some legitimate business like sweeping the floor or tending the flowers, and is there so very much difference in placing the flowers on a stone altar in a St Mary's, to putting them on a Standing Stone? I have never set up a Standing Stone but I have helped shape up the stone for a modern altar and there was very little that was spiritual in our feelings as we worked.

Of course the church as we know it is a comfort to man, but it appears that man always set up something to mark his belief and after all does the church tower or spire differ so very much from the Standing Stone pushing up through the earth? Rather than lose one church in all the county I should say let there be others put up wherever a few people gather together to live in harmony, but don't put them on the corner site of the busiest cross-roads : choose the site where the soaring tower reaches furthest towards the sky.

Nor is the Church very encouraging to its followers now; for one thing so many of their biuldings are kept locked to the real worshipper, and they have the real excuse that people steal, although that surely shows that the Church has failed in its teaching to cause such a serious weakening of the respect due. I have had an old studded door set in a stone porch which my people in the stone trade actually made centuries ago, locked in my face because the parson was in a hurry to get to his tea. The cycle has turned full circle and worship has once more become the function of the appointed priest who sets the hour and the order in which it is done.

And for all my interest in their churches I have seldom had a parson offer to show or explain to me what had been put in his charge; most of them show, and some of them admit, that they are professional men doing a professional job in which they have learnt the external observances. They know how to deal with the trained worshipper and would welcome him in scores, but there are few less courageous men than the usual run of country parsons to-day, and it will be a long time before they refill many of the empty seats where at one time the ordinary people found something that gave them courage and comfort of heart.

Despite the poorness of what might be called the box-office returns of the Church, there is one thing that is heartening

Mill at East Stoke

to see if you are lucky enough to be near a country church when it "puts on" something that attracts people to its door. It may be one of those nestling in a chalk valley or standing in a green meadow with the flat old river bed stretching on either hand, or better still a small rocklike church near the edge of the sea whose squat tower has been a landmark for thousands of seamen during many long centuries.

And although going to church service in our country has come to mean, in most people's minds, a trickle of drab sober people with blankness and disapproval on their faces rather than anything hopeful or at all spiritual, the awe of God long ago became a thing merely to pay lip service to, and they were going to a dark cold church through a drizzle of rain in keeping with our fogbound culture. That is what going to church meant for millions of us, and if we know anything about our past social history of not so very long ago, it was not the people who made the Church like that, but the Church which deliberately brought that atmosphere about. Blame the Puritans if you like, but it damped people's hearts and caused them to take their pleasures into a kind of underground movement.

But now there is a great difference, because despite our gloominess about our weather there are many glorious spells of good warm sunshine when it is good to be in England and Dorset in particular. And if you come across an old warm church set so perfectly in the environment it has itself helped to create, no more and no less a part of the scene than the crowding farm and manor and barn, the cottages and bit of the village street with an inn; if you come across that, when some special thing has called to the people, say a harvest festival when the thanksgiving is not too long delayed because the plural parson has to fit it in at the most convenient time for himself, then you might see a country church service which is not drab and unduly sober.

Yet it is not the Church which has altered but just that the people have again found courage to be gay, and much of that springs directly from the fact that the women are no longer afraid to wear bright and many colours. Less than thirty years ago we thought that colours should be quiet and there was an unwritten rule that only certain colours ever went together.

Women prided themselves that they could wear only one, and that within a severe range of shades. Now, thanks to something, probably an eye on the sales returns, we are offered all the best and brightest colours there are. Cheap and machine-made as the stuffs are, they are one of the most promising things which have come back to us, mainly because the sheer delight of them has given our women the wish to be gay.

Watch four girls cycling towards our imaginary church service : in the distance there is a sudden moving patch of colour weaving towards us against the soft greens and browns of the background. People can say that the girl's taste is wrong because she may wear six different colours, but the weaving group as it sways up the hill is a success and as they come near they are laughing and happy because their own brightness has heightened their joy in life.

And the small children of both sexes are good to see, whether they are sitting quietly inside the church scattered about like bright flower petals, or screaming in play outside when every possible colour streaks across and across in a dance of pure good life. I once saw something that brought that goodness of life to mind for all that my cynicism suggested might be behind it. I met a bishop walking on a high Dorset road and he was moving in a light blue cloud of flowing stuff with his cross and his staff glittering palely in the afternoon sun. Beside him walked a brown tweedy farmer and a blue-jerseyed fisherman and straggling along behind was a small crowd of children dressed with all the bright colours we have been given back. And the bishop's black head-dress and the few women's black clothes set the balance which made it a good sight. And when that old man smiled and raised his hand to me in greeting or blessing, I felt that the countryside was good and also that the Church could really mean something in our daily lives. God was not something that was shut up in a box until the lock was unfastened and the light switched on.

Still again brought into being by the Church which seems unaware of what it could and should mean to us, I once looked down on something very close to what we can believe happened around the Standing Stones of long ago. I saw a white-clad parson apparently blessing the fields and the stream, for war had once more shown that the almost uncouth word fertility meant something more than sex, and the holy things of the Church had been brought out in procession and shown the fields and barns which it was their business to make prosper.

It did not matter that the man who carried the high wooden cross was a rather poor sort of man, he too was a frail human at times, but while he carried that cross he was serving something higher than mankind no matter what name we give it. And as the parson turned away to do his job well in all the corners, his white splash of movement was followed by many gay colours which should be seemly to any god which helps nature. Chief amongst them was a group of Land Army girls who have done so much to bring colour to the fields, and surely their dress has been the most attractive uniform of any of our women's services; certainly the well-cut short greatcoat has been the most merciful to the figure and the somewhat girlish hat not quite so much an addition as any of the other hats and caps.

I must ask the other women to forgive me, but I do love to see the Land Girls; everything about them is so suitable for the work they do and for the countryside, and they fit in the picture as Robin Hood might if he came back. Nor are they only workmanlike and doing a good job well, and rightly no woman wants to be just that all the time; if one of them has a good figure and she is dressed in her pale breeches and green jumper and stockings, I declare that they show a woman in a very attractive light.[1]

But it is not only their decorative value which I wish to put forward—although I have more to say on that—for many times in the early winter mornings I have been overtaken by a covered lorry and when it has exposed its rear the space has been filled by the prettiest picture a man would want to see as the Land Girls go off to work, and as they stoop over a potato field in that back-breaking work they look like a flock of gay birds. Yet again, recently many of them have adapted a pure white scarf as their field headdress and this gives them

[1] Since this was first written the uniformed Land Girl has become something of a rarity.

something of an austere impression which they are far too human to strive for, but the trend is right and gives hope for the future because those young women are feeling their way towards what is right in the right place.

But the greatest success of the Land Army is that they have largely broken down the countryman's resentment, although that should not be so very surprising because women once had a great part in agricultural pursuits. And there are many farmers who have employed them—I know several sour, hard, money-loving men who have never given an inch to anyone or anything in all their long lives, and yet they have come to speak well of the girls who have been forced on them.

In fact the very success of the girls has had its drawbacks for them. If farmers have come to realize that they are doing a good job and are willing to work hard, some of those men have also come to look on them as almost as good as a man about the place, except for the difference between forty-eight shillings and three pounds ten shillings a week.[1] And undoubtedly many of them have worked willing girls too hard and too long; you can see the girl in her off time and think it good to see how clean her life is and how it suits her English face, then later towards the end of the day's work the bloom may be gone and her hands gently tremble with exhaustion. For so many of them are too young to ease up, lest they are thought to be slackers. Being young they apparently soon recover when the work is over and the bloom comes back, but some of them have been driven too hard with the shortage of good food on the land which produces so much of it.

Surely when it comes to gratuities and such rewards the Land Girls have been treated as shabbily as country things usually are, but some day we may again have men in power who know where so much of the country's real wealth is so hardly won. Power and those who seek it now pander to the towns which contain the bulk of the voting strength, forgetting that the country should come first, as it could and would go on even if town life became impossible, whereas a town would not live a week without the fields to feed it.

There is scarcely a person in the whole nation who has not

[1] 1945.

felt the pinch of the food shortage this time, but a moment's reflection proves that we have never got right down to rock bottom, because in any country which has really experienced famine or even been anywhere near it, we always read of how the towns make expeditions or raids into the countryside to obtain food. We have read it about every country on the Continent which was occupied by the enemy and the enemy countries since they were beaten; always the townsman has to turn to the countryman he so often derides in normal times, to save him in times of real stress.

That is the law of nature which towns would do well to bear in mind, and it has not operated in this country all through the long war years except in a few cases where it was convenient and which do not alter the rule of that real stomach-driven urge of existence. There are thousands of country dwellers who have literally had to live on their ration of things that were in short supply, either because they lived far out where to reach a shop was something of an organized expedition, or their working hours were so long with un-imaginable cycle rides to and from it, or because the village shops were allowed so small a quota of the few extras there were.

I know what I am talking about in this matter because I have lived both in towns and right out in the country. In the towns, of course, there was not the advantage of fresh garden produce but such things were usually obtainable there, and it was always possible to find something under the heading of "teas" and that term could be stretched to almost any length. Anyway there was always a cup of hot liquid of some sort and an occasional feed of fish and chips for the real sturdy queuers. British Restaurants and works' canteens were a thing of the towns and something was done to make up for them by giving farm workers an extra cheese allowance, but it is not everyone who lives in the country who comes under the heading necessary to obtain that, and it is not exaggerating to maintain that the food situation proves that as a whole the country has not yet come down to the real pinch. When it does you will see people swarm out to get the swedes and turnips and potatoes which the countryman works a lot harder to produce in his shorter spare time.

Of course the man who could afford to live in good hotels could manage to live pretty well, but that could be either in town or some country inn; the pinch came when he had to move about on his business and if that was out in the hills and villages he might actually go foodless until he got back to a town. I have done that and been thankful to get a loaf of bread from a bakehouse or van to fill up the empty space, known to so few people, that can come in a man's body, but I can assure you that the standard loaf by itself is a very uninteresting food.

I had never intended to write about food again, especially as Dorset has not got any real native thing except the Blue Vinny cheese, and are we ever likely to see that again? And my reason for leaving the subject of food alone was because once I wrote about it and mentioned the satisfaction I had sometimes got out of making a real man's-sized supper on bread and cheese with a big raw onion, washed down with a quart of stout or beer. Such a supper has something about it for the man capable of it, and he should be able to exclaim with some real heart- and belly-felt gusto, and perhaps dream some glorious dreams afterwards.

But I have paid enough for writing of suppers like that, as I found that when anyone invited me to a meal, any meal, I could expect to find onions taking part in it; perhaps big baked or boiled ones at lunch, or a good meat pie saturated with the flavour, and once a great unpeeled raw onion beside my salad plate when there was no other onion on the table. And fried onions are apparently served at all times and with anything, sometimes crisped up toughly and sometimes a wet soft mess of grease.

Of course all this comes under the heading of the host's kind intentions and must be appreciated as such, while it is accompanied by a triumphant smile, "Oh, we know how you love onions, we have read what you wrote about them." Nor in face of such consideration with the meal before me can I in decency point out the great difference of such onion dishes during normal mealtimes and the state of a hungry man at bedtime. Then the fumes of the newly cut onion, *and* the stout, jog his jaded senses and juices, and his whole mouth and throat is outraged by the combined foulness until the somewhat rotten flavour of the strong cheese is as mild as new milk.

I can still enjoy such suppers at the right time and hope to for some years to come, but that does not mean that I like living on an onion diet or that onions are necessarily anything to do with Dorset, and any other food that I exclaim about shall be such things as a wonderful chicken cooked in some cunning self-basting dish which returned all the goodness of all chickens. Now that was a dish worth writing about, as was a plump steak slowly baked with several potatoes and tomatoes and the whole smothered with field mushrooms and I believe a touch of Worcester sauce and other things all mingling their flavour together.

Juicy joints have their points too, as have baked trout or scollops stewed in a sharp sauce. After all, bread and cheese and onions with stout or beer are a meal that a lonely man can get for himself in a few moments, and perhaps at a time when the violent jerk it can inflict on him may have to console him for the lack of more delicate delights.

It is to be feared that Dorset has nothing outstanding like the Scotsman's haggis, for in spite of all the hilarious jokes about that dish and my being a Dorset man, I have found it good eating and believe that it should have a good food value. There used to be what was called a Purbeck pudding which as a child I used to eat solely out of an exaggerated kind of national feeling, but have long ago decided that to call it Purbeck was a serious insult as it was a sodden mass of soaked stale cakes baked between thin pastry.

And although there are plenty of Pudding Corners and Pie Crust Lanes, they do not necessarily mean that Dorset people had a high standard of living. I know a short row of cottages prominently marked as a prosaic Providence Terrace, but which is always called Pie Crust Corner because for more than a generation now a large family have lived there who at week-ends, when they have money, squander most of their substance in big feeds. One of them has told me seriously, "I tell you, you can't get up round our corner sometimes for the smell of cooking. I tell you we believe in living well up there." He forgot to mention what everyone knew, that later in the week they might not have bread to eat.

The Providence Terraces, Jubilee Buildings and Victoria Places are by no means confined to our county, but it is interesting to notice how often they crop up in every small town and village and how in nearly every case their style dates them as much as the actual date, if it is fixed up on them as it usually is. They have written all over them that they are the expression of some provident Victorian who often lived in one of them himself where he could keep a watchful eye on his neighbours and tenants. Probably a happy man that he had achieved the stability which that age thought it stood for.

Those Victorian landmarks are as different from the peasant growth of most old cottages as they are from the present-day semi-detached Council house type and the box bungalows. The old cottage that we still have was seldom put up by peasants but it was still the type and is rarely hard on the eye, no matter how hard to live in; it fits in because it usually grew out of the ground on which it stands, but how often has it a damp course to keep it dry or head room to give a man air, or windows to give enough light? And if there is a supply of running water is there a drain to take it away? It is one thing to live in such a delightful cottage during the week-ends of a good summer, but quite another matter to spend a whole lifetime fighting against all their drawbacks.

The Victorian structures are one degree better in that they have water and drains and nowadays gas and electricity, but how often have they any room with the slightest degree of comfort? Unless one counts the front room or parlour, and Victorians never used that except for very special occasions, and therefore it was alien to cosiness. The lived-in part of the house was usually a very draughty place where all the washing had to hang, because Providence Terrace often meant that the essentials were very cramped for room.

For all their unsightliness, and their greatest aesthetic offence is that they will never mellow into anything else, the Council house is usually warmer and drier and, when the rent is not too big for the one family to raise, the tenants have more space of all sorts. And even if their general flimsiness makes it possible to share cooking smells and the wireless programme with the neighbours, they escape that wretched back-to-back idea where the whole row of outside sanitation stood, or literally sat, with elbow to elbow except for the plaster partition.

I take the risk of being severely sat on by many of those who damn all modern building in the country—so often the very people who have a wide choice in where they live themselves—because I believe the price, although great, is worth paying in better living conditions for those who have the misfortune of having to live where they can. And of course so much of the blatantness of the new building is unnecessary if only more use would be made of the local material of each district.

There is a friend of mine near the Hampshire border who built his house from the land around him, and had to fight almost every difficulty that could be put before him. Stan had worked in a timber saw mill and bought up all odd and spoilt boards he could get until in time he was ready to set up his house. There was no question about his having permission to build a house but there was great objection to his using boarding of different widths. He had spent years of his spare time sawing and shaping it but still a plank about two feet wide had to go next one half that width. The result was something that might have been approved if he had used it in such parts as the gable ends or been able to describe his house as half-timbered. But it was all timbered, and he had not put his boards through a machine to make them all alike and therefore acceptable to our times. He rightly saw no sense in wasting an inch or two of good stout planking. The local authorities bothered him as much as they could until the greater problem of war gave him respite, but he is living in a house which with reasonable care will be good and sound for several hundred years; it is not built with any view to being a thing of beauty, but there is not one thing about it which is an offence to the eye in any way.

And Stan is the nearest thing to Massingham's English peasant that I know. Most of his days are spent in the woods felling trees and leaving them lying around looking like huge ancient sea animals stranded there by some freak of nature. That is the way he now has to earn a living, but his real way of life is running a few animals on a few acres of a smallholding; he would rather spend his time hauling with a couple of horses as he used to, and although his team might be odd in shape and size he could get more work out of them than some better horses were willing to give.

Perhaps willingness was the most striking thing about Stan's animals, willingness to work or fatten up for the butcher, and it was all done by caraway seeds, and an occasional dose of worm oil. The little mare of his team was a sturdy creature who did her share of a day's ploughing and when he took her out of the traces she reared and jumped and flung up her heels in sheer high spirits. Of course there were men who said that they would give her another hour's ploughing until they had taken that out of her, but their horses never had a jump in them after a day's work. The gelding he had bought as a bargain because the animal was in a bad way. Certainly it could scarcely drag a sand cart out of the pit until Stan had had it a few weeks; then instead of having to coax it to make the effort he had to get up and ride and hold him down tightly as they came out on the hard road. There certainly was a great change in what that horse was willing to do after being brought back into good health.

The bullocks which Stan was fattening were like most such animals and were willing to eat and chew in blissful ignorance that their good life was all a means to an end, but they really shone as if the fat on their bones polished their coats and they still rushed to the food as it was put out to them for all that the edge of their appetites might have been taken off.

And the secret was just caraway seeds, mixed with their food and which made them eat heartily, for often some animals will lose their appetites when they are too well fed no matter how good and wholesome the food is. That and Stan's horrible worm oil which may have been just a country-man's magic. I am not at all sure that the preparation of that was as simple as he said, but he used it and certainly his animals were a picture to look at and full to the brim with life. I will give it as he told me.

When ploughing he hung a tin can on one of the handles and as he saw a big earthworm he stooped over without stopping and picked it up; when he had a horrible mess in the can he transferred them one by one into a clean bottle and when he had filled that he just corked it down carefully and put it away. That was all, and he could show the result as an almost clear oil-like liquid. He declared that it would make any horse eat its head off and come out in those rings which are said to show that a horse is in the best of order.

He was a great believer in the caraway seed treatment for humans too and ate all he could himself. He certainly was virile enough in many ways, but it became hard to get food of any sort to fill him without having recourse to anything that made him eat more. I could not find out if he ever tried the worm oil on himself but believe that he had enough faith in it to make even that possible.

There is one domestic arrangement which I have never seen equalled in any other part of the world, although it is said that other south-western parts can show the same thing. And it may be better to leave the reader to decide what points there may be in the arrangement.

An ordinary small country cottage, built to house only one family even if it was in the days when families might mean anything, may have the usual little house up at the end of the garden as it should be, well away from the house and as secluded as may be. It is often a snug retiring place so very different from the embarrassing upstairs convenience of the modern house where the retiring occupier often has his own relief shattered by encountering a pained face outside and slinks away to the sound of savage bolts being shot home. The business is different up the cottage garden; a gentle stroll to see how the seeds are growing or the apples ripening and a quiet withdrawal with no harsh rattle of bolts. And the furnishings of the place may be different, for despite it being a one-family concern there may be seats for two side by side; I have mused on how much of the fable of the three bears is founded on real life, for companionably close together there may be two different-sized seating places, and I have heard of even three. Yet the progressive trend of human thought can be seen even there, if privacy in such matters really is progressive thought, for one of the covers may be permanently fastened down.

Yet who could object to a small little low seat built specially within reach of the maternal guiding hand? I have liked to think of all the generations learning some of the niceties of life there, perhaps even the grounding of team work instead of the hectic rush of stamping feet. There must still be many women whose gentlest memories of their mother are woven around the quiet moments up in the small house at the end of the garden.

Chapter IX

WILD LIFE

WITH the rest of the British Isles it may be said that we have no climate but plenty of weather, which is not much use when you are trying to pick a fine afternoon for a picnic but it does make for interest. We are fogbound. Are we? Well not compared with one or two foreigners I have met. We are always wet and damp. So we look cleaner than most people.

One afternoon as I was pushing a bicycle up a long hill between high overgrown hedges, I was idly thinking of all the different people who had belittled our climate in so many different ways. Other countries had hotter suns, or drier airs, fresher winds or colder snows, anything that was better, or perhaps worse to my mind. It seemed that British weather was drab and dull and uninteresting; everyone knows what has been and is said about it. Whereas in truth its very uncertainty and sudden change ought to be at least more interesting than the bitter cold and blasting heat of some other countries where the weather is supposed to be reliable for months ahead.

Anyway, between those hedges I was moving through the heat of a mild oven and the white blaze of the sun was burning the skin of my shoulders through several thicknesses of clothes. Those who say that an English sun never burns are right in one way because I knew that at the top of the hill I would come out in the open air where there would be a fresh breeze that I would feel beneath those same clothes, but where I was and at that time the direct sun was almost frightening in its power. If hot countries mean such conditions all day long there is everything to be said for our weather.

But the heat of that particular hour of that afternoon was exceptional; there was thunder about and the north-east was building up a towering grey and black cloud which might or might not move overhead. That was part of the fun; I might get overwhelmed by a few minutes' downpour which would ignore a reasonable raincoat, or have a grandstand view of it passing by the hilltop. Or even more as I hoped, that solid-looking blackness would disperse without venting its power on the harvest waiting all around to be carried.

For twenty minutes the threat remained, apparently waxing and waning as grey arms pushed out from the mass and retreated, but in that time I had crossed over the hill through the expected cooler air and got into a valley where the road was lined with trees on one side. At any moment the rush of wind might thrash those trees about until the sheer weight of water held them down; there was no shelter there, quite apart from the slight danger that lightning might choose to strike the very tree where a wet man was crouched.

Then the English weather asserted its right to be unpredictable and it started to rain without any wind. There was time to dismount and put on the raincoat in great hopes that the threat now overhead would remain just a threat. And the next corner of the road opened up some farm buildings perhaps a quarter of a mile away. There was the promise of shelter there, but as if the cloud above saw a victim escaping the wind arrived and the water was turned on.

It was a race; the hot dry road became a swift stream and the lightning played down as if to make sure of me first; the thunder could be ignored as the empty sound it was, but I arrived at the farm buildings in a blaze of what might be music and a marvellous display of fireworks and fountains. Fortunately some big barn doors were open and I rode in regardless of what welcome might be there : an irate farmer might object to being startled, or his dog defend his possessions to the last.

But of course nothing like that happened, the barn was empty; nor was that important as I stood looking out. The sheer weight of falling water cut off the view a few yards away and the harvest standing in stooks opposite seemed to cower down into the mud from which it so recently had proudly drawn itself up. Certainly it was the sort of weather a farmer could pray to escape.

Yet to the onlooker with no direct stake in the value being destroyed before my eyes, there was something grand in the effect. The thatched roof poured a transparent curtain of water behind which the lightning played, and the sweeping rain literally lashed at the earth as if it was not content just to pour down. Of course it was just a thunderstorm of which the weather forecast had warned us, and while I was thankful to have escaped the worst, as it eased up, the thrill was taken out of it. Instead of still being an interested onlooker I became a thoughtful person who hoped the storm would be followed by a clear spell rather than be the break-up of the day's weather.

At such times a man's thoughts wander while he waits, and as I watched the stream of flood water running by it was surprising to see how uneven such a tarred road surface could be. It was just a country lane where the little traffic ran chiefly in the same place and had apparently worn two hollows where the wheels came; probably the tar had merely been brushed over the old original gravel surface and I was looking at the wear of wheels of past generations. There are still plenty of country lanes like that which have not yet been given a camber and the tarred surface has set in the shape of the old wear and tear.

Anyway the main current of my new river flowed where the wheels ran and it was like looking down on an overflowing river in miniature. I saw how the big bubbles caused by the heavy raindrops came gliding into view and sweeping past, and I wondered if any of them remained unbroken long enough to survive while in sight. It was not easy to keep any particular one in view nor see why it should deliberately seem to shoulder its way out of the main current to cross over a shoal where it rocked dangerously in shallows hardly able to float its light burden.

Yet time after time I watched a bubble cross a troubled shoal to regain the main channel which swept it swiftly away, although so many of them disappeared on the way. I could pick out one thirty feet away on my right and watch it surmount all the dangers to which it was subjected until it became lost to me the same distance away on the left. Sixty feet of adventurous travel for a thing less substantial than the silk of a cobweb, yet of course many of them disappeared as I watched them and it dawned on me that although I was

watching the apparent destruction of air and water, the atoms of which they were really composed were not escaping.

For I was living in a world which had not yet become used to the atom being shattered, and my air bubbles were displaying surely the weakest kind of explosion of which we know. Yet the day will come when some man will find a way of smashing the atoms of which my air and water is made up. Some day either by accident or design some man will touch it off and perhaps the whole force of nature as we know it will change.[1] We have all seen how quickly a poisonous bomb crater recovers and have been told that signs of grass soon appeared in Japan where the atom bomb was tried out, but when all Dorset can be put through an upheaval that will put any natural earthquake in the shade as we have been promised, will it have to remain a bare solitude where an occasional investigator explores or will the chalk and clay and stone and shale make a new geology for other men to write about and find traces of vaporized bones to prove that the Dorset man really existed. And will men have to write of a new botany when life starts again?

Of course all that was the idle thinking of a wet man who wanted to get home and change, but the new and now tremendously important need for a world nationalization pushed itself forward. What was the use of holding tightly on to the quality of being British, although that virtue of never admitting that we were whacked has so recently paid such handsome rewards to the whole world who trembled for us and themselves after us? It is no use playing that idea down : Britishness saved the world, that stubborn streak in our ancestors which no others have got yet although the newer nations may one day be glad they have it in their stream.

If all that will have to be put aside what place has this series of County Books, and why am I hoping my volume will make Dorsetness stand clear and stubborn in the light? But I will start by coming to the rescue of Devonshire, although it will end by putting that other regionalism of the town and country before the light. Can we Dorset and Devon and town and country men boast and brag and scorn each other without

[1] I have since been given to understand that water and air, and most of the things we know, are simply a kind of atom ash, from which the activity has long since departed.

Bridport

bringing an atom bomb on our heads? I hope so, as it is more pleasant to play with bubbles.

A newspaperman said that he had made the pleasing discovery in a small Devonshire village that they called the latest engine of war, with unconscious irony, "this yer platonic bomb." Now I take it that at least he was a man who had become a Londoner, a townsman, even if he still claimed to be Devonshire, someone who went to a small Devonshire village at the week-end and heard them talk of this platonic bomb, and with the ingrained conceit of the smartened town wit he jumped to the ignorant conclusion that the yokels were mixing up their syllables.

And of course that is what the smart Londoner does assume : that the cider drinkers mumble in their cups and their ears are too filled with wax and hair to get it right, even if the newspaperman carefully explains. I have seen it done so many times and it is all so cheap and easy. But I could point out that that is the great joke; no one will ever see any enlightenment break out on the countryman's face because that is their way of living up to the part expected of them.

Anyone might playfully mix up the words atomic and platonic because the connection is not too subtle, but whereas the Londoner would do it with great care to see that no one really thought that he was making a personal bloomer because his greatest fear in life is that his wit should be thought clouded, the countryman in that Devonshire or any other village plays his part and looks as unconscious as the suggested irony. Unconscious my foot! That newspaperman was having his own foot gently tweaked.

Anyway his town-sharpened intelligence should have told him by now that the old idea of ignorant people getting words wrong has not much force. It used to when we had to pick them out of print and absorb other people's pronunciation, but most of us received our first inkling of the atomic bomb from the established voice of the B.B.C. and we got it first smack, and if we countrymen mix it up with Plato it is deliberate.

I may as well relieve the reader's mind and get the author out of that thunderstorm where I left him. Although the storm passed away, it left the roads of the hills as swiftly running streams and on reaching lower ground I found a temporary flood too deep to ride through.

There was nothing unusual in that, perhaps, but swimming strongly up the road was a white and ginger cat which turned back rather than face me. It returned to dry land and stood looking as sad as a wet cat usually does and I wondered what had made it go against its accepted instincts and enter the water. Cats swim strongly, as I had just seen, but in this case there was not the slightest reason for it as it could have walked along the roadside bank as I proceeded to do, nor did it follow suit but stayed there looking unhappily across that water. The only conclusion was that it knew that road so well in running along it that it could not leave it for the safety of the bank.

And cats often seem to move about uneasily after a thunderstorm; that afternoon I met many of them prowling on the alert, and I have noticed more than once that as soon as the storm is over they insist on going out and appear to be inspecting the damage. But cats are strange creatures and quite unpredictable : I once came across one caught in a wire snare and leaping in the air as high as the cord would allow, and although I knew the danger I could not leave it there.

My intentions were to merely get the peg out of the ground and let it go with the wire still around its middle, but when the leaping spitting creature realized that I was going to help, with teeth and claws bared ready it turned its head away and let me feel the cruel wire where it was gripped. It seemed impossible that even a cat could live with its waist compressed to about the thickness of my thumb, yet in time with many soothing words on my part the wire was eased and pussy walked away apparently none the worse. The unpredictable part is that on the very next day I was along the same path and there was the same cat in the same sort of wire snare, but this time the noose had tightened above its breathing parts and poor puss had paid the price of not taking advantage of experience.

And that is what has surprised me so often about animals. For all their cleverness at times they can be such dumb brutes. I am not going to write much about the fauna of Dorset since, for an observant countryman, I know very little about when the cuckoo arrives and how often it sings between successive breaths, nor have I the ear to know the difference in one thrush song and another. Nor have I ever seen a live badger although for years I lived within half a mile of where they carried on a lot of work and I visited the site many times. I have seen them shot and poisoned and one dead in some brambles where boys had caught it unable to tear its tough hair out of the innocent-seeming blackberry thorns. And I want to see a live badger one day, as men have told me that he looks like a native bear and there are many hillside thickets which should have a bear in them. An old friend of mine once met a bear on a road that I know—and I believe every word that he said—it was in his youth and he was a shepherd courting a nice girl some distance away.

With the recklessness of youth he used the hours of darkness to travel backwards and forwards, and one bright moonlight night with his spirits heightened by love and feeling that the world was well, he suddenly became aware that something was overtaking him. He stopped in his tracks as it was unlikely that anything else should be abroad on that road at that hour, and when he looked back he could see as far as the corner and the thing was still coming on out of sight.

To him it sounded as loud as a team of horses and then round the corner swung a bear and trotted right up to him. It seemed as startled as he was as they stood there face to face in the moonlight. He claimed not to be frightened as much as amazed to see that his bear had eyes as big as saucers and we can guess that his own were opened wide. But of course the situation could not last and had to be broken off when the bear, which had been as big as a donkey, shrank to the size of a badger and he shooed it off.

Was he right in claiming that he had seen a bear in all that a bear was and not been very frightened? To him it had been as big as a donkey and he had stood face to face with it at a range of about a foot. He had even heard its lips part and seen the reflection of the big moon in its eye—for the moment it had been a bear and he had not run away.

And that experience made him sure that all stories of the night and ghosts and such things were merely in the people who experienced them. If he, a good strong shepherd not

afraid of anything, could bring a badger up before him as
big as a donkey it was not surprising that weaker men had
wild tales to tell. So, in his newfound arrogance he challenged
his father on his deathbed to come back and haunt him and
the old man threatened to do that. But although as a shepherd he was out at all hours of the night over the fields his
father had also known so well, the old man never came up to
make himself known.

I see that I called a bramble an innocent-seeming thorn,
and we are inclined to look on them much the same as the
thorn which pricks the dainty finger of a lady as she plucks
her rose. We look on the blackthorn with a different eye
because we were brought up with the idea of the crown of
thorns, and our sloe bushes could have supplied that. But the
bramble can be put to a more sinister use when a man finds a
rabbit down a hole out of reach; then, while we can be sure
that the rabbit is down there pressing his silly head into the
end of his bolt hole and tucking his rear in tightly, the man
cuts a tough old bramble and trims the thorns off the end he
is going to handle. Then pushing it down and making sure
that he has reached his prey he twists it about until the cruel
spikes have gripped in the fur and the dumbly protesting
rabbit is drawn out.

I have seen people wince at that description and then throw
on their furs to go out; they love their warm furs which probably once spent a day or two held by the foot until put out of
their misery. But we humans have strange scruples until we
are personally touched.

It is difficult to work up much compassion for the maggot-
like rabbit, and it is a pity that the Normans introduced him
in their time as the creature was not a native of this country.
We could do without him but do not believe one-quarter of
the outcry that newspaper farmers arouse against him. Every
farmer would like to be free of rabbits on his young corn,
especially when they come on his land from another man's
woods, but few would like to cut them out altogether and not
one will look kindly on a man who helps in the good work
and takes one for an occasional dinner. Not that the thing is
worth much in the way of food, as dogs and ferrets will starve
to death on a rabbit diet and it is certainly a tasteless dish on

its own. But it does enable a countryman to keep up his self-respect by poaching at the risk of being fined; I know several such men who do it for the fun they get out of irritating the local farmers and the village policeman.

And if I have insulted the humble rabbit too much I can also tell of one which did not run true to form. One evening while lying overlooking the Channel we were watching the rabbits of all ages playing on the short grass when a stoat appeared amongst them; most of them disappeared and the stoat approached what looked like an old doe. It was a big experienced-looking rabbit and instead of running away or coming under that strange influence which stoats have on rabbits, it waited until the enemy was near and then kicked at it with the full force of its hind legs. It was the stoat which left the field of combat.

But it is quite true that in most cases the rabbit just gives up when the stoat decides to get it. I have seen a stoat appear and one particular rabbit seem to lose all power to bolt, as the others did, and only be able to hop weakly about until the stoat unhurriedly approached and took its time about getting the grip on the neck. Yet there is no more doubt about the bloodlust of the one than there is about the terror of the victim. I once saw a nice half-grown rabbit coming towards me and it was crying instead of leaping ahead out of danger as it ought, and close behind was the evil bloodsucker who was also too intent on the business to see me. The tragedy took place within six feet of me and the sheer terror of the rabbit was matched by the ecstasy of the stoat as it drained its prey.

Sometimes the stoat can be a victim of his own powers. Once I was working in the edge of a wood and we heard the death-squeal of a rabbit out in the field. The old woodman there was too clever to rush out quickly but he soon went out and picked up the rabbit while the stoat ran off, and soon the same thing happened again and we had two rabbits, nor was it surprising that later we saw the white and brown hunter capture its third victim, although it was less willing to give up this time and threatened us. And then just before going home we heard the same heart-searching cry and there was the stoat with a fourth rabbit; once more we went near and slowly the now really bloodthirsty animal had to back off, yet this time it did not threaten us but cried like a beaten child and we were hard by while the old woodman addressed it.

"I don't like to do this, but surely you can catch one more, and we're just going, whereas I can't catch one half as easy as you can."

It seemed right that he should placate the stoat if he could and in any case he would never hurt the thing that caught a dinner for him; but to rob is the law of the wild and we can be sure that the stoat would have no mercy on us, as he is built entirely for murder. Pick him up and examine the needle-like claws and teeth and watch the vicious curve of his body when he loses himself in his blood feast; or only watch him when he performs his mad dance which looks so delightful until you see that every leap is a pounce and the wicked muzzle is a grin of hate.

By comparison the fox is a mild-mannered animal for all the killing he will do for mere pleasure; but he is well known for being a wily brute who seems to smile at his thoughts. I have little experience of him as a quarry in the hunting game, but have met him scores of times in many different situations. Yet here again I have been surprised how unwary a fox can be for all the cleverness people have wished on him.

One day while off the track in a wood I sat down against an oak and smoked a cigarette and almost at once saw an old fox coming towards me in full view. I had been pushing through the hazel undergrowth such a little time before that the fox must have been near enough to be warned that something was in the wood with him; another man would have heard me for all that we humans have lost most of our power of acute hearing. But here was a cunning old fox walking slowly towards danger and as he crossed the place where my scent must still be warm on the ground I fully expected to see him sniff and become alert. Most pet dogs which spend their lives lying before a fire would know a man had walked there, yet this wild creature, whose mere survival rested on his alertness, did not even drop his nose and passed me while I was smoking at a measured twenty feet. I certainly saw the quiet smile on his face as he strolled along about his business, just as a small vixen once sat down waiting for me on a corner and almost flirted with me. Some people would have declared that she must have been a tamed fox which had escaped but I knew her kind and quietly bade her begone while she was well off. Which she did without the slightest concern in her situation.

That a fox stinks is very much of an understatement, but I am not going to accept the explanation that it is because it has dirty habits compared with, say, the badger, which cleans up its sett, while a fox will lie in filth without turning a hair. The smell is too pungent to be just filth and taints the very air where it has passed. I have known some very dirty, hairy farm dogs whose matted coats reeked to heaven on a wet day as if there was years of dog in it and wet dog is bad, but those dogs did not fill the air for yards around as one fox will. The fox must have something of the same ability in that way as a billy goat, and that is bad under any conditions.

I remember once stopping in a sunken lane to look at a distant view of the sea and I said, "There's a billy goat over that wall." My friend might have been willing to allow me second sight, yet was sure that I had not been able to look over the bank and wall into the field, so she leaped up and declared me wrong, there was no goat of any sort in sight.

Then it became a question whether I could discover unseen goats, so we set out to trace this one and walked half a mile before finding it. There it was, a black, evil-eyed brute looking at us with too great an interest while its dark lips delicately played with a leaf. That was the only delicate thing about it and it was still a question whether I had smelt the thing at half a mile or merely where it had walked along that sunken lane the previous week.

There is still one more beast of prey in Dorset and with perhaps less pleasant connections than any of the others. We have plenty of adders, and the less harmful but still unlovable grass snakes. I think that perhaps Hampshire can boast more numbers but we still have enough and in suitable weather it is not surprising to see several during a day. As they remain totally unmoving if they can while humans are around many people have been near them without knowing it. And when a snake does decide to move off quietly there are few things which can so correctly bear out that the word to glide is to move smoothly and easily and flow gently.

Stone marking where Charles II fled near Bridport
Brownsea Island across Poole Harbour

A snake in a hurry leaves no doubt about it and yet it is often possible to decide what it is by its movements. The grass snake seems to slide forward without much effort, as if the raised head somehow pulled the rest of its length up to it; while the adder will go all out as if it was living up to the description of a flashing snake. Head down with chin on the ground the adder's whole length vibrates, and it has gone like a stream of quicksilver. Yet I have seen big grass snakes at Gad Cliff which have found a way to use the terrain as a means to attain almost unbelievable speeds.

At Gad Cliff it is easy to believe local men who suggest that some of those grass snakes have lived there undisturbed for ages and so grown to immense size. There is a wild place of fallen rocks, some of which are as big as houses and surrounded by luxuriant growth of all kinds, and being almost inaccessible no man may go there during a whole year, making it a sanctuary of wild life. I have seen as many as seven adult foxes there, but as foxes venture out where men live they run a risk that the snakes do not. Thousands of rabbits live there and also come up over into the fields above and these rabbits have their runs down the steep slopes with the long tough grass sloping downwards, and while I have never caught a snake making its way up against the lie of the grass I have seen them shoot down.

It seems as if snakes have an intelligence that they are willing to use, for when disturbed on the top of Gad Cliff they hurry along until they reach the top end of a rabbit run and then pour themselves into it. Several feet—we swear to as much as six feet—of brown liquid lets itself slide several hundred feet downwards at a speed impossible to guess at. When that hard dry grass lies downward on a slope in the hot sun it is impossible to walk on and in the runs every stalk helps to guide the snake's own super-streamlined length to achieve a speed that looks greater than if it was falling through the open air.

Once on Gad Cliff an adder leapt aside at the last moment and, instead of disappearing as it was well able, stopped to challenge me just within reach of my stick. This was unusual and I was well pleased to be able to examine it. Its length lay immovable as a bronze serpent, but it held the threat to move like lightning in any direction. The whole thing was terribly alive for all that its eyes were fixed on me without a flicker and for the first time I came under the sinister influence of a watching snake. It was not pleasant but I waited as I had never seen one of the almost black adders before. It had the usual markings but they were merely a darker shade of the same colour and its eyes were distinctly a very polished jetness.

Nor can I satisfy those who say that there is room in the country for adders to live, because for all its speed my stick moved even faster and I was able to handle it. Again its blackness was startling and it measured the accepted eighteen inches which many men say is never exceeded, but I had measured one which was just under thirty inches and there was no doubt that it was an adder and not a grass snake.

I know a few stony fields where the snake life is considerable and once saw an unusual thing there of which I might have doubted my own description if another man had not seen it and our descriptions agreed. We were examining an outcrop of stone, when under our eyes appeared a golden snake not more than a foot long without any markings, and it was not a slowworm as we had plenty of time to see that it had a neck and shaped head which no slowworm has. Its thickness was impossible for any foot-long snake that we knew, for without exaggeration it was larger than my thumb and that is not a small one. Most snakes and adders of a foot length are about the thickness of a fat fountain pen.

And while we can agree that grass snakes are harmless as far as they are non-poisonous, it is nonsense to say they will not strike, as once I accidentally trod on the tail of one and its other yard of length whipped round and definitely struck hard at my shoe before flashing off. It was as hard as if a man had jabbed at my foot with the end of a stick, and I was glad to have had on a stout shoe, as if its teeth had marked me the psychological effect would have been unpleasant for all that I knew it was harmless.

There are men who seem to have a fascination for seeking out adders and may kill scores in a summer, but I have never been able to discover a man who has seen the half-believed phenomenon of the mother adder swallowing her young when in danger. I have seen what appeared to be a dozen or two needle-like things which looked like young adders and although we waited and watched carefully no mother adder came to give them the doubtful shelter of her belly. Surely our zoological experts should now be able to prove that theory once and for all, as there are thousands of English adders captured alive and sent to London.

It is not easy to suggest that the different shades of adder colours are the result of their environment, but on one part of the Dorset coast I could give a good guess at the environment of certain lobsters brought ashore. Those brought in at Chapman's Pool may come from three different fishing grounds, and perhaps it will be necessary to point out to some readers that the lobster only gets its red jacket when it is plunged into boiling water, for while they are alive they can be a mixture from black to light blue with yellow touches on their tails and claws.

A lobster which has had its environment on the shale of the Kimmeridge Ledges will come into the boat an almost complete black like the shale under water, while on the bottom that is strewn with the tumbled Portland beds the colour will be lighter with much more blue, and in deeper water ten miles out they may be a delicate light blue in parts with much more yellow about them. And any lobster or crab caught near one of the rusty wrecks will be found to have taken on some of the rust colour of the iron.

Some years ago we had a good example of the lobster's ability to take on the coloration of its environment, when many thousands of tons of newly dug, and therefore white, stone from the Portland beds were taken from near St Aldhelm's Head and dumped outside Poole Harbour to form a trainbank to guide the tidal scour out into deep water. This new rock barrier was put in a district that had no natural rocks and so no rock dwellers like the lobster, but Poole fishermen soon discovered that lobsters had come there to live. They started what was a new line of fishing to them, and while the stone was new and white the lobsters caught were almost white with merely a suggestion of the blue in the thicker parts of their shells.

I think that environment accounts for the occasional letter that gets into the Press about an albino lobster; somewhere in the neighbourhood of where it was caught there may have been some repair work to a groyne or jetty or sewage pipe and that particular lobster had its home where the new cement or stone caused it to be colourless.

The lobster is a fighter but can easily be deceived and made to loosen its hold, whereas a crab must be smashed to pieces before its claw will relax. I once saw an experienced fisherman accidentally put his hand in the grip of a big lobster and instead of pulling away as anyone might instinctively and making the thing grip tighter, he quietly reached over and pulled the other claw and at once it let go the hand to defend itself.

Nor will a lobster attack a man although they will defend themselves stoutly during the "adder months" when the snakes ashore are active. During those few warm weeks it is no light matter to put your hand in a pot with five or six lively lobsters scrambling madly around, but unless you put your hand in the way the lobster does not come after it. There is one thing on our Dorset coast which does seem definitely to attack, and that is the dog fish which they call a nurse. Occasionally a nurse gets in a lobster pot and as they have room to turn around in the circular pot they will follow a hand around and keep their business end towards the danger.

And although a conger eel will bite very viciously, I have never heard of one attacking even when loose in a boat. Usually if they get loose of the hook they slip over the side before anyone can do anything about it. When one is brought aboard in a lobster pot it will go round and round like greased lightning and if a sharp enough knife is placed in its way it may disembowel itself, which is about the only way to deal with it; but do not ignore it even then as I have seen a severed head make mincemeat of a man's hand some time after the head had been cut off.

Now I can tell a story about a conger eel which may make certain people scoff, and there may be a psychological angle to it for all that. A man found a good-sized eel in a pool left by the tide and considered it a catch although it appeared dead. Few people would have eaten it but he did and gave some away to another man, and as neither of them could tempt their families to eat a dead fish the two men had a big feed. Within a day both men were ill as might be expected, and in fact they may have expected, and strangely both of them had marks on their backs that looked like the skin of an eel. It was probably just plain fish poisoning but there were people who claimed they could see the eel shape in the dark patches.

Of course we can have some strange beliefs on the Dorset coast. I know a young woman who had a severe bout of fish poisoning and when the ugly results healed on her arms it was possible to see that the scars were very much like great coarse fish scales. She either expected to carry the mark of the fish and therefore the scars assumed that appearance, or we looked for it and therefore saw what we expected. I would not attempt to answer that although my eyes have seen those fish scales on her fat arms.

There are a great many people who will say that they do not care much for fish as a food and I once was willing to be sympathetic to that idea. But there are few better foods when the fish is fresh, and for some years I ate and enjoyed great quantities straight from the sea. In that way a person is spoilt for eating any shop fish, as the two things have no comparison no matter how advanced the methods of preserving it have become. A fish loses something in a matter of hours, and minutes are better between the sea and the pot.

Nor does it seem possible to over-eat on fresh fish, and perhaps great quantities of it are needed by the complete fish eaters as they all appear to have voracious appetites. The fish themselves are never satisfied for long on each other, and a conger eel will eat more than his own weight and size under your eye while you pull in a net. Incidentally fish have a better intelligence than birds and rabbits when surrounded by a closing net. Rabbits or birds will throw themselves against it and get thoroughly tied up in the meshes, but I have more than once seen a shoal of fish inside a net and yet not try to rush it until one of them had discovered a broken mesh and the whole lot queued up and poured through it like the water itself. There was no pushing and shoving but thousands would go through the hole in less time than it takes to write it.

Naturally the language used in the boat would be appalling until the hole was dragged in with the last fish attempting the hazard at the very last moment.

And although fish will give up soon after being taken from the water without any messy killing to upset people with a tender heart, sometimes those people get a bit of a shock when carrying home a string of rock fish. One rock fish that in August and September is taken out of the water with all the vivid colours of a rainbow and is called the harvest cunner, is a very stout fellow for his length and has a big air sac inside him; it is this sac that chooses the unexpected moment to relax with a distinct grunt which has made people drop their dead fish under the impression that it has groaned in distress.

The fish-eating birds have an appetite in keeping with their food and put away an amazing amount, and they do literally put it through themselves as the whitened rocks of a sea-birds' colony shows. A cormorant will dive off a rock and reappear with a fish that it has great difficulty in getting down and repeat the effort seven times with scarcely a breath between, before taking a little rest and voiding a few times, when it is ready for another great meal.

I once saw what looked like a fight between a seagull and an eel which probably weighed twice the weight of the bird, and anyone who has handled an eel knows what power they have and the impossibility of getting a hold on it, but this gull presently got the head in its throat and after a great effort swallowed the whole two feet of lashing fish. There it stood bulging with the strong coils inside it throwing it about and unable to take off, although of course if I had insisted on frightening it off it would have thrown up its dinner none the worse for having been eaten once.

There are some tremendous gatherings of cliff seabirds in Dorset like the guillemots, razorbacks and puffins, and it is always startling to come face to face with a puffin in his own home, as his colouring is so unexpected every time you see him. The latest war has played havoc with these birds again but as there seem to be teeming millions of them, and nothing seems likely ever to destroy their nesting places, they will make up their strength even if man's efforts continue.

Less likely to survive there are a pair of peregrine falcons that I know men sought to rob every year despite the law. And as every man's hand seems against ravens the old pair that I used to know may be gone now. For some unknown reason every man with a gun used to shoot at them and more than once one of the birds flew about with hardly any flight feathers; one spent most of a summer with only three in the right wing and yet seemed to fly without any hindrance.

We also get our full share of migrating birds both coming and going, when the cliff fields are swarming with little birds apparently loath to start out or tired after their journey, for despite what some naturalists say I have seen tired birds come to land at the first opportunity. And most people who have lived near the sea edge have seen that strong flier the homing pigeon come staggering in over the waves to drop exhausted on the first foot of England, sometimes too tired to eat or drink until it has rested; it is then that they fall easily to hawks and even the glutton of a seagull.

Nor amongst the wild life of Dorset must we leave out the cats which have taken to the wilds, and here it does seem that the domestic animal gone back to nature has gained something in intelligence, for most keepers will agree that such a cat is very hard to come upon and seldom makes the mistakes that the completely wild fox may make. But of course when man really decides to do so he is capable of outwitting any animal and these renegades find themselves nailed up with the other killers of the countryside.

In recent years naturalists appear to have learnt a lot more about the migratory habits of butterflies, or at least their knowledge has become more available. It is rather surprising to find that these wind-blown creatures are capable of even ocean flights, and the English Channel is supposed to be nothing to some species; for instance, the objectionable cabbage white can, and does, cross it to help out our own native-born stock.

Several times when lobster fishing off the Dorset coast where it is just over sixty miles to the other side, I have seen thousands of these butterflies making north in their apparently feeble flutter. We just used to bring common sense to bear on how and why these were out so far from land; we were perhaps ten miles out and the time was mid-morning with a gentle breeze in the butterflies' favour. And every time that I saw them was after a hard northerly dawn wind which not one person in a hundred except fishermen knew anything about.

During spells of perfect summer weather when for day after day the sun beats down with scarcely a cloud to mar it, the hour before dawn can be anything but summerlike, and a few miles off shore the wind can have more than a nip in it. It is then in the first light that butterflies may be seen being blown over the cliff edge with wisps of hay from the fields, so it is not really surprising that we used to think that the butterflies we saw later were returning to land when the wind had turned in their favour.

Apparently we were wrong, they were Continental migrants on their way to our happy land, but there are still one or two points which are worth examining. At mid-morning, we will say as late as eleven o'clock, they were ten miles from land heading north towards it and moving very slowly as if it was quite an effort, as it probably was. We used to watch one sink lower and lower as if it was just about to collapse on the sea, but never saw it actually touch, and at their speed we reckoned they still had another two hours' flight to go. Now we are told that they were coming from France across the Channel where it is at least sixty-four miles wide between the most outjutting headlands in the straightest line.

We knew that at dawn some six hours earlier there had been far too much northerly wind for butterflies to make way against, and as we can presume that the wind reached all the way across the water at something of the same power, we know that the butterflies were not on the way then. So where were they? At their apparent speed they had not left the French coast since the wind had turned in their favour, yet there they were well on the way to Dorset. Was it surprising that we thought they were just waifs of the dawn wind going back to the cabbages in our back gardens?

CHAPTER X

NEAR THE STOUR

THE town of Shaftesbury is well up in the north-east corner
of Dorset and only just inside the border. In fact it might be a
Wiltshire town and is sited on the chalk which has come
across Hampshire and Wiltshire to meet the crevasse where
the River Stour finds its way from the Blackmoor Vale to the
sea at Christchurch.

We can claim the Stour as a Dorset river but the bulk of
its water is collected up in Wiltshire and it passes out of our
county north of Bournemouth. But it flows through very
historical country which was well occupied in our early days
before Rome came that way and has been well populated ever
since. The Stour has scarcely a straight mile in all its length
and many times it almost turns back on itself as if it would
like to give up; and although it drains a great area of chalk-
land it never seems to grow as big as it might.

It also goes perilously near Somerset where that county
sticks a corner into the Blackmoor Vale, and of course it lends
its name to several places although some of them are not
actually on the river. There are some more good-sounding
names in this part of the county, for what could be better
than Child Okeford or Margaret Marsh? And who played
the fiddle at Fiddleford; was it the ferryman or did he once
have to accept his fee in a tune?

Shaftesbury is not on the river and at one time was a very
dry town, having to rely on the good graces of Enmore Green
for water, but for all that it had a considerable place in high
life. It had a famous Abbey which attracted different royal
adventures but ended in the Reformation which scattered so
many established Church institutions. The greatest asset was
of course the murdered Edward from Corfe Castle, who had
caused the heavenly light to shine down there in Purbeck, and
it might be in order to wonder why the spot where Heaven
disclosed itself was not made the place of pilgrimage. Or did

L   145

it need the publicity of the great funeral procession to bring it to fruition at Shaftesbury?

The body had lain in state at Wareham and then the pomp and glory started until all the great people of the south were following. The affair was being built up as it went slowly through the countryside and it is not surprising that it was thought marvellous or that miraculous cures were accomplished at the martyr's tomb. Yet it is strange that such a useful spot has been allowed to be lost down the years and no one now knows where the holy bones are; while down at Corfe Castle the exact place where the deed was foully done is pointed out on a bridge which did not exist at the time. The knowledge of just where Heaven came to earth never seems to have been as important as it should.

King Alfred founded the nunnery at Shaftesbury and that had the usual intriguing history and to be the Abbess must have been an interesting and perhaps exciting career for some of the able women who landed the prize. It may seem a long cry from there to Robert Bruce in the Highlands of Scotland, but his wife and daughter were confined in the convent and perhaps were there when they got the great news of his victory at Bannockburn.

An occasional nun was stolen from inside the walls as was to be expected, but one man in 1285 took two so that it hardly appears that they were very hard to steal, and as his punishment was not so very fatal and final and he merely had to swear off nuns in the future, it looks as if 1285 was more enlightened than some earlier and later periods.

The Mayor of Shaftesbury should feel that he has a considerable honour in his keeping as he is one of an unbroken line since 1352. But Henry VIII was the end of the town's glory as of so much else. Since the Abbess marched out at the head of her nuns, the place has had nothing to live for, and now is just a pleasant country town dreaming of its past which still butters some bread for its inhabitants. And while so many people think of how great and good some of those Abbey foundations were, and perhaps would like to live again under the warmth of their influence, it should be remembered that although there was ease and plenty and gracious living in and around their walls, all the wealth that made it possible was drained out of the countryside and the sop that was flung to the beggars and pilgrims was a very small part of what fattened the Church.

Shaftesbury town may still sigh for its Abbey, but it was a heavy burden, and there is still the lighter hand of the Church on the town in some of its names : Parson's Pool, Angel Lane, Magdalen's Almshouses and Bell Street set the tone of the place and are far in front of our Jubilee streets and Veronica roads.

Sherborne also has its roots in history as at one time it was the capital of Wessex when Wessex was a kingdom of its own. St Aldhelm was a bishop there in 705, and to be a bishop in those early days did not only include learning and scholarship, as three bishops of Sherborne died in battle fighting against the Danes. It was in St Aldhelm's time that the school was founded there which makes a pretty long record as schools go, but of course the original ideas have been much changed and St Aldhelm would not recognize some of the aims of to-day.

Fortunately Sherborne Abbey survived Henry VIII mainly because the man who got it sold it back at once to the town for use as the parish church. And all the many alterations and additions to the building have left us a very good church with even a bit of St Aldhelm's first work. But although the town is conscious of its past greatness it does not seem to expect that back again, as perhaps Shaftesbury does, and it is scarcely interested in Sherborne Castle, which has had as lively and interesting a history as most such castles, and met its fate like Corfe Castle when Cromwell refused to let it stay as a thorn in the side of the growing trading era of England.

And over the hill towards the Somerset border in the village of Trent they have an authentic hiding-place of Charles when he fled from the battle of Worcester. There is a story that while he was lying there he heard the church bells ringing to rejoice in the report that he had been killed, which annoyed him. With agreeable royal favour Charles rewarded the Wyndham family, who had sheltered him in the Manor, but forgot the promised reward to the woman who rode pillion with him to provide the necessary touch to make him pass as a servant, and fourteen years later she was still making a petition as she was tired of waiting.

The vague great semi-circle of the Blackmoor Vale is the dominating feature of this part of Dorset and most of this well-watered area is the best farming country. Here there is little sign of men who scratch a living out of the soil and much sign that farmers are well-to-do and well-fed men. England may not flow with milk and honey to any great extent but the Blackmoor Vale would furnish a considerable river of milk.

But even here there are odd corners and strips which to the lay eye look as if they are not put to full use, but neither the Vale nor Dorset is the only part of the country where land and men are kept apart. Any thoughtful person moving about may take note of all the land which looks forgotten. The war years with their restrictions on every man's ways have made a great difference and I deliberately refrain from calling it waste land as there is hardly a waterlogged corner of tangled bushes or rough hillside which is not put to some use at some time. I personally know such pieces of land which supply little in the way of food, but cattle have access to them at certain times and do keep open winding paths between the bushes if only to seek shade in summer and shelter in winter.

So technically it is not waste land as the owners or renters would point out quickly : yet again the war years have proved what could be done with much of it. I have no intention of stepping into the arena where such things are fought out. Most farming people can pick out flaws in the workings of the War Agricultural Committees just as those bodies can show many individuals where there is room for necessary restrictions and improvements.

But this lack of putting good land to full use is hard to reconcile with the genuine land hunger of so many people who never have a chance now to give their hearts and bodies to making good earth produce to the full. Even Suburbia in all its various degrees is a pale reflection of land hunger although much of it is diverted into the smoothest lawn or the brightest flowers in the whole road, while the barns and all the outlying sheds have become the box of a garage which is made to fit the car without leaving room for the owner to potter about. So much useful work is done on the real land when the stress of weather makes a man keep in the cover of his buildings; he may be bad-tempered because so much work is being held up outside but he can get pleasure as well as satisfaction amongst his own tools and possessions.

Even the boundary stone of a man's plot can be set up in Suburbia in the shape of a bird bath or sundial, but few men can set up a boundary stone in the country with the feeling that henceforth what is inside it is his to do his best with. I am not going to set out all or any of the reasons why we no longer have a "bold peasantry," but surely Suburbia and the building societies have proved the value to the country as a whole of having so many people with a real land stake in it. Would the owners with so many thousands of acres really suffer in the long run if they let the small man produce so much more out of some partly used acres?

I know some of the answers. Big and still bigger businesses sometimes claim to show bigger profits in money because they can ignore boundaries of fields and even men's limitations. But the whole value of land is not always tied up in money profit, and even if it is, why is the smallholder always expected to be able to pay so much more rent per acre than the bigger farmer? It does not matter if he rents from a landowner or a County Council or even a farmer who has a long lease himself and therefore can sub-let an odd corner.

I have known smallholders who paid three pounds per acre every year for land which was less than thirty shillings in the bulk, and it will be found that the three pounds an acre was usual when thirty shillings was a high farm rent which included all the farm buildings and dwellings, whereas the smallholder often started from scratch without even a fencing post in place. So if the big business of farming with thousands of acres paid the highest dividends how on earth could it be expected that a man could get twice the amount out of every yard of his few? The thing does not make sense, regardless of the great loss in valuable human interest which so few wage-earners can be expected even to understand now, and the neglected pieces of land which are just waiting for that little bit of personal interest that would make them flourish.

And I know the answer that there are poverty-stricken smallholdings with shiftless people on them. Of course there

149

are, as there are poverty-stricken landowners with shiftless ways—although their way of life may not seem to suggest it. But at least the smallholder is struggling against a burden of heavy rent which no bigger farmer would even start to think about, and there is little doubt that to-day such a man and his family are often looked down on by less deserving people.

Far outbalancing the failures and those who just hang on to a hard way of living because they have lost their courage, there are many small places wrung out of very unpromising situations. They do flourish in their own way without a waste yard; and apart from and above that, there is the confidence which is so hard to achieve unless a man is allowed some initiative to develop his own life. Some of those wage-earners who have to travel daily to jobs which give them subsistence have to pass pieces of land which might produce more if the two could be brought together, not perhaps in hard money, but certainly more of that something which the country finds need of in times of crisis.

If my ideas are entirely wrong and the independent man on the land is gone for good, so much of history both past and present is mistaken, because when some really decisive happening has occurred it has always been good policy to do something to appease the land hunger which seems to be part of most of us. All recorded history mentions the question of settling the returned soldier. Far be it from me to want to see another pitchfork army arise as it has so many times, because the day of settling anything in that way should be gone. Although this last war has proved that there is nothing at all wrong with the nation as a whole, a few more small men on their own would far outbalance such things as surrender of shooting and fishing rights.

Another answer that I know is that the estates, so often grabbed under the various Enclosures, have given us the splendid layouts and views which are so much a part of the countryside, and that to allow the settlement of small people would spoil much of this. There is something to be said for that because haphazard sheds and fences can become a litter all over the face of things, but the most dreadful shed becomes toned down and soon fits in with the general greenness of everything.

Any local authority can point to some "awful place" in their district and from that show reasons why smallholdings are not to be encouraged because some of them offend all the by-laws there are, and anyway the menfolk often have to go to the nearest town to work so that they can pay at least double the rent any big farmer would pay for the same acres. And the women may grumble because they have no laid-on water or light or only two buses running at the end of the lane. The life is hard and an endless struggle because when a cow ails or a horse has an accident the whole structure is threatened.

But the most "awful place" is not very offensive to the eye and is never permanent because in a few years after it is abandoned it has mouldered away. The local history of any district is full of such abandoned struggles. I have seen traces of occupation in many places now far from habitation or even road; a chimney foundation or merely a hearth beneath the grass, and how many people have said, "How did that apple tree come to be planted out in the fields here?" A little search might show other evidence of gardens and dwellings there.

It was in the country that people lived until they were cheated and driven away from the real reason for living there, and the urge to get back exists even in people who deliberately send their children away from it. And when the world wakes up to the fact that even the food found in tin cans has first to be grown in humble soil, there may be more chance that the land will get back under the guidance, not necessarily the possession which scarcely matters, of those who are willing to tend it.

There is a trend towards living in the country but hardly one in a hundred want to live a countryman's life, and even the person who builds an unassuming house in a sheltered spot usually wants to bring much of the town with him. They love the pretty flowers and the cute birds, but the very air soon becomes urban when the constant tradesman's vans and the householder's private car have turned the country lane into a built-up and lighted area.

It has nothing to do with Dorset or even the countryside in particular, but some day the modern way of living must become top-heavy and overdo itself. We take every trace of mineral out of the bowels of the earth and skim the surface of all the fertility we can coax or rape out of it; we strive for the great achievement of a car for every man so that he can get from place to place, and some want to fill the air with machines, so that if it is taken to the bitter end there will be nowhere to walk nor air to breathe. We take all the water out of the rivers to wash all the cars and streets and shop windows, and some people want then to remove all hedges and "uneconomic" trees, and when the whole balance of nature is upset they wonder why many of the good things of life are not so good as they used to be.

And when people point out that the trend towards that has been going on a long time and *they* see little sign of collapse yet, they forget that the town mentality had not achieved much say in what lay outside their urban bounds until several generations ago. Nor is a hundred or two hundred years much as the countryside knows time—although with their greater speed of things the Americans have already succeeded in creating their famous dust bowl which may yet make their garden of Eden a desert—because the balance of nature is not the rise or fall of the yearly cuckoos or the number of lovely sunsets.

The school which says that England should and could be made a garden, in the sense that many a mansion has laid out an ordered and decorated garden where there may be that negative marvel of a flowering shrub for every month of the year, and an artificial waterfall with golden fish in a pool below it—these people should remember that such a garden can exist in almost any environment as long as there are plenty of more or less natural conditions surrounding it.

But if all springs are made to run where directed according to a man's whim, you are going to alter the actual face of the earth and we have already enough experience to know what that can mean to the rainfall. And even the boldest of garden planners can hardly believe that he can have his ordered beauty if he prevents the air from dropping its moisture, nor will his twelve flowering shrubs, from as many other lands, do much to bind the soil or replace the fertility they take out, or anything at all to appease the hunger they may bring to him. Nor do such gardens make any allowance for the domestic stock which has its great place in the scheme of things; those famous gardens which millions of people have paid a shilling to "view" do little towards keeping a pig or educating people in the real understanding of what growing things do mean to mankind. It would be far better for everybody if people would pay their shilling to "view" a good smallholding and then come back every week to see how the sow's family was progressing. Anyway I can assure them that the sow is every bit as interesting and more personally attractive than some of the things glimpsed in the Big House garden.

But there is no truer thing than that beauty is in the eye of the beholder; some of us must accept that many people do not see much in a flourishing family of pigs. People can trip round the ordered gravel paths of a Big House garden without soiling their shoes and it is so easy to exclaim over the things that everyone else exclaims over. Yet much that is accepted as beauty is merely the obvious, like a big glorious skyful of sunset colour or the glades of bluebells which are recognized and visited like shrines, and a glamorous parade of racehorses or the white wings of a yacht race.

This sort of thing is safe to exclaim about and no one thinks you are a bit strange to refer to them, but a sky that only shows the setting of the sun by a moment's gleam of pink on the tip of one cloud overhead can be just as startling; to meet a grey shire stallion on a hot dusty heath road is to see more perfection than the most famous racehorse. There again it is in the eye of the beholder, of course, and some people can see beauty in the lines of a motor-car rushing along the miles of a bypass which has been given over to ribbon building.

I have startled people by declaring that sometimes the pylons which carry electric wires over the country—so often without stopping to leave any power in the rural areas—can show a real beauty. Not the pylon that rears itself outside so many country windows, nor the one over the roadside hedge; they are too often just steel erections placed where they are most suitable to the owners and of course too near for our purpose. But at times when you see them from high ground, stepping across the river and lifting high above trees, then they can be confused with the spire of the village church which everyone claims is a thing of beauty.

I could not take you to some point overlooking the Blackmoor Vale and make you see ten or twenty tall spires receding into the distance and hinting at so many snug villages with lovely churches. Something would not be right and we might only see some pylons, but they are worth looking for in wide wooded valleys and if people would forget for the moment what they are there is beauty in them. And why should what they are be so certain to destroy any delight an eye might find in them? They are the spires carrying the light of one of our modern gods, tall, delicate, silver fingers which might have wind bells and harps placed on them for the delight of the ear as well.[1]

That is enough to damn me in the eyes of many people, but remember it is all in the eye of the beholder. Nor do I forget that it needs the kindly light of a sinking winter sun to make the trick work best. But all beauty is a trick of the light and the eye which have to work together. Often a great stretch of recognized coastal beauty is hidden by the glare of the sun and water while the rock pool on the shore gives up all its secrets of colour and form. Later when the quieter light throws the coastline into a sheer sweep of relief the pool at our feet is just a cold dark puddle in which neither colour nor form stirs.

Dorset has all its share of the recognized and accepted beauty spots, but any local guide or boarding-house keeper will disclose them and it is not for me to speak more for one part than another with regard to the touchy subject of of beauty. There are people who say that there is nothing like the misty distances of the Blackmoor Vale and there are plenty of viewpoints on high ground from which to see it. But neither there nor down the Stour valley is there much of

[1] Nineteen forty-eight saw a spirited controversy regarding the continued use of the wireless masts on Bulbarrow Hill. I must say that as I saw it in 1948, the Bulbarrow type of mast in itself is a thing of beautiful graceful lines and the designer should be given due honour. I should like to always be able to look out on it from my window, a fairy lacework in certain bright lights, and a dimly solid pointing finger when the sky is dark. The people who suggest taking 100 feet from its height have either never seen it, or are completely unable to visualize the mutilated stump they would leave.

that feeling of standing in a cleft that goes on and on; it is rather that you are surrounded by high land.

Two outstanding hills overlooking the Stour are Hod and Hambledon Hills which obviously once controlled the river passage there in Celtic days; they are both fortified camps although the strategy which built them there is not so plain to the eye. They could not have had much effect on the whole in disputing the river crossing as has been suggested, because no enemy would be tied down to crossing the river in their sight. But it is likely that they were sited to deal with the passage up the river of any invaders pressing inland from the coast.

But it also seems possible that they were built as places to retire to for the people who lived in the higher ground of the Cranborne Chase; all that part was densely populated and if people were driven out of their settlements there was every chance of making a last stand with their backs to the river. And if the river was a national or tribal boundary as was likely, the hill fortresses were the outposts of the Cranborne Chase against the strength of all those who lived across the river, for both sides are smothered in earthworks and burial mounds.

Not much further down the river where the hills pinch in more, Blandford Forum with its background of the ages sits on the bank without any of the conscious dreaming of past glories such as might be found in Shaftesbury and Sherborne. Blandford has been a market place and river ford for a very long time and yet has not many of the relics that so often prove to the most casual eye that a town has a long history. It is said that the place was very subject to fires on a big scale and as recently as 1731 their Great Fire destroyed everything except forty houses. So it is not much wonder that the town has none of that charm of real old streets and houses.

My chief memory of Blandford is the great brick erections of the breweries, and Blandford ale is said to be very good. It must not be thought that I am fitting the cap on Blandford if I now mention one thing over which the brewery companies are letting themselves down in the south-western counties. Anyway the companies will not care, as the beer business is a flourishing one and likely to remain so. I too agree that beer is best although not worth a shilling a pint.

Although some brewers do not seem aware of it, I consider that they have been entrusted with something worth keeping beyond selling beer and making great profits. The country pub should never be lost until at least it has been surrounded and overwhelmed by the town's heavy hand. Yet every year cosy little pubs are "enlarged and improved" until the local men are pushed into the background if not turned out altogether. I have met new landlords who admit that they have pushed the "locals" out to make room for passing trade.

Also I have known passing motorists talk of dreary little public-houses where the countrymen mumble in their cups and which I know from personal experience to be cosy friendly houses where there is good company for good men. But there again such things are in the inner eye of the beholder, as to me, and countless others, there are few things more dreary than some smart town public-houses where they may boast that there are three hundred in the room, and the pace is fast.

I have a real bone to pick with some brewers in Dorset, and that is in the way they are making all their sign-boards one uniform enamel plate. "The Swan," "The Fox," "The Castle," "The Globe," are all treated alike. A blue plate with the name in printed letters of white with no attempt to produce the sign which must be much more the original than the printed word. It is not so bad when the plate is fixed flat on the wall, nor does it really matter for the Railway Arms and Station Inns, but I have seen this raw sheet of tin swinging from outjutting arms that are good works in themselves and once held aloft a work of art.

Nor is it likely that the enamel plate is cheap in its first cost as there could be no real mass production of "The King's Arms" or "The White Hart." But of course they are practically indestructible and will glare coldly for the next few hundred years. I know a Swan Inn which is a good house to look at and has several centuries of good life behind it and which it still carries on; it is a house worth keeping and the brewers spend a lot of their big profits on it, yet out over the street they have placed their enamel plate where not so long ago a board painted with a white bird used gently to sway. The thing is wrong and I am surprised to find that men who will expend a lot of money on keeping an old house in intelligent repair can allow the old board to be scrapped.

I do not suggest that they should pay vast fees to some well-known painter to paint their Swans and Foxes and Arms and Black Boys, rather they should hunt out some local person with an eye and hand for that sort of thing and get him to put his own particular Swan on the board. That is the point; the picture should be Mr Smith's down the road, and he should be given credit for it and be someone worth knowing when you become a customer. His Swan will be something to be proud of no matter how easy it is to pick faults in its perfection as a drawing; it will be a work of art or the man would not attempt the effort. And the fact that it will not last as long as the ugly enamel plate is no drawback; for many years it can hang there getting fainter and mellower until only the old people can still see the bird, but it will always be a good thing.

North and east of Blandford Forum and its brewers the Cranborne Chase stretches towards Salisbury Plain, of which geologically it is a part, and although it is still quiet country there is little to hint that it was perhaps the last part of England where the rule of the law reached. It was not much more than a hundred years ago that it was finally "cleaned up" in the real sense of the word. For centuries the Chase had carried a heavy head of wild deer and the preservation of them caused many battles and skirmishes with men who sought to thin them out without permission.

But poaching was a comparatively honest affair, even if it caused an occasional broken head and transportation, and there is still latent ill-feeling between the families of those who informed and those who suffered. Nor were the smugglers all damned men who handled the stuff put ashore at Poole and Swanage; smugglers and poachers often had sympathetic understanding from some of those whose job it should have been to run them down. But there was a time when any cut-throat could lie low in the Chase, and the law did not reach him. All kinds of dirty work have been hatched in the once secret corners, and probably there are hidden hoards of stolen wealth still lying there now gripped in the roots of some great tree. And no one would ever find the mouldering bones of the cheated partners and unfaithful mates who bled into the grass there, nor the holed skull of an odd Preventive man.

To-day any Sunday school could spread its litter in any part of the Chase in complete safety, and if there is just a little poaching there it is only for that alien the pheasant. The glory of the Chase is departed and the law of nature seems to have been tamed when the law of the land arrived.

The Roman road from Old Sarum to the west strikes down for Badbury Rings which is one of the most effective of Celtic works; it appears the perfect defence of a flawless site and has probably been held often against great odds. It certainly is a place that should make the most sluggish imagination work and has given rise to several legends about the romantic adventures of King Arthur of the Round Table. But Badbury Rings were old when King Arthur walked in Dorset, if he ever did, and Merlin worked his spells across the Channel. The busy hands and keen brains of the Celts who built the fortress were much more important and interesting in making Dorset what it was and is.

There is the story that somewhere on the hilltop will be found the golden coffin, the legend of which crops up several times in Dorset. I have never been able to discover even a hint of anyone expressing a theory about how this story got started, yet casually a man or woman will still drop a word or two about it as lying in this wood or that garden. All these things must once have had something to start on and I have come across the golden coffin enough times to make me believe that there must have been good reason for it to spread and survive as long as it has.

Of course the people who have passed it on by word of mouth for scores of generations were only doing what I am doing now. I have received a hint that it lies somewhere in the village of Worth and also in Downshay wood, and in repeating it here will cause someone to rake up hints about it which they have almost forgotten, and the legend will go on another step. I do it completely without embarrassment, as I have great hopes that some day a great heavy golden coffin will be levered out of Dorset ground. I like to be a link in a chain and would hate to be the last link in any way.

The Roman road turns away from Badbury Rings as if the legionaries had given up any idea of finding the golden coffin if it existed in their day, and swoops down to cross the river at Shapwick where the Stour runs through the highest of the hills. From here it is not far down to Wimborne Minster, which is another place which has found benefit from the Church.

It is not peculiar to Dorset to have towns which find considerable substance in their age-old connections with the Church, but it may be reasonable to speculate how much the power of it has left its mark on the Dorset mentality which does seem a thing apart. We had many centuries of being well under the thumb of the Church with intensive pressure applied from Norman days until Henry VIII at least; during which time the Church sucked the country dry mainly for selfish direct reasons and to the benefit of Rome; and so long as the towns around the Church establishments had a small share in the good things attracted there, it was not surprising that they looked on it as worthwhile.

The Church did encourage martyrs and mystics and seers of strange things, and while there were many pagan thoughts and even observances carried on, at the same time it is natural that there was rather a mix-up in men's minds. A Church establishment drew raw men inside its circle, men who had been cradled in an environment not very far removed from the Celtic hilltop towns, touched by Pagan Rome and then warmed by a Saxon brand of Christianity which travelled a long way to enter Dorset by the back door.

The leaven of Norman latinized culture had something besides clear open minds to work on and the result was, perhaps naturally, not always predictable, but it did give us something in our outlook that is not hard and fast and allows us to wander off the beaten track. A Dorset man does not sharpen every idea into a fine point which injures somebody, if it be only the man who uses it.

Of course, since Henry scattered the Church we have been tempered in the Puritan fire and then survived the shattering effect of John Wesley and Victorian smugness. Yet we still love our religion which has everything in it from the permanency of the Cerne Giant to the mournful respectability of a

159

church or chapel organ moaning for a few minutes once a week.

Wimborne seems quite open about drawing substance from having the splendid Minster in its keeping. Yet it does not appear to be steeped in its Church connection like Shaftesbury and Sherborne. Shaftesbury might easily discover a wonder-worker or a great scholar in its shadow, while Wimborne would be content to draw a royalty from a publicity agent. But their Minster is a remarkable and attractive church, even if it misses being a grand building; it seems to give a lot of weight to decoration and holy relics rather than to realize that such a pile of stone carries its own sense of power.

North of Wimborne, near Horton Heath, it is possible to be directed to Monmouth's Ash, under which the fugitive was picked up when making for Poole where he had every chance of being smuggled away to France and Lady Wentworth. But of course the original tree has been gone many a year and these replaced relics are only effective to those who are willing to be hoodwinked. However, I am informed that Monmouth's Ash is still an ash tree, which is unlike the Larmer Tree up on the Wiltshire border, that for hundreds of years was an elm under which were held the Cranborne Chase Courts where the business of the Chase was thrashed out in very open court. Larmer's Tree is still pointed out, but, by some wizardry, it has become a youngish oak—which is rather apt to spoil the effect.

White Horse, showing King George going away from Weymouth

CHAPTER XI

THE DORSETS

MY earliest memory of the Dorsets was always very hazy and secondhand, but lasting for all that; an older sister used to remember an uncle who had nursed her on his knee so that her face was close to a red jacket. To her he had been a redness and that was all because he had then gone off to the Boer War, while I never saw him at all except through her eyes and the armchair in which he had sat. But to a small boy he could always be brought there on the left side of the fireplace, even if the red coat was very faint and the outline merged into the general shabbiness of the kitchen.

And of course when I saw men in the flesh wearing the red jacket it became a normal boy's ambition to fill it out some day, only to be superseded by still more colourful coats as a widening horizon brought them into view. But the lure of that red coat was and must still be a great thing to be taken into consideration; not only do Teutons like to dress up, but our Celt, Roman, Saxon, Norman blood can respond. Soldiers and all Service men should not only have the best pay and conditions but they should be allowed to outshine the mere civilian.

The Dorsetshire Regiment rightly or wrongly makes the county a shire and if they wish it that way it is not for anyone to question them, although it is likely that the decision to add the shire to Dorset was taken by people very far removed from the county. It smacks of Victoria and it was not until 1881 that the two regiments were amalgamated under that name. But they have made themselves into a famous county regiment since then, adding to a long record of honourable service stretching over nearly two and a half centuries from 1702.

Originally they were the 39th and 54th Foot, the first being in both the 1726–7 and 1779–83 defences of Gibraltar and being the only regiment of the army to have this record,

Hardy's birthplace, Higher Bockhampton

which has given them the Castle of Gibraltar in their crest. Then in 1801, by capturing Fort Marabout in Egypt, they won the Sphinx surmounting the word Marabout, which is a unique honour in the British Army; but "Primus in Indis" is the proudest thing on the badge and is worth a history book on its own.

It not only means that they were the first of the King's regiments to serve in India, which is worth recording, but several years later, in 1757, at Plassey, they were the centre and hard core of a force of 3,000 men, mostly native troops, which stood face to face with some 55,000 including 15,000 cavalry and fifty heavy guns manned by French artillerymen. Threes into fifty-five makes the odds over eighteen to one, which may seem hardly possible, yet the battle ended with the British force holding the whole of the enemy's camp, baggage, guns and stores. That's what the 39th meant.

No wonder they are proud of being First in India, and a five-foot Dorset infantryman has the right to walk off a troop-ship in that country before any other army man. But of course they have not been glamorized; there is no need to flatter the pride of a county regiment, they are always there and always have been there and the equivalent will always be available to be used and then ignored. If they had restricted their ranks to men of mere height, they would have had songs sung about them, for size in soldiers catches the eye as much as anything.

Size, horses and kilts are the soldiers' surest way to the public's regard, and the Dorsets have served as light cavalry when General Sankey put them on mules in Spain and earned them the nickname of "Sankey's Horse." Also they have had considerable experience as marines afloat which makes them something of handy men to have around.

But they were at home on the water and have another special anniversary to keep up which does not fall to many army regiments. They already had another nickname of the "Flamers" after burning the American base and town of New London with its naval stores and twelve ships, when in 1857 they were caught in the Indian Ocean on the *Sarah Sands* well afire with the stern blown away. The ship's captain had given up hope and most of the crew had taken to the boats, while the holds still contained a lot more gunpowder; but the troops fought the fire for seventeen hours until they saved what was left of the ship and then got her to Mauritius after twelve days of gruelling work at the pumps. They had earned a second claim to be known as the "Flamers," and their achievement was read out at the head of every regiment in the army.

The main siege of Gibraltar was four years of the usual dirt, filth, hunger and scurvy and exposure to all the rigours of climate. It is the history of all soldiers and the garrison had to fight off the combined Spanish and French fleets on the sea, and overpowering numbers from the land approach. Yet the end was that the defence, weakened by four years of toil and fighting under shocking conditions, came out and cleared the enemy both on land and sea. That again was what the 39th meant.

It is interesting that a man who had considerable effect on bringing about the abolition of flogging in the army was once a sergeant-major of the 54th—William Cobbett, who became a famous social reformer and died a Member of Parliament. It is not many sergeant-majors who have the makings of reformers in them, and knowing that Cobbett had been through the mill proves that his "Rides" were not merely the outcome of social theories.

In the early nineteenth century the line of thought which was followed by authority is shown by what happened when a mutiny broke out in the garrison of Gibraltar. The 54th did not join the mutiny but behaved with unflinching loyalty and discipline; the rights or wrongs of the mutiny or the loyalty is not to be questioned here and now, but the result somehow again smacks of the hand of Victoria. The Duke of Kent gave to the Officers' Mess plate to the value of four hundred guineas, which somehow seems to be a strange way to reward the rank and file for all that may have been behind the term "unflinching loyalty."

The Boer War saw the Dorsets the last to leave the hill at the Battle of Spion Kop. They marched and fought for several years while they learnt how to wear down the enemy. And in all actions in which they took part in that rather unsatisfactory war, they got the highest praise from every high officer who handled them, gaining a name for the Dorsets

163

and upholding the grand traditions of the old 39th and 54th. The regiment again had a Mounted Infantry Company, but they had more conventional mounts than the mules of Sankey's Horse of affectionate memory.

Nineteen-fourteen saw the 1st Battalion early in France in time to line the Mons Canal where the Germans, flushed with success after success, stubbed themselves against the British "contemptible little army" of lasting fame. It is well known that the super-excellence of the British infantry rifle fire saved the Channel Ports then, and Germans still believe that the line was held by machine guns and not rifles.

The Dorsets like all other regiments lost heavily in the fighting retreat to the Marne, and also when the defence turned over to attack. Four hundred Dorsets fell to a division of Jaegers, and they were a mere skeleton when they were taken out to be reinforced. By the time poison gas was used in the spring of 1915 the Dorsets were on Hill 60 and many of them died there silently, putting to the test whether discipline would stand up to another new and terrible weapon.

The 2nd Battalion was in India and in October 1914 was sent to Mesopotamia as the only white unit of an Indian Brigade. There not only did it have a lot of hard fighting but broke much new ground towards learning how it could be made possible for white troops even to exist under the condition of flies, heat and general unpleasantness.

In reading the history of the regiment it is more than interesting to see how often the Dorsets were "first in"; there was the Leipzig Redoubt in 1916 and again in 1944 the entry into Germany. It is a great pity that the people of the county do not know more about their own regiment, even if they are not all six feet high and wear no kilts and ride no horses. Anyway, many of them did ride the modern horse, called the Bren carrier, and it would be possible to write a colourful story about them which might make people realize that there was and is something exciting as well as sturdy in the county men.

Nineteen-forty found the 2nd Battalion at Dunkirk, and although only 240 survived to reach the coast they arrived still a fighting unit and eight of their Bren carriers were last seen going in to fight it out with nine tanks. Individually the men still had their tails up when a sergeant and two privates asked and received permission to swim over a canal they were defending, to obtain enemy identifications, which under the circumstances might hardly have seemed to matter much.

The 1st Battalion was at Malta and made a special point of not letting low rations interfere with fighting off air attacks, clearing bomb damage and keeping aerodromes as serviceable as possible. Some even turned their hand to servicing aircraft in the general shortage of everything, but that redounds to the credit of the fliers who had to fly aircraft manhandled by the Dorset footsloggers! Malta was a battle in which everyone who took part can be proud, and we can be sure that the hundreds of the Dorset's forerunners who had died at Gibraltar looked across with approval.

But there is something in being islanders for all of us. Our own British Isles, which the world thought lost in 1940, how small they must have looked on the map to Germans and others of that kind, especially with that open flank on the south-west. Even some of the rest of the world still outside the conflict breathed easier, because when this last little fighting spot was rubbed out the trouble would be over for a while until Hitler was ready again for another of his one by one.

Yet history ought to have shown that when there are a few British on an island or rock, here at home or elsewhere like Malta or Gibraltar, it is going to take a lot to shift them off and they will stay there just that little bit longer than anyone else. The proof seems assured when it is remembered that the weight of the German might was turned against all Russia rather than attempt to crush the real kernel of resistance.

The 1st Battalion of Dorsets at Malta followed the tradition : after taking all the dirt there, they were in the beach landing of Sicily, then Italy and finally Normandy. The shades of all the 39th and the 54th, and the Dorsets who have died all over the world, must have looked on and said, "I told you so, we can take the dirt and then give it back. Them boys down there ain't whacked yet. Good old Sankey's Horse-and Flamers-and Dirty Dorsets."

Nor is the impossible beyond them, for they shared in that in Burma where, almost unknown, and certainly unsung, they accomplished a feat of arms as well as endurance past normal understanding. There is a Regimental Memorial to many good Dorsets at Kohima where they won and held a vital and all-important road junction on the road to Imphal; it was a typical bit of dirty work which so seldom gets sung about, but one more good sound thing to have in the regiment's firm structure.

If the Germans had dared in 1940—and that small word "if" will always be the keystone of all history of the future—if the Germans had dared try the cleaning up of the last fighting corner of Europe, then the Dorsets would unescapably have had a big share in the lively time that would have come about our doors, because with the Canadians they were some of the very few fully armed troops still left here. And the Dorsets have a valued connection with Les Fusiliers de Sherbrooke of the Canadian Army.

The Dorsets' claim to be the first infantry to enter Germany is because at 4.35 p.m. on 29 September 1944 one of its patrols was across the River Maas in contact with British armour and U.S. airborne troops. We can be sure that in the years to come there will be other such claims but it is quite in the tradition of the Dorsets to be the first again. Primus is one of their second names. We see it again at the Barnard Battle School where the Young Soldier Battalion has come to the front to become the demonstration battalion. Long may the Dorsets remain Primus.

But I received a slightly sobering contact quite recently when I travelled in a train with some Dorsets coming on leave from over the water. Without being bold enough in the overcrowded compartment to open my own mouth I listened with a real mental smile to some good Dorset men's voices, and they were happy because they were going home. Then after a stop and change I found myself in easier conditions with just two other men of the regiment, and after deciding that they were good types such as I knew well, we got talking together. Neither of that couple belonged to the county, they were just two men whom the army had "pushed around"!

We must accept that all the Dorsetshire Regiment does not speak our way, but the dialect is well worth while because Dorset was something when Wessex represented a kingdom, and William Barnes was not wrong when he suggested that if the kings had stayed there the Dorset way of speaking would have made everything else a dialect. Perhaps he was not on such sure ground when he claimed that we spoke the oldest British tongue, but there is no room for doubt that we talked correctly, whatever that means, at the time when the American continent was being opened up.

The way people of that continent speak to-day proves that —despite all that has contributed to that colourful English tongue. The first people over there, at least those who set the tone either in numbers or moral quality, took our way of speaking, call it west country if you like. It may not come through all the nasal twang and slick phrases, but it is the basis of it all. When I listen to some American speaker on the air he so often sounds like a Dorset man who has gone over there and picked up a touch of something else. He may not approve of my saying that but he cannot deny that much of his way of expression went from over here.

Nor is that entirely a one-sided idea of my own. I speak with a very definite Dorset burr, and many times I have been taken for a Canadian, sometimes embarrassingly so. Once a waiter at an expensive dinner singled me out for attention in a way I could not understand. I was merely a guest of the party, yet he hung over my shoulder whispering about places in New York and Canada where he had worked. He seemed to think we had something in common while in truth I knew precisely nothing about what he was hinting, and after a long time I told him so.

"But you are a Canadian," he told me flatly, "I know you by the way you talk."

My reply, "No, I'm a Dorset man," not only made him recoil as if I had suddenly looked up and sworn, but he left me severely alone after that and glared across as if I was to blame for his mistake.

Another time was when I had to talk hard to prevent myself being arrested as a Canadian deserter from the army (that was not in Dorset), and while it was flattering to find that I still looked good enough to be thought a Canadian soldier, it was surprising to find that the burr of my voice apparently had more weight than the truth of my identity card. Incidentally, I escaped from that embarrassment by remembering that I knew a policeman of the same county force. Some fifty miles away a country copper was notorious for his drinking habits and could lower an amazing number of pints in an amazing short time. I knew him, and by expressing the proper amount of awe for his achievements was able to prove that I was no stranger from a far country across the water. My identity card was pushed back at me and almost, although not quite, I received apologies, but "I thought that I had the so-and-so when you opened your mouth." A few generations across the Atlantic have not destroyed all the good points of our words.

Some people smile at the Dorset way of talking without realizing that they themselves sound just as uncouth and unnatural to us. They would be on surer ground if instead of objecting to the accent they pointed out the different grammar that we may use. I say different rather than bad grammar, because that is a thing that does change with the years, and after all we in this country have not got any official body to say what is or is not acceptable. A Dorset man may be merely a bit behind the times when he mixes up his tenses, but he is not wrong.

I myself have no objection to any kind of accent although some of them are ugly to my ears, and some sound affected, and if the grammar is understandable there is no reason to worry about it. That well-known jibe that a Dorset man might say, "You didn't ought to have let her went," is not so bad as can be suggested. After all, "didn't ought" *ought not* to suggest anything else, and if she has already gone, well, she "went."

And to write as it would be spoken it would be necessary to put, "Thee disen ought t'ave let 'er went." But it is impossible to write in dialect. Barnes did so with some success but many of his words as written do not produce the sounds I would make. Of course since his time the great increase of movement has resulted in much bastardizing of our speech, but such advances, improvements or otherwise, must always go on in such a living thing as a people's speech.

Certainly Barnes would say that I spoke an impure tongue, and while I know that he was a great scholar as well as a dialect poet, I should have to maintain that my way of talking

Stinsford Church, where Hardy would have wished to lie
Bere Heath

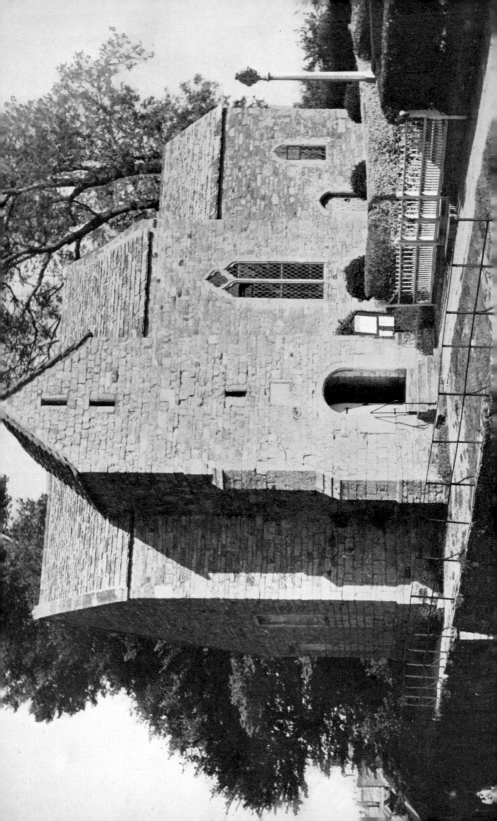

was pure of its time and place. And that is what matters most; a thing carried out of its time and environment is no longer pure because in refusing to move it has itself become alien.

Barnes wrote of the "old woak" and I have heard many people speak naturally of woak trees and woaken tables and coffins; nor is woak for oak so very uncouth, as some of our words, like "one" for example, use the letter "w" without putting it in the spelling. But my experience is that we would more likely use the letter to say the wold oak instead of Barnes's old woak, it is quite in order for me to say that "the wold man is dead like the wold oak tree," and even that he is "going to be buried in a [not an] woaken coffin," but even to me it would feel something of an effort to say "the wold man is dead like the wold woak tree and is going to be buried in a wold woaken coffin."

I say that it might seem an effort to me, but that may be because much water has run off the chalk hills since Barnes's day. Yet he must have known that all old things in Dorset are wold. And in the wolden days as now everyone used the word old much more than oak in the daily round, he may have liked the idea of the woaken man so like the woaken tree, but his "old woak" does not strike as true as "wold oak" would to me, and to be really consistent he should have written of the "wold woak."

Few things are more pathetic or irritating, according to how you look on them, than when a person who has had the advantage of some education gets up on public occasions to give a rendering of local talk. I have never been able to decide how much of it may be a compliment and how much is patronage, but it seldom is convincing and anyway the locals can do it so much better because it is purer with them. An even worse offence is when a local man who, perhaps, has reached some position in his small environment talks Dorset in an exaggerated way when he is talking to less fortunate people, just to show how far he can condescend to their level.

Why there should be so much pother made about accents is hard to say. The worst way to speak is that of many people who attempt an affectation which seldom comes off. But few of us who were brought up in dialect can escape some such

169

thing as we have to keep two senses of values in mind, and it is easier to slip up in two versions of one language than to be bilingual.

I once knew a chemist who made great play on the fact that I had lived in the village of Worth, and as Worth is high up on the hills we speak of anything happening as "up Wor' " instead of saying the whole of "up at Worth." And this chemist liked to speak of "Wor' " in supposed ridicule, only he was so afraid of spoiling his own affected accent that he merely made a noise like Wa-a-a. He would say, "You know, up Wa-a-a, Ha-a-a." Certainly we never called our village any such uncouth noise, it was Wor' spoken to rhyme with burr.

There is something I like very much in such things as "nit fish, nit fowl, nit good red herring." There the word "nit" can mean, "not" fish, "neither" fowl, "nor" good red herring; it is "not," "neither," "nor," just as you wish, and much depends on the intonation used. Dorset voices have a way of moving up into a rather high pitch at times which has nothing to do with emotion, despite the definite burr which is formed in the throat.

Of course much of our way of speaking is just laziness, as many a good man who literally has not a lazy bone in his body sees no reason to make any effort with such an unimportant member as his tongue. We slur many words together without opening our throats at all, and as lazy people have got to make the most effort after all, we have to reach high for some things if we want them. I am sure that is why we use a long-drawn-out "ah" instead of a "yes," and then have to actually take the "yes" from the roof of our mouths with the tongue.

Of course the machine age is going to destroy good dialect voices, not only because we, or, still more important, all the new young people, hear so much standardized speech over the air and pick up the less worthwhile things from the screen, but because the age calls for so much more technical language in everyday talk. The most benighted of us can hardly go through life with a vocabulary of about two hundred words now and expect an ordinary day's work to call for only half of them.

Every day calls for the effort to attempt a new word and
such words as we only guessed at thirty years ago; it would
be pointless to try to repeat here any of the words that have
come into ordinary conversation during the last few years,
and thanks to receiving them over the air by spoken voice
they do not stand much chance of being rendered into dialect.
The B.B.C. may leave me my wold man in a woaken coffin
for my lifetime, but my grandchildren will never use it except
perhaps in a little affection for the poor wold man of wolden
days.

In another thirty or forty years when all my generation
have gone and we were the last of the golden age—using the
word in keeping with the speech is a silver idea—it is going to
be very difficult for people to realize what life was before the
voices of the world were available at a switch of a knob. Even
I have already spent far too much of my life lying abed unable
to sleep because a neighbour's wireless set went on and on
indefinitely—and I admit that I have been kept awake by a
nightingale's song and by some cathedral bells whose sound
was said to be tremendously tuneful—but the bird or the bells
did not belch blaring music while the alleged listeners shouted
"conversation" above the noise and even chopped firewood.

If that can happen in a country cottage, where the wireless
set relies on the recharging of the leaky batteries, how bur-
densome life will be when the full power of the grid system,
which crisscrosses every field, becomes available to every
hamlet at the same cheaper rate it is in the towns. An American, Nathaniel Macon, used to say that the American nation
should be built up by men living where no man could hear his
neighbour's dog bark, and while that is rather out of the
question in Dorset I do wish something could be done towards
seeking a way to blanket other people's taste in the wireless
programmes. Spending £500,000,000 on seeking a new
energy is all very well (perhaps a few noughts are missing or
added but a few scarcely matter any more than what money
symbol is placed before them), but it is to be hoped that some
effort will be made to protect a few of us, who want and need
protection, from too much machine energy.

Since I have been writing of the Dorsetshire Regiment the
War Office has decided to end recruiting on a county basis for

the county regiments, the overriding reason being given as the necessity of the military service itself. Yet the change will cause no loss to the regiments concerned! On this kind of assumption and announcement anything under the sun can be accounted for. The overriding necessity of this or that service has always been the excuse of those who have a horse to ride or an axe to grind.

Of course it was a necessity during the war to put a Dorset man where there was a place or need for him, but for the future, which we hope will not be so entirely a military affair, there can be no necessity to put him in the London Rifles or something like that. It seems far more likely that the necessity is a clerk's necessity to make things easier for that side of the army, a very poor thing to balance against the hard-won and really valuable traditions of the regiments. But of course it will be so much easier to do the book-keeping if the man from a Dorset chalk village can be treated as just a figure in a clerk's ledger without having to bother about fitting him in the Dorsets, even if he wants to be.

So it appears that there will be even less Dorset speech from the men with Primus on their crests, and with the standardized or average speech there will be one more step towards a standardized Englishman, a unit in a ledger. And how easy it will be to run everything. Even the B.B.C. instead of widening their programmes will need to have only one, the clerk's ideal age.

But perhaps our standardized machine future will still leave a few odd fellows to poke around and take an interest in things and people who are not so terrifically efficient on paper, until perhaps we may have a rarity value. I may not be the last of the aboriginal Dorset men, but it is going to be harder to rear them quite so closely bred.

And although the Dorset of which I have had personal experience has been entirely in the first half of the twentieth century, there is no point in trying to hide the fact that much of the charm of the county and its people is founded on what has gone before. And while both we and Dorset have retained perhaps more of it than most others, it may disperse under the onslaught of the second half-century when we are promised so much more speed and paper efficiency. It is now the end of 1945, exactly 1900 years since Rome destroyed the then very ancient town of Maiden Castle, but Rome is a mere incident now on the chalk hills while the town site is still there in its original layout.

It may be said that I have returned and returned again to Roman Dorset because it has left such a great mark on so much there; but always to me it has been the mere impression of a heavy hand and a few words and names left by a passing tide of conquest. We never absorbed Rome, neither did it alter our own foundations. Fortunately the science of archæology has become intelligent and not merely content to destroy its subject in study and then to shut the result up in dusty tomes for learned men to discuss. I have the Reports of the Research Committee of the Society of Antiquaries of London dealing with Maiden Castle, by R. E. M. Wheeler, in which my Celtic forerunners have been made to come to life, and Rome, the Dark Ages and all the rest can be seen as just passing phases. So, perhaps even our own new destructive Age will not be able to wipe out the visible connection any more than it will be able to destroy the blood.

It has long been my ambition to reconstruct Maiden Castle as a town in going order, and the Reports make the attempt possible. A reconstruction may also help to interpret Dorset and Dorset people to others. So many of us have one foot at least figuratively still in the hilltop towns and there is always the comforting feeling that we could retire there in comparative well-being when the rest of the world has lost the race with its machines and atomic energy.

CHAPTER XII

THE TOWN OF MAIDEN CASTLE

1

FOR untold generations men saw the River Frome flow slowly to the sea before any one of them ever dreamed of bridging it; to them it was a valuable barrier because no man wished to come near his unknown fellow, and every river or other natural obstruction was one less worry. That secure flank or back-to-the-wall feeling comes to most active men at some time in their lives, although it may express itself in many other ways than by a man standing with his rear protected by a river of water.

Long after men achieved enough mutual trust to live in groups they still could not trust a stranger near, so it would never enter their heads to build a bridge over a river, which would invite strangers to cross and approach. Early man did not build bridges nor show much evidence of knowing how to swim; he treated water with respect, and hoped his enemies did too.

The Frome always had its beginnings in the chalk springs of Dorset, some of the springs breaking ground where very little chance could have caused them to run to the north into the wide plains of Somerset instead of south to end up in the English Channel at Poole Harbour. Chalk has an appearance of coaxing a stream along as if it did not want to give the water a chance to see how easily the friable chalk can be damaged. A rocky valley may seem to throw the water along until it is upset in itself and just tries to escape down to easier country. Only in wide, fertile, flat country do the river and land appear to get on well together and flow along in harmony as if they could tell the world a thing or two.

So the Frome and its tributaries are guided down to near Dorchester, where the River Cerne joins in. The Cerne water has come from the country of the great Cerne Giant and perhaps has picked up the meaning of that big fertility symbol. The Frome, now a respectable chalk river, gives up trying to push through to the nearest sea in Weymouth Bay, and is content to make the much longer journey east to Poole Harbour. Along the whole way the chalk remains the real controlling influence, but has retired on both flanks until the river has forgotten it and flows on quietly until it reaches salt water in Poole Harbour.

When the river flowed the whole way without a bridge, there was already a town of great age lying two miles south of the bend and near the junction of the Cerne, but well away from the water because those who first planned it did so with an eye on hill defence. In 2000 B.C. the south of England had settlers' communities of agricultural people with their system of fields and flocks and herds, but there great suspicion still existed between these groups which may have been tribes grown out of family gatherings.

An agricultural tribe settled on its own fields is the first step towards civilization, and this was a great mental step away from the conditions where one man with his mate or mates roamed unceasingly in search of natural food, and drove off his own sons as soon as they grew near the state of rivalling his unquestioned authority. As long as a man fought or fled from his fellows there was no chance that any personal advancement could be shared and therefore carried on; and yet until a man did show others how to increase the natural food there could have been little opportunity of their drawing together for mutual aid.

It probably took some comparatively gigantic catastrophe to force people into coming together, just as a forest fire or widespread floods will cause animals to share some strange company at a pinch when the danger forces them to crowd on to the last bit of clear land. As the danger retreats the animals recover their mutual distrust, but as the human intelligence is always ready to advance, it is likely that instead of dispersing each into his family group again men stayed together, and soon discovered that as a whole they were better off. In the same circumstances of an enforced gathering, a man with more power may have forced the others to stay with him as a bigger example of the family group, but in some way all men have gradually overcome the futility of roaming alone.

Civilization in all its many shapes was not a thing that

sprang up in one particular nation or part of the earth. The Egyptians, and later the Greeks and Romans, possessed, or rather achieved, a great advancement which crept north and west until it took in the islands of Britain, but the people here already had achieved a great amount of their own. Some of their engineering and astrological knowledge, of which there is ample proof, was by no means inferior to any other. There were at least two things against Britain being able to make so great a show of civilization as the Mediterranean nations : there is no evidence of a teeming slave population to carry out great schemes of building, and even more important, the climate and soil oppose the preservation of any evidence except that which is bulky and practically indestructible.

Yet a British civilization, in the sense of advanced thinking, left such evidence as the engineering feat of Stonehenge, which in itself proves an extent of astrological knowledge. Such things did not just "come about," any more than an Egyptian Temple or the Greek language or Roman Law; the hard stone is all that our climate has left, but to those who can see it the work of man's brain is there as well. Too often the war reports of Julius Cæsar are taken at their face value, yet they are sometimes second-hand at best.

At least two thousand years before the Romans reached the country, some man had chosen a hill two miles south of the Frome as a place to build a settlement, and seeing it to-day one can get a good idea of what he was looking for. First he wanted a hilltop that could be defended and enough clear land to grow food. Apart from the necessity of defence he would have to keep to the hills, as all low-lying land was forest-covered and every watercourse a swamp, and the only way to move from district to district was to follow the ridgeway roads well up on dry land. It was as if, besides living on an island surrounded by the sea, the people were tied to islands in the forests and swamps.

People had lived on the river in smaller camps, but the need for more space would be one reason for sending them up on the open hilltops, and perhaps the fact that the site of Maiden Castle is just off two ridgeway roads may mean that people wished to get away from the danger of strangers moving through the country.

176

The Gatehouse, Cerne Abbas

Before the cutting of the first turf, and it is likely that they carried out some such ceremony with more meaning than is done to-day, even although the idea has survived into an allegedly totally scientific age, some man walked around the site with the plan of the finished structure already in his mind. He had chosen the eastern knoll although it was some ten feet lower than another just to the west, because this chosen site had the steepest slope just outside where the new walls would be placed.

It would be well to get an idea of the size of the work they were going to start. The first enclosure was to be some ten acres in extent and surrounded by an earth wall. The material would come from an outside ditch as much as seven feet across and five deep; it was a big job for anyone to face with the comparative lack of digging tools; every bit of earth and chalk was levered out of place with such things as deerhorn picks, and perhaps carted upwards in baskets. The idea of every bit of loose material being picked or scooped up by hand is not quite as impossible as many people think; hard-handed men can use their hands as shovels in a way that needs to be seen.

But the ditch did get dug and the wall one day completed the rough circle. It was perhaps the first town on the site, and the Neolithic builders had every right to feel proud of their work, although it is not likely that they had a moving-in day, as they would be living there long before the work was finished.

A man's home was where his fire was, and he had no trouble moving his effects, as they merely consisted of a cooking-pot and a few tools. On such work as this he would work all the daylight hours except those needed to bring food up the hill, and a small fire in the shelter of the new walls would be a considerable protection for him. So the people would begin their town life as they got on with the job, and although they were doing it under the stress of some kind of pressure, the importance of securing their crops meant that all the usual field work had to be done at the same time.

It would have been no use building a strong defensible wall if during that time they had neglected any of their food-growing. Life at the best meant stretching the available food a long way, and nowhere on the whole site is there any evidence of storage to any extent at all comparable to what would be necessary to any modern people. So food must always remain the big thing in their lives even while building against some definite threat. It speaks for the advancement they had made that they no longer just moved away from danger. They had achieved a standard of living which made it worth while staying there to hold on to and continue.

There is much evidence of how these Neolithic people lived in their new town, and also evidence of how the chalk material in the wall crumbled and slipped down, of how the ditch gradually became shallower until the place must have begun to look shabby. All that may have been the natural neglect of shiftless people who had inherited a well-constructed earthworks from more energetic forefathers; they may have been able to convince themselves that their town life was still secure behind strong walls, but they also began to dig their hearth pits outside the walls in the ditch itself. Whole families must have lived outside, and that points to other things as well as neglect.

In all periods of history there are times of danger when men draw together and plan defence; when they prepare in time they may complete their defence as they were able to complete the walls of the first Maiden Castle, and when they are too late it is seldom that they leave much evidence. But even the most dangerous way of living becomes everyday life in time, and people can forget to keep everything prepared. The obvious neglect at Maiden Castle suggests something more than that, and it may just be that there was a period of peace when it was no longer necessary to remain behind strong walls.

In any case the site was later almost if not quite abandoned for a while and certainly was no longer a stronghold, because it was chosen as a burial-place for one man. But the mound built over him was something unusual even for those days; it was no less than 1,790 feet in length and some 60 feet wide, a super Long Mound by any standards.

It was the custom to bury the great dead of the time in grand solitude on a lonely hilltop, and this super Long Mound placed on the site of Maiden Castle was for no ordinary great man, or they would not have placed his grave on what was

178

then a town site or a site that was likely to be used again. It is certain that those Neolithic people had no more use for the place, and while agriculture of their kind is an industry which does not boom and lag with some fickle demand, because the demand of hunger is always there, it is not likely that the fields around went out of use, if only because such fields had been too hardly won out of the forest.

So apart from some natural disaster wiping out most of the people, the reason for abandoning the town was likely to be some improvement in the political outlook of the south. The pressure that had sent their forefathers to the hilltop behind strong walls had somehow been eased or absorbed, enabling them to live somewhere outside; the evidence proves that they were not suddenly driven away and had stayed on there after the neglect of the defences was far advanced. Nor were they nomad people who might move off with their herds; their mode of living was centred on and around the hill.

There must have been more peaceful and settled times. They were again able to live in the lower lands nearer their fields and the forest which supplied so much of their needs, they could live near water instead of carrying it up the hill and could build fires without carrying the fuel long distances. There seemed every reason for leaving the town which was always as bare of necessities as the naked hill before anyone thought of living there.

But there is just as much reason for peaceful and settled periods as for periods of stress—even more so in the comparatively simple and uncomplicated political structure of those times. A strong raiding party ravaging through the country could threaten the whole stability of a district, a year's harvest successfully destroyed could strike an almost fatal blow. On the other hand, one strong man working for the good of a district would have been able to bring about great local improvements in the order and safety of everyone.

Was it such a man, or rather the heir of such a line of men, whom the people honoured above all by giving him the greatest Long Mound for his burial, which they built in and across the abandoned town site because he had shown them that all that that stood for was behind them?

We can dismiss any idea that he belonged to some rich and

powerful family who had the power to buy up or commandeer a city lot and use it as a very desirable vault. In the stark realism of Neolithic society there was no room or even the extra substance for a wealthy or leisured class. A man might be powerful but it would have to be useful power, and strictly confined within the limits of ordinary life as led by the people as a whole.

Whatever the reason of his important burial, it was not that he was an old wise man whose long years of service had endeared him to the people, because he was not more than thirty-five years at death; nor was he some gigantic warrior who had achieved sheer physical success from mere bulk, because he was of the normal stature of his kind. His position seems to have rested on the personality of the man, and the treatment offered to his body more than suggests that his brain was taken away and used for some special purpose.

Probably it was dedicated to the greatest good for the greatest number, but someone insisted on having it, because the medico of the day only obtained it at the third effort; and although that may suggest that he was a bungler, his failure was in the field of anatomy and certainly not in the technical sense at all. His flint cut neat enough holes in the skull but not in the right place to obtain the brain.

Also the legs and arms were broken in several places as if to ensure that he could never walk or strike a blow again; and all this may appear to prove that he had been taken by some enemy and utterly destroyed to make an end to all his works, and his brain eaten to provide them with the knowledge of how he did it. And that perhaps his people merely obtained and honoured his broken remains by taking them up to the hilltop and building the Long Mound over them.

But it could not have been done that way. The work was carried out there on the burial-site, and the head treated first and then the body, the legs and arms being severed before being broken.

Whatever the circumstances of his death it is evident that he lay there in his Long Mound undisturbed for a long time; the hilltop was given over to him with other mound-burials dotted about on other hills in the neighbourhood. The fashion in mounds changed in shape, but the living did not dwell on the hills with them, and if they still lived inside strongholds like Maiden Castle but built in the valleys, the wear and tear of life on that busier level has swept them away.

Even if they lived behind strong walls down on the level, those defences could hardly compare with a hilltop site, so the conditions must have been relatively more easy and peaceful. But there is also a theory that Europe went through a prolonged dry spell which not only impaired the usefulness of the high chalk fields—too long a rain shortage would destroy them completely—but also made some of the swamps and river bottoms habitable. These conditions forced the populations off the hills but made the lowlands available, and that could be the reason why the first Maiden Castle was given over to a burial-site. But it still seems preferable to hold that the cause was more local, and depended on the waxing and waning of civilization and what it then stood for.

Perhaps the increasing and excessive rain of some gigantic weather cycle drove the people back up on the hills again, for they did return to the old site despite the Long Mound lying across it; and it is certain that they returned during the early part of the Iron Age, in which it might also be as well to look for the reason of the return. Iron placed a tremendous power in the hands of those who possessed it, and power has always made men seek out other people's land and possessions. What is more likely than that pressure was once more exerted on the already age-old move to the westward? The people who actually came to these islands may not have deliberately wanted to come in cold blood, but any real movement of populations causes some pressure in the most distant static areas.

Britain received the miracle of iron as did all countries in the old world, but it is safe to say that some of the effects of that miracle were felt long before any piece of iron was seen here. Iron brought in a new age just as surely as some other discoveries such as steam, radio, and flying. Maiden Castle may have been rebuilt and reoccupied in the search for safety in the new age, yet long before any iron weapon was used there.

The walls of the first town had been little more than a heap made of the material thrown up out of two ditches, one inside and one outside. The new builders had advanced their engineering knowledge throughout the seven-hundred-odd years during which the people themselves seem to have become Celtic instead of Neolithic. The new walls were not merely a heap of material, but both back and front were retained by timber with comparatively massive posts set about five feet apart. This evidence of the use of real timber suggests that they did have the new and efficient iron cutting tools.

This wall was a real obstacle in itself, in that it presented an upright surface which needed actual climbing, and was not just a difficult slope which must be faced in full view of the defenders standing on it. It stood some twelve feet in height and the same in thickness, and the new ditch outside protecting it was not only steep but as much as twenty feet deep and fifty across. Taking into consideration the platform running between the wall and the ditch, any suspicious-looking stranger coming near was at least sixty feet away before he even passed the farther tip of the ditch, and such a distance spelt safety with the weapons of the day.

While kept in good condition the walls must have been impregnable to any attack, as all the time the attackers were in the ditch they were exposed to everything that could be thrown down on their heads; and even if they could fight their way out of it and reach the wall itself they were then exposed to hard fighting with opponents standing above them. And although it is not likely that the attackers developed night fighting even for the sake of surprise, the advantage of darkness was much reduced as long as the slopes of the ditch were kept in something of their original whiteness. On the darkest of nights a patrolling sentinel on the walls had a good chance of seeing any movement of darker objects against the chalk.

The new wall had roughly followed the line of the first rampart—the contours of the hill decided that; but having less rounded corners and no inner ditch it enclosed about sixteen acres instead of something more than ten. And it is remarkable that, with strength and defensibility the chief purposes in building it at all, it should have both a western and an eastern entrance. For the sake of safety it would surely have been better policy to make people walk all around the outside and enter by one gate, trading public convenience for military convenience.

Yet probably there were people who insisted on a way out at their end of the town, although the western side with the slightly higher ground just beyond was always the weak spot of the early site. Nor was the western entrance just a foot-path for the convenience of those who worked outside in that direction; it needed a gate nineteen feet wide to close it. A lot of modern traffic could pass through such a gateway, and it does appear unnecessary even if the flocks and herds did sometimes come inside at night.

And the eastern entrance was doubled with two gateways, so that, on a peaceful day when there was no danger near, the town must have been wide open and the townspeople can have felt little restriction on their movements. That the danger of these wide gateways was soon apparent is shown by the fact that a new work was carried out to run flanking ditches and walls outwards to give the eastern gate protection. It was an afterthought, because this work was built on or cut through the scarcely used road metalling laid outside the gate. They had to sacrifice an open space that appears to have been where the cattle were either kept at night or penned up in small pens for some kind of market.

The period during which this open space had been so used could not have been long, but long enough for new engineering ideas to reach or grow in the town. The new short walls run out from the gateways were built in the same way but, instead of being held in place by the big timber posts, they were faced up with dry stone walling. This step from timber to stone may suggest that the timber had not been quite good enough to support the sagging weight of loose chalk, or that these builders of the second Maiden Castle had put up their walls under the threat of close danger and therefore had used the available timber; or again, that they were newcomers to the district who had perhaps driven out the native people with the aid of the new iron and, not knowing the resources of the district, had not discovered that there was a valuable outcrop of stone over the hill to the south and only two miles from the site.

In any case, stone was first used to retain the bulky chalk walls of the gateway extensions, and also, to back up and strengthen the main surrounding walls when these were made thicker, stone seems to have come into fashion; and that may

183

also have come about through the use of iron tools to aid the work in the quarries.

There appears to have been only one worn and metalled street inside the walls, and that did not run from the eastern to western gateways, but bore off to one side to the highest part of the town. And it is of great interest that although they had included part of the now ancient Long Mound inside the walls, they apparently respected it by not building into it. It must have been somewhat in the way as it occupied some of their limited space; they may have fought bitter controversies about leaving this relic of old days; on one side, wanting to do away with what was to them after all only an earth monument to some unknown man of the dim past, they could point to all the sites for their modern desirable homes which this monster grave occupied.

But the side in favour of retaining the Long Mound as it was held the day, and during the occupation no pits were dug in it nor hut posts placed on it, although the flanking ditches from which the material of the mound had been dug were taken over and used. So people lived right up against it with apparently no overwhelming awe of it as the abode of the spirit of the dead, and that shows it was not only fear and superstition that prevented them from incorporating it in the town. The property sharks of the day had not reached the stage they have since.

This Iron Age town thrived for some hundred years or so, and then expanded in an amazing way which needs some explanation if that is possible. In the end all towns have spread outside their original walls, but usually only after a considerable period of peaceful conditions, even if those peaceful conditions in the district are obtained at the cost of allowing the walled town to become strong enough to force its will and laws on the unprotected countryside. And even then the first dwellings outside were always mean hovels where the very poor could live, as, not being valuable enough to have shelter wasted on them, they could take the first risk; and when such people had lived outside long enough to prove that it had really become safe, then the more valuable townspeople might venture out and so begin the spread of a film of town right into the country.

But Maiden Castle did not gradually spread in that way, and there is no evidence that it had become safe to live outside the walls. The population might have swollen until it burst the walls, but even so that could not account for an earthwork enclosing about sixteen acres suddenly needing the great enlargement to forty-six acres.

The greatest natural expansion of the smaller town could not suddenly have provided enough people to defend the new bigger one, and the very fact of strong walls still being necessary proves that they only built to a size they could defend within reason. Natural growth might have made them take in double their area still without needing to defend double the length of wall, but in some way they were able to jump straight from a village to a considerable town by any standards.

The whole thing hints strongly at the town being overwhelmed in some way, not necessarily a military defeat and occupation. The newcomers could have been kindred people wanting to join up for mutual aid, perhaps only economic aid because town life was showing some advantage.

There was no outstanding change in military methods at the time of the enlargement—they still needed only the one wall and outer ditch; nor, because the actual construction was different, does that in itself mean that the work was under different guidance. The first wall had been timber-retained and upright, presenting a surface to be actually climbed, whereas the extension was a mere steeply-battered heap of material, and the slope of it was merely brought up from the bottom of the ditch. It was no longer a barrier in itself but a difficult obstacle to rush, and it provided that the would-be rushers arrived at the top of the wall in no good condition to grapple with the defenders waiting there.

This again suggests that there was no shortage of defenders for the considerable new length of wall, although the old type of upright wall had proved rather troublesome to keep in good repair. Where the new wall abutted on the old and covered it, it has left proof that the chalk filling had burst through the timber facing and trickled down both back and front, so forming a working plan for the battered construction of the new work. This type of sloping wall needed constant

attention as it was inclined to trickle down into the ditch, and
it was often refaced and added to in height, with later stone
walling built behind to strengthen it.

Here then was the hill town ready to house its greater
population who must have cleared extensive new fields for
their support. The neighbourhood must have teemed with
busy people during such events as harvest-time, and with the
continuous work needed on the walls, the digging of dwelling-
pits and building it is likely that there were no idle hands in
normal times. The thing should be and was a going concern
under the conditions of the day, and only some new development in the way of living was likely to upset it.

2

HAVING established the town on the hill in the greatest form
it would attain, it may be as well to notice the place it was
likely to hold in the whole scheme of life in the south of
Britain. First, it was off the beaten track of any regular trade
route, and this appears to have been deliberate, because the
site was by no means the only one in the district nor the best
natural defensive hill if that had been the only asset looked for.

The planners had chosen to settle midway between two
routes, one two miles to the south running along the high
ground from Purbeck to the west with a spur down to Abbotsbury Camp near the coast, the other a more important trade
route which crossed the Frome where Dorchester was to be
later. This route had direct connection with the important
cliff-top town at Hengistbury Head to the east in Hampshire,
and there is plenty of evidence that Hengistbury had trade
connections with the Continent, and was in fact something of
a cosmopolitan port.

The builders of Maiden Castle had not sought to control
the trade which crossed the river there. The earthworks of
Poundbury on the river were never a permanent dwelling-
place, and were either a shelter for travellers on the trade
route or a strong place where Maiden Castle people could
retire if surprised while at work down by the river. From the
river crossing one route soon climbed to the top of the ridge-

way to escape the low-lying swamps and went straight west to Eggardon and into Devonshire, while another branch turned northwards to Ham Hill and eventually across the Somerset plains to the lake village of Glastonbury and the caves of Wookey Hole.

There was a considerable density of population living in many towns and villages scattered between these places, but nearly all of them were sited on chalk uplands which supplied the only open spaces with the added advantage of lending themselves to defence. All down through the Cranborne Chase, which is a continuation of Salisbury Plain, the hill towns appeared on almost every hill, and in the west beyond Maiden Castle into Devonshire there must have been as many people as the land would support.

Some of these sites have proved that the people welcomed trade, and therefore travellers if not strangers, much more than Maiden Castle did. New cultures as disclosed by "foreign" goods were strangely absent in the early occupation of the town, as if despite or because of comparatively greater size it was self-sufficient. Perhaps even then the urban atmosphere was working to make the townspeople draw apart from the rural countryside, and nothing is more certain to lead to a people's real loss than the idea that they have advanced beyond their neighbours' way of living.

It seems that Maiden Castle did not share the advancing outlook that constantly moved westward, because new ideas are found at an earlier date in other smaller and more distant villages which could not have held such an important position in either size or situation, and certainly did not have such importance given to their defence works as was eventually given to those of Maiden Castle. Perhaps the townspeople did get an exaggerated idea of themselves as they certainly were not of another stock; they were an example of a remarkably pure breed which their aloofness may have helped a lot to maintain during a long line of unbroken generations.

But the Celtic people were a pure breed as a whole, as is shown by the unusualness of any change in shape or measurements of all the bones discovered. A woman with a larger nose formation must have been just as noticeable in life as she was when her bones were uncovered; perhaps she had wandered off the trade route at the river crossing and been accepted and perhaps even treasured as a new kind.

The rather small, lightly built people did not have a very long expectation of life, as is understandable when the conditions of life are taken into consideration. More of them died under the age of forty than surpassed that moderate span, and some of them had already survived some ugly injuries. Nor do they bear out the popular idea that the nearer to so-called natural life and diet the better the dental health, as for all intents and purposes their life and diet was near enough to nature, yet even this short-lived people had lost many of their teeth during their lifetime.

Apart from the regularity of their measurements they could have been taken for small Englishmen of any time—except that to-day there are so many variants of the breed; and also that the early man but not the woman had somehow developed a slightly longer forearm. The idea of an early naked savage painted with woad, and usually imagined as some hairy monster with a heavy undershot jaw, is very much off the mark no matter what soldiers' stories the legions carried back to Cæsar. A townsman of Maiden Castle would not be noticed as out of place if he could take part in the life of any modern town to-day. And if his bones had been laid down with others in some charnel-house of a London plague he would have measured up well to complete the average.

There is one thing which has always to be borne in mind about such towns—the inhabitants were entirely dependent on the produce of their fields and what could be picked up from the chase. Certainly there was a lot of forest land which must have contained much that could be hunted, but the density of population was rather high, and game did not have a good chance of surviving between towns where it was within reach. And people who have to shut themselves up in walled towns, for whatever reasons, are not inclined to venture on hunts farther afield into the unknown where they might get caught by nightfall.

It is more than likely that many people grew up inside the walls of Maiden Castle and died there without ever spending a night outside, and people would live their whole lives within sight of it and yet work out in the fields every working day.

Nor is it likely that a man looked for a wife in another town as long as his home-town could supply one, and in any case the other town was not likely to welcome him there for that purpose. In the event of a man somehow obtaining a wife from, say, Ham Hill or Abbotsbury, whatever her feelings it would mean a final farewell to her home place and family, and her best policy was to forget all that and consider herself as entirely of Maiden Castle.

Her people might occasionally discuss her going for a while, but there would be no slipping over for the afternoon to pay a visit; a stranger from another town would not find it comfortable or easy to gain admittance past the gates. And always there was the restriction on movement in that it was necessary to complete all journeys in daylight hours.

In being entirely dependent on their own food production it not only kept them tied to the locality and very local in their outlook, but there was very little of anything to export to other districts in exchange. Whoever the traders who set out from Hengistbury along the route to the west, they needed something portable in exchange to make the trip profitable, and if a people are only living from hand to mouth on what they can produce in their nearby fields, it is going to be a long time before any new line in goods is going to reach them.

Maiden Castle might exist for a decade or a generation and never in all that time have a jar of corn to spare or an ox that could be bartered for a new idea in pottery. It needs something beyond the bare necessities of existence to promote progress of any kind, and there was very little beyond bare necessities to be found on a bleak chalk hill.

A society which is based on a primitive agriculture does not only suffer from the lack of anything surplus to trade for outside ideas, but in a harsh climate, where there are no bountiful tropical conditions to supply much of the necessary food, the individual himself is so occupied with labour that he has little time or opportunity to develop such ideas as do strike him. It is said that necessity is the mother of invention, but people whose whole life is spent in toil give little attention to anything not directly bearing on the task in hand, and the urge of necessity does not strike them because they feel that their life is already full.

For instance, a busy agricultural community like Maiden Castle would never feel the need to develop communications in any sense; the act of writing would never start in such circumstances; the idea of a postal service would never be felt; and even a daily news record has little part in a life spent working in time with the four seasons. Many such people in modern days have got through life quite satisfactorily with nothing more than a local weekly newspaper, and that only interests them as far as it deals with their own village or relations.

The town shut behind its earth walls could have continued through all the ages as it was, living off its fields nearby and finding all its few other wants in the forest. If the rest of the world could have left it alone the Neolithic people would have been there to-day; it would have had periods of getting down low after a spell of overcrowding, but the very thinning out would have strengthened the new growth. Of course such a thing is impossible, although it has been tried out in a few cases since modern society has discovered that there is at least the charm of novelty in an original way of life. No one can prevent some contact reaching across such an artificial barrier; those inside start a demand for some of the things they think they are missing, and the outside world has never yet been able to resist the chance of improving less advanced people even if the intentions are always for the best.

And a walk through the eastern entrance of Maiden Castle, after being passed by the guards about the ramparts of the gates, and up the worn metalled street bearing towards the high ground of the original knoll, would have shown a lot of room for improvement. First, the street meandered off to the right for no apparent reason except to reach the high point, and although most roads of any respectable age did meander in that way for no reason that can be discerned now, it is not considered correct when laying out a new township where the space is going to be very confined.

But the architect of a housing estate might be wrong to shake his head over that street. Perhaps it was a well-thought-out plan to leave a clear run between the gate and the highest point, as a lookout posted there could see quite a lot and during times of peace, when there was no real need to guard the gates continuously and all the townspeople were outside at work in the fields, it may be that the only watch was kept on that spot of vantage.

It would be the dwellings that would call first for improvement as many of the inhabitants were living in pits. Some were pits roofed over to keep the worst of the rain out and others were pits sunk in the floors of huts. Which came first and which was the most satisfactory would be hard for people to suggest unless they had lived in these conditions, but most people are quite ready to maintain that the pits existed first and that the huts naturally grew out of endeavours to fashion a roof that would shed water. A pit was man's attempt to produce the natural caves in which he first found shelter after leaving the water.

That is all right for a theory, but by the time man had progressed such a long way that he could live in an organized state like a hill-town, he had left the natural cave era far behind him. Anyway the natural cave population was very sparse as the real natural caves of any period are comparatively few and far between. The poor water-animal man, seeking to surround himself with the darkness and solidity of a cave to replace the comfort of eternal water, must have died in his teeming millions as most water things do before he floundered into one of the few caves.

He was too elementary then to dig a pit for himself, and his next step was to leave the shelter of his caves and crevices to take to the forest, which could supply almost the same degree of dimness and that sense of being confined. He stayed in the forest, and whether he did experience a time when he took to the branches is not so very important here; what is important is to remember that during all that time he was a gatherer of natural food and not a tiller of the soil. And such a creature would be on the move all the time as soon as the little natural food had been gathered in a small area; he would not spend his time and labour in the wasted effort of digging a pit which he might leave next day.

Another thing against the pit idea during the dark forest era is that in a thick forest it is almost impossible to dig such a thing for the mere mass of tree roots, and much of the darkest forest was swampy where any pits would at once fill with water. Pits do seem ruled out for the deep-forest dweller, even if he did still have a memory of his caves.

A few twigs and leaves bent round the branches of an over-hanging bush seem a more obvious effort to find temporary shelter, or some branches leaning between big tree roots and in time thatched with grass; a hut of sorts until, greatly daring, some advanced thinker put up his own posts instead of using the live wood as it grew. After that man was indepen-dent because he had discovered that he could create a house quite apart from the trees if he wished.

Perhaps that was why he at last forced himself to face the open spaces, and when he did discover that he could improve on the natural food supply by cultivation, the need for a more permanent home would also cause him to build better. The possession of a field, however elementary, prevented him from moving off to avoid meeting others of his own kind; contact was forced on him, and in time he learnt that there was some-thing to be gained by the growing trust between himself and others. Civilization had taken a great step.

But huts of a sort are much more the obvious thing for elementary men; and although the first townspeople of Maiden Castle were quite familiar with both, it is too easy to say that they dug and used the pits before they knew how to build huts. Considering that man had been a forest wanderer for a long while, he had advanced a lot by the time he knew a method of or would be willing to labour hard at digging in the ground.

So, roofed pits or cellared huts, the dwellings in the town were up-to-date; the family in the pit could feel snug com-pared with those who still shivered as they crouched around a few embers in the hut overhead; the same few sticks glowing in the pit gave much more heat and the warm hearth would keep the family in comfort until the morning. The search for warmth was only slightly less acute than hunger in the harsh climate of an exposed chalk hill, where the rough damp winds in off the sea are the most noticeable feature of the prevailing weather. Knowing such sites on a warm summer afternoon has no comparison with even a wet summer night spent there, and at any other season the chief impression is that the weather is frankly miserable. It is no wonder that those who

192

Acoustics in Norman chancel arch, Tarrant Rushton

could burrowed down into the chalk to escape the searching wind which would blow through the most carefully built hut.

Instead of the hut-dweller feeling superior to those who still huddled in the ground, the man in the pit was the possessor of a modern home with the latest ideas in comfort. When he had eaten the evening meal he could stay crouched around the embers of the invaluable fire, and when sleep overcame him he was already abed and his bed was likely to stay warm all night. For they never threw out the ashes of the hearth, and some pits gradually filled up with them and the household rubbish which accumulates even in a home which has no furnishings beyond a cooking-pot or two and the owner's few tools.

A layer of ash a foot in depth represents a very long period of occupation—perhaps the upbringing of a family, because the fuel was all wood and the resultant ash from a wood fire is very little. Also every bit of fuel had to be brought at least from the edge of the forest which was beyond the considerable area of cleared land, so it is not likely that a man was reckless with fuel except what was needed for cooking. He would not throw on another stick just for the comfortable look and feeling of a fire, and he could always scatter the warm ash and lie in it.

In fact they must have bedded down where the actual fire had burned, because a respectable pit, which presumably housed at least the members of a family and the dogs, was often no more than five or six feet across on the floor with the sides overhanging to form a smaller entrance. This did not give much room to do more than crouch while a fire was burning, and while cooking was in progress some of those homes must have been too warm for comfort; the hungry man and children would stay around waiting patiently or fretfully according to their moods, but they would be loath to stay away and after nightfall there would be nowhere for them to go.

The cook must have often been a very harassed person but she did have everything at hand; it had to be because there was no other storage space. She had the crude stone mill there and the grinding of the meal was a hard labour alone, the few grains of corn that could be trickled through the hole in the

O   193

upper stone would result in a very small amount of meal at each filling, and unless someone else poured the corn in, the milling process was a slow two-handed job.

Although they had small bowls and perhaps could share out a portion to each person in them, they could not have been very particular about the manner of eating and had nothing in the shape of spoons. No matter how hungry a man might be he had to wait until his food was cool enough to bear holding in his fingers. Civilization has now at least taught the most refined person how to achieve the remarkable feat of possessing a mouth and throat and stomach which will easily handle food and drink far too hot to be held in the hands. That alone might have surprised a Maiden Castle man who was waiting for his stew to cool enough for him to grab the juicy mutton rib-bones.

There was one thing denied to the pit-dweller who had laboured hard and long to dig down eight or ten feet into the chalk. He did not one day decide that at last his home was habitable, and have a moving-in party where they could sit round the first fire there and enjoy the nice, clean, gleaming room. Because housing space in the town was more than crowded, as soon as he had dug out a shallow hole it was inhabited; it was too valuable a shelter to leave until he had finished the work. So a new home was a very gradual affair; each night they slept a little deeper and there was no limit to the depth. Occasionally a pit never got very deep, as if a man grew satisfied when he got his head below ground level and started his permanent hearth there, and when time passed and the hearth level rose he went on living there after his head had appeared above ground level again. He would suggest that it was comfortable enough when they curled up on the warm ashes.

But some of the pits were as much as eleven feet deep, as if a man had liked digging; otherwise there seems little point in going down much deeper than would cover a standing person. Depth alone did not provide more space even for storage purposes when the occupants must have covered all the floor-space and built a fire as well. And although they were restricted in size owing to the relative weakening of the sides with every extra inch of width, they did not hit upon the idea of linking two smaller pits with a comparatively strong tunnel or connecting doorway. In that way they could have kept the strength of two smaller pits and yet had some degree of size.

Perhaps the crowdedness of the town would not allow such two-roomed double homes, but they were sometimes very reckless in sinking one pit very close to another, with the result that the dividing wall collapsed. They knew how to support an upright side of a pit by building a wall of stone, yet they did not go a little further and support an overhang with pillars, which would have started them on the road to digging caves out of their pits, and even if such caves had been very shallow it would have been a great improvement on an open pit covered by some kind of roof.

That there was no attempt at undermining of any description may help to bear out that Maiden Castle had remained cut off from the outside world to a very great extent for a long while, because Neolithic people had a good knowledge of mining in other parts of Britain, where they had sunk deep and sometimes extensive mines into the chalk to trace the best flints for weapons and implements before the Iron Age. The Stone Age had lasted longer in Dorset, and the intervening Bronze Age was less developed, not only through isolation, but because the poverty of the culture had prevented the necessary trade in copper, which did not exist anywhere near Dorset.

But the tradition of mining for flints ought not to have been so dim that no one trusted to burrowing beneath the surface, and away in the north were people who understood living in the caves of Wookey Hole. Some knowledge of it ought to have filtered into Maiden Castle if they had any contact with the outside. And there is still the theory of cave-dwellers digging pits because such pits were the outcome of their remembrance of a cave existence. If there is anything in that a mere open pit would not have satisfied them.

That most of the pits were roofed, or were merely a kind of cellar inside a hut, is shown by the way the walls did stand up to wear and tear in such a friable substance as chalk. They were protected from most of the weather, because many of the lips or edges of the entrances show a remarkable lack of wear even of people scrambling up and down, while there is proof that the pit below was continuously occupied over a long period. People going in and out must have taken great care not to damage the edge even with the ladder they used, as a very few weeks of careless use would have ruined the bottle-neck and resulted in a mere sloping hole often joining up with the home next-door.

Despite the lack of space, that appears to have occurred only occasionally, and then one pit was usually abandoned and filled up, as if the idea of communal family life was not very acceptable. They would live a crowded town life with neighbours within a few feet of them and hardly room to walk between dwellings, but each family seemed to insist on the privacy of its living-quarters. The length of time that some pits were tenanted is shown by the depth of ashes gathered in the bottom, as it takes some years to produce a foot of wood ash covering a floor-space of six feet diameter, remembering that fuel was valuable because it all had to be brought so far and that only a small fire was possible if humans stayed in the place with the fire.

Yet some were occupied without break until there was several feet of ash, and then perhaps left vacant while chalk and earth trickled down and formed a slight layer. Another tenancy might build up another layer of ash, to be succeeded by the rubbish and débris of other dwellings nearby until a new occupier took over. Nor was it impossible that an old pit would be filled up with the material dug out to provide a new one nearby, pointing to the owners being absent yet also that the new people did not take over a home already provided.

Sometimes there were as many as twenty different stages before what had been a deep pit had become a shallow depression no longer capable of housing anyone and only used as a cooking-hearth. Yet with all that use the overhanging entrance remained much narrower than the bottom after people had climbed in and out thousands of times, and even greater care was taken when a pit was sunk into one of the few pockets of clay formed inside the town.

Considering that a pit was a man's whole living-space when at home and that all his activities had to be carried on in it, it is remarkable how few things were mislaid and lost on the floor, although the great scarcity of possessions made each thing too valuable to be easily forgotten. And it is evident that most of what came under the heading of rubbish was carefully picked up and carried away, otherwise the occupation layer of ash would have contained far more such rubbish than ashes. Such things as meat bones were sometimes flung over the shoulder and occasionally a dead dog or infant buried in the floor, but such behaviour could not have been general or the occupants would have driven themselves out of hearth and home in a very short while.

That they did not and yet allowed the ash to collect proves that they deliberately left the ash to provide warmth, because the very small handful of wood ash resulting from a day's cooking could not possibly have covered up the rubbish collected during the same day. A mutton bone, a broken pot or even a discarded garment contains much more bulk than the fluffy ashes from a fire. It is more remarkable that the ash layers are sometimes as pure as they are than that they are mixed up with earth and chalk, as the state of the surface above-ground must have been appalling during wet weather and a lot of chalky mud carried down on the feet of a family.

Of course the conditions must have been very foul at times; the family and the dogs sleeping crowded together were enough in themselves, if anyone had seen the slightest objection in the minor smell of humans and dogs. That a pit was lived in after a dog or an infant had been buried or forgotten in it shows great hardihood or a chronic shortage of housing, and the one case in which an adult woman was found in the bottom of a pit hints at some crime of passion. It was not usual to bury adults inside the town at all, and that in itself makes it appear to be a secret hiding of an unexplainable corpse, and a man levelling up the bottom of his pit would not appear suspicious enough to attract attention. Also she was a woman in the prime of her life—about twenty—and such women are the most likely victims of crime.

Although there is nothing left to show it, certain pits must have been lined in some manner to hold water. The chalk itself of course was too porous, yet they had definite water channels connecting up to form a catchment area between dwellings and guiding the water into one pit. This may have been some kind of street drainage, although there is no sign of the silt which would have remained in such pits as the water seeped away, and the town of about five thousand people must have provided some kind of water storage as there is no well inside the walls. Rain catchment on a careful scale would have gone a long way to supply the needs of cooking, and at all times except during acute danger the people would have gone out and down the hill to drink. The fact that such rainwater would also collect the filth about the town would not unduly worry those who had to use it.

That such a large gathering of people should elect to live on an apparently waterless hill has caused much speculation as to whether there were springs there at one time, and also on some of the many other hilltops where such towns and villages were situated. It does appear rather short-sighted to go to great lengths to build strong walls on a bare hilltop, with all the attendant labour of carrying everything up to that height—a labour which would continue for as long as the town existed—and then to find that the very defences might pin the defenders inside with no water available. The five thousand people of Maiden Castle would have been reduced in a very short while under a close investment, and it is not feasible to believe that military knowledge was so short-sighted.

Either such towns had a better catchment and storage system than appears possible or the evidence bears out, or there had been so far no hostile element capable of collecting enough strength to invest the walls completely. The sit-down siege did not play a part in those days, partly because of the numbers needed and more because no one liked the idea of staying outside during the nights. The methods of war of the day were sudden attacks which, if they succeeded, brought valuable gains, because the victors gained the shelter of a wall and turned the defeated out into the night. Or if such tactics failed, the baffled attackers melted away to regain the comfort of their own defences, which were not likely to be more than a reasonable day's journey away. Early man did not like the hours of darkness even for his own ends.

The chances of Maiden Castle having to surrender for lack of water were not great, and therefore it is not necessary to assume that the splendid invention of the dewpond was already known; and in any case the town could not have spared the space needed to lay out enough dewponds to provide for the whole people. And although it is well proved that springs broke out at a much higher level, and there is good evidence that the climate may have been wetter, such a higher level could not have included the hilltops where so many sites are found.

At the most the spring level is suggested as sixty feet above the present one when every drop of rain that falls is conducted as speedily as possible down to the sea again, and even with no change in the rainfall such efficient drainage compels the water down from the hills. When the same amount of water fell on any given area it eventually found its way to the sea as now, but took a much longer time to reach there through the choked and waterlogged valleys; and not only was the water level of a valley always much higher, but the great extent of water-bearing land in ratio to the natural drainage of the hill was bound to have an effect of forcing the water upwards.

Yet there is little chance that a spring ever broke surface inside the walls of Maiden Castle, and although the inhabitants would not have to go as far as they would to-day, they did have to leave its protection to fetch their supplies apart from the casual storage of rain.

Except for alarms and excursions caused by the outside world, towns like that must have been comparatively comfortable, as the greater part of everyone's life was fully occupied in work outside the walls during normal times, and during the dangerous hours of darkness they were snugly down out of the cold around their hearths. The few needed for a nominal patrol of the walls were able to call others when needed as a shout would reach most of them, and if the gates were closed at night there was little chance of being rushed in enough numbers before the whole town could turn out and man the ramparts.

They at least had security as far as such a thing was then known, and such conditions should have led to some kind of social life. But there is little trace of such a thing, and either they remained each family living for itself apart in its pit while united in the town for protection, or their social activities were carried on outside in some amphitheatre away from the town.

Nor did they leave much evidence that they had any religious beliefs that needed any apparatus. It is only conjectured that they held fertility rites in the spring and harvest rejoicings later in the year, and perhaps leading personalities sometimes went up the River Cerne to visit the Cerne Giant, or the double stone circle at Poxwell some six miles south-east towards the sea.

3

THE generations that had dwelt so long behind their town walls in cultural isolation must have grown to believe that their way of life would go on for ever—that is the price such people have to pay. The village, the town or the nation that sees even the immediate future pictured in itself and its outlook is left behind and receives a nasty shock in the natural course of things.

That during the two thousand years or more in which a town had been on the site there were changes in the people, and one occupational lapse when the turf grew over the ramparts, does not affect the fact that people lived there in seclusion and that seclusion must have been deliberate. A small place like one of the many other hilltop villages scattered over the south might have carried on just as long an occupation because it was near some good water or had some fertile fields within reach, and yet remain unimportant to others except as just another village. But Maiden Castle must have been known as a large town and so had an importance for centuries; it could not remain aloof unless that was the policy of its inhabitants.

There is no doubt that there were changes in the people even if they were not violent changes brought about by conquest. The Neolithic people had gone to all intents, but there is no way of deciding how much the subsequent Celtic people were composed of the old stock. A town had existed there long enough to see a pure race evolve, and in any case a few generations are enough to produce a complacent form of mind in town life. It does not matter how many times they changed their blood, if at all; what would matter was the relations the town held with the outside world, and the continued occupation behind strong walls proves that those relations did not alter much.

They probably thought they were keeping up the standard of their defences by the different improvements carried out on the ramparts. The work was done in spurts as if the chalk crumbled down into the ditch for a long while and the people were indifferent for years. There was little patching and repairing, which would have been the obvious thing to do; a small gang whose duty it was to keep everything in order could have carried the rubble up again as it rolled down and all surfaces would then have remained clear. But when any repairing was done it was on a large scale, and in that way the rampart was added to several times for its whole length; sometimes walls of chalk blocks were built and stone walls were added behind for strength.

It would be interesting to know if these sudden spurts, in which most if not all the people had a part, were caused by threats from outside influences or were started by a nervous body working from inside who were shocked to see how the ramparts had shrunk and the ditch filled. Probably a mixture of both, as despite the degree of organization they could achieve at times, there was a strong tendency to let things slide in both senses of the word betweenwhiles.

A man might walk along the walls for years and never see anything below him outside except his own fields slowly merging from fallow to plough, to green and then golden harvest, and so back to stubble again. And perhaps he himself could scarcely remember seeing an enemy outside near the ditch, while his son growing beside him had never seen a dangerous stranger, and certainly did not fully understand what the defences might mean to him one day. At such quiet and easy times, which must have occurred, it is not strange that a townsman gave little thought to clearing out the bottom of the ditch, or care overmuch if the rampart walk was getting worn down by the feet of the patrol.

And the labour involved in the mere act of having to produce a living out of the not very rich upland soil did not leave much time or energy to gather up an odd basket of rubble occasionally and bring it back up the steep slope to the top again. So repair work was not done as it was needed but only under some kind of pressure, and the periods of neglect were quite long enough for more than a generation of the short-lived people to live out their life without sharing in the active work of defence.

They were due for a shock, and although there is no way of deciding if it came on them suddenly, from what can be seen of their alternate neglect and work, added to their aloofness, it may well be that they saved themselves by the skin of their teeth and were just able to hold the ramparts against a new weapon. In some way they were introduced to a new sling which could fling a more dangerous missile at a much greater range.

The sling itself was no new thing to them, as it had been the Neolithic as well as the Celtic weapon, and it is held that the slightly longer length of the man's forearms was due to their constant use of it. Certainly the bow had no comparable standing with it during the Iron Age as there are few arrowheads scattered about, and no armouries of them left to be found later, whereas sling-stones are found everywhere with many hoards placed in strategic positions. A man might have a few hundred stored in his pit or his hut, and several thousand were not unusual, while at the eastern entrance over twenty-two thousand of them were heaped ready to repel attacks on the gate.

For many centuries the rampart slope and the outer slope of the ditch had sufficed to keep the enemy far enough away to be more or less harmless. Many times such an enemy had ventured to the edge of the ditch, and although a sling was dangerous at that range the defenders in their very advantageous position above were able to control what happened. There was no danger as long as the enemy were kept out of the ditch, and the man on the wall would find that comparatively easy as long as he did not have to keep down himself.

But suddenly in some way Maiden Castle learned that that ditch was not enough, nor even two such ditches. They deepened and widened the first one below the rampart and added two others on the south side where the slope is rather gradual, until an enemy was standing some hundred and forty

yards away from the man on the heightened wall. That was a
long way to throw an effective sling-stone uphill, while on the
steeper north side, though the enemy could approach a little
closer, his range there was cut down even more by gravity.

It can be presumed that the townspeople not only built their
protection against the improved weapon but adapted it themselves, so that the farther rampart was within their own range
from the main wall. And this is proved by stone platforms
being built near the entrances, which were completely re-
modelled until there was a long way to go before reaching the
gate after entering the defences. The platforms were a new
thing in that they were towers enabling special slingers to
swing a longer sling than could be used on level ground.
Armed with equal weapons the defenders always had a tremendous advantage, so with their new multiple ditches and
ramparts the townspeople could once more feel safe after they
had mastered the new sling themselves. Perhaps they again
grew to think that life would go on for ever as they knew it,
and they certainly had put a tremendous amount of labour
and good engineering knowledge into the new work, which
does show that they considered their way of life was worth
while.

It had been during the remodelling of the eastern entrance
that another odd woman was popped into the ground in what
looks like another hidden or hurried burial. During the actual
work on the rampart she had been curled up and placed in the
bank like another basket of rubble without any attempt to
supply her with the usual grave-goods to help her on her way.
Either she was one of the gang at work there who had died a
natural death and, owing to the rush and strain of getting the
work finished under the threat of outside danger, her fellows
could not spare the time to give her the ordinary burial so
just covered her up there and then in the knowledge that she
helped build up the rampart as much as a few baskets of
rubble; or there was a quarrel there, again perhaps under the
strain and stress of hurried work after having almost completed the new defences; by that time nerves might be raw,
and in a quarrel the woman was more or less accidentally
killed and the evidence hidden up quickly.

It was only these possibly irregular interments which took

place inside the walls or even in the outworks, as it appeared to be normal to bury the dead well outside, although they did not take any undue care over where or how they disposed of the corpse, except in the exceptional cases of those given a hilltop mound as a monument.

It was the custom to place grave-goods with a corpse, and even small children were supplied with a small bowl of food; apparently the idea was that the dead had to undertake at least a short journey to some other land and needed sustenance on the way. It may have been the crude idea that the dead person actually needed the food, but it is more likely that it was a mere formal gesture.

By that time the pot of food may have been an empty gesture and the pot as empty as the gesture, but some were provided with a joint of meat, and it is not likely that they placed the bare bone there. One man had the ribs and legs of a sheep lying with him, and another woman not only had most of a sheep but a dog placed in the grave near her head. Sometimes the meat was placed beside the body, but often it was being grasped in the hand, yet it was seldom that weapons were placed ready at hand except for an occasional sling-stone which might have been accidentally included in the grave filling, as were the odd bones of earlier interments. These odd sling-stones could have been deliberately placed there with the sling which soon disappeared entirely, as the sling was their main weapon, but neither arrows nor axes were used as grave-goods, and it is probable that fighting was not the most important object in the lives of these agricultural people. But even if they did not consider that a man would have to fight for a place in the new land, they also decided that he would not have to till the fields for his livelihood as no tools were given him.

A dead person was not laid out at length on his back nor put down at any recognized regular depth; often the work was carried out in a rather casual way, needing a hole just large enough to curl the body up on its side. Such methods of escaping work were not necessarily due to mere lack of effort because using deerhorn picks and the hands or mutton shoulder-blades as shovels was hard enough work as it was. That they had no undue respect for and were not deterred by supernatural fear of the dead is shown by what happened when they disturbed a grave in digging a new ditch. They just hacked off the part that protruded and left the rest in the bank without weakening the structure by removing the bones to a new resting-place.

. Without any such intention on their part, every time they placed a pot of food with a body they supplied a register which, while perhaps less detailed than a parish register, is much more permanent. By the chance of such a custom a man can be dated to at least the period of a certain type or shape of pottery; he might be given a pot made earlier, although bowls in everyday use do not last long into a new period, but he could never be given a design or quality that came into existence later. And some types of pottery did not last long and can be placed with accuracy.

It is not likely that every time a new or improved example of pottery did find its way into Maiden Castle it was received with rapture, as the townspeople were definitely retiring and thought themselves self-sufficient. And although they did possess a few examples of the good Glastonbury pottery from the lake village away in the north, either poverty or lack of interest stopped them obtaining or developing something in the same line. Their local pots were rather on utility lines, and although sometimes friable they had at least one improvement which did not come in the usual and accepted way from east to west—it was perhaps a local trick made necessary by the quality of their clay. Instead of making a separate handle and attaching it to the pot they pinched out a handle from the thicker shoulder of the rim itself. This made for strength but not easy handling, as it could be grasped only between finger and thumb, but to overcome this handicap they supplied two such handles at opposite sides instead of one. It was some centuries later that this was discovered or newly invented again in the country that lay to the east of Maiden Castle.

They did make somewhat feeble attempts to copy Continental decorative designs, but the urge of art for art's sake was never very strong, although in striving for a cooking-pot which was economical in the use of fuel they did obtain vessels which were good to look upon. It was not until very late in the history of the town that they had the benefit of the potter's wheel

205

to help them, although this almost obvious invention was well known in the world elsewhere, and even after wheel-turned pots were made on the spot the old method was carried on side by side with it. They either carried on stubborn tradition to great lengths or the needed precision-tools were still not available to make enough wheels.

The earliest inhabitants of the town had not yet discovered that the bottom of all utensils should not only be flat to stand upon, but must be dished or hollowed so that only a rim comes in contact with the surface on which they are placed. It will be found that the bottom of everything like cups, bottles, in fact anything that is picked up and replaced often, is made hollow in this way and therefore seldom rocks about on an uneven surface, whereas if the bottom is flat and level the slightest piece of grit under it makes it unsteady. Yet it may be incorrect to say that this was unknown in Maiden Castle as their cooking-pots were made in the most efficient way to stand in rather than on a fire. By having a tapering bottom, which was sometimes almost carried to a point, it was possible to place fuel well beneath the sides, which is the only economical way to make a small wood fire do a lot of work.

But such pots always need supporting, which is not so much of a drawback amongst the hearth-stones. The limitation in initiative is shown when they used the same rounded bases for small food-bowls and cups which were not likely to need standing up in a fire. The demand for a cup that would stand firm on a level surface was not so obvious as might appear, as there could have been few smooth, level surfaces in the whole town —certainly there were no tables; yet every time someone put down a bowl of food or cup of liquid he had to place it in a depression or prop it up against something. It was surprising that some earlier potter did not think to flatten the base of a drinking-vessel so that it would stand alone.

One failing of some of their pottery was that on such a chalky site the clay picked up particles of chalk, which did not bake with the clay and later dissolved out. By the time of the Iron Age new styles had reached the town, and some of them were perhaps based on metalwork rather than pottery proper; the strengthening was placed where sheet metal needed it, which is not necessarily the same for pottery. For instance, a pronounced rim is a weakness in a pot when it falls over, as the rim strikes the ground first with all the force that the weight of the pot provides, whereas a round-shouldered pot without a rim rolls over and may rock backwards and forwards but does not strike anywhere with a jar. The strongest pot is as near egg-shaped as possible, without rims or protruding bases, and the earliest pots of Maiden Castle are nearer that shape than later ones. So perhaps the later, better-finished work lost something of utility in exchange for new shapes and ornament.

In fact, the heavy rim tended to disappear at one time until it was represented by a mere incised line just below the lip of the pot; in theory it was still there for those who demanded it but was no longer a danger when the pot fell over.

What was an advantage was the dished or hollow bottom, so that a full pot of food stayed upright when it was put down. It is likely that when a man first owned such a pot he still automatically tried to prop it up in the old way, and perhaps through confusion of both types being in use at the same time, more than one person lost a meal when an old rounded pot quietly rolled over in its own way.

The potter's wheel must have been a startling introduction to the hand potters, and soon after its use this was apparent; pots appeared in many shapes with perhaps only the potter's imagination as a limiting factor. Pedestals began to appear and shapes which can only have been more decorative than useful; at last culture had caught up with the stubborn people of Maiden Castle, and whatever pleasure they got from it was paid for in pottery breakages. Some of the new types would not have worn well on a hunting trip or lasted long when carried out in the fields. At such times a man would hunt up one of the old pots that looked and behaved very much like a coconut.

The townspeople of the Stone Age, which had lasted there well into the Bronze Age because of the lack of bronze and the poverty which prevented much trade with the outside world, knew well how to work in flint, and some of their axes were efficient instruments for fighting purposes. For cleaving a man's skull or inflicting any severe cut, a flint axe with the keen edge which they knew how to produce would have few disadvantages compared with a bronze or early iron axe. And although it is difficult for us now to imagine anyone doing any other work with it, the heavy timbers used in the early town could have been cut down and shaped with no other tools.

As always, the man trained in the use of the latest type of tools may have a certain real contempt for the worker trained in and using older and apparently clumsy tools, but that feeling is accompanied by a much greater sense of almost awe that anyone can complete good work with such tools. Usually the modern machinist, using highly developed machine tools which will hold a good edge indefinitely, is secretly amazed that anyone can do so much work with hand tools with practically no cutting edge, and he realizes that he himself could do nothing with them.

So perhaps the Stone Age tree-fellers swung their flint axes with a freedom that does not seem possible now, and instead of the brittle edge breaking off at the first stroke, the hard oak was cut out in good-sized chips. It is a great pity that timber has not lasted in a condition to show what kind of axe strokes were possible, but axe cuts on good-sized bones prove that men were not afraid to use their hard-won edges on hard material.

A few of the good stone axes found in the town had originally come from as far away as Cornwall, and although this appears to suggest some extent of trade in weapons at least, those Cornish axes may easily have been the spoils of warlike adventures, with no way of deciding if the Dorset men had raided down into Cornwall or the Cornishmen pushed up into the mainland. It is known that Cornwall was developed in a very early age, with a sea trade in the valuable tin found there, and such development has always led to internal pressure which causes people to spread outwards. Any such pressure was certain to be felt in Dorset, although the townspeople of Maiden Castle were always able to maintain their aloof position between the eastward movement from Cornwall and the westward movement from Hengistbury and other coastal towns in the east.

A well-made flint axe is the result of some very delicate work when it is remembered that there were no hardened steel hammers to chip along the cutting edge. The best hammer they used must have been another flint, and a work-

208

man using a hammer in careful work has the face of his hammer always in mind, yet the Stone Age flint-worker could never rely on his stone hammer face for more than one blow.

Yet an axehead is a clumsy work compared with the care needed to shape up an arrowhead; some of these are scarcely thicker than leaves and seem to have been copied from a tree leaf. But not only did they somehow break off these delicate flakes—they chipped the sides into keen cutting edges and gave them a point like broken glass. Some of these arrow-heads were deadly missiles and would not require a direct hit to inflict a terrible gash, while a man in possession of a good flint knife could cause some shocking wounds at close quarters, as every flint cut or stab would sag open in an ugly way and not tend to close up like a steel wound.

That a flint-worker took advantage of every lucky shape of a broken flint is not the whole thing, as although a broken flint cuts like broken glass, a weapon or a tool had to have its cutting edge placed in suitable relation to the rest of its shape. Even small flakes used in the hundred-and-one domestic ways about a home are often found with the cutting edge retouched up as if they were someone's favourite knife, and regular sawlike teeth were not beyond the worker's skill.

Perhaps even older than the flint culture, implements of bone were in everyday use. Strong, pointed splinters of bone must have always suggested themselves as stabbing weapons, and a good leg-bone was valuable material after the dogs had gnawed it. Leaving enough of the rounded bone to form a handle, which could be shaped to fit the grip, the mere rubbing away of half the hollow shank-bone on the slant produced a pointed weapon or a useful tool. And a big hollow bone or oxhorn could be made into a comb when one end of it had been sawn or worn into teeth. These combs had no likeness to the modern flat comb as the teeth were on the end and ran "with the grain."

Perhaps these combs were not hair-combs, although it would be strange if long-haired people did not use them as such. It is suggested that they were used in weaving to arrange the weft of cloth, and if so this evidence of weaving, with the many loom weights, goes a long way to confuse the value of at least part of Cæsar's war dispatches on the invasion of Britain.

P

Ramparts of Maiden Castle

His description of woad-painted savages does not fit in with townspeople who wove, and presumably wore the cloth they wove, and some kind of weaving was carried on there long before the Roman Empire started out on its way. Nor does the presence of lightly made brooches suggest the wearing of animal skins as clothes, as although they are often ornamental these brooches had a good utility use before the days of buttons and buttonholes. But they were too lightly made to hold stiff heavy skins together.

The many iron ring-headed pins may have been more suitable to fasten skin clothes together, but they were accompanied by the evidence of weaving, so it can be assumed that by then the townspeople were wearing cloth. While the wearing of rings has no bearing on whether or not the people were clothed at all, it does show that they did like to have some kind of ornament, as they were found still wearing finger and toe rings several thousand years later. One woman was wearing a ring on her third and fourth fingers but these two rings were made in one piece.

Perhaps the glass beads of various colours had reached the town along the trade routes from the outside world, as anyone who understood the secret of glass manufacture enough to produce such things would have left other evidence, as glass is practically indestructible. Beads were also made out of almost anything that had a natural hole for threading or were shaped in a way which made it easy to pierce a hole.

While the wearing of beads and brooches is not proof of a high degree of civilization, the possession of dice shows that they at least knew how to count up to six, and the people who can do that have opened the door to much higher mathematics. These dice were not the usual squares of bone marked from one to six, but were oblong pieces of bone with the two ends left plain without the numbers one and two; the numbers started at three and must have been made in this way for some reason to do with whatever game they played. As people who can make an oblong bone with two plain ends did not do so because of any limitation in their intelligence, the square would have been just as easy to make.

Perhaps they were not dice for tossing at all, but were men used in some kind of dominoes—that they were not exactly like the modern domino men of to-day does not prove any-thing, as the rules of a game can and often do alter for no apparent reason. A townsman of Maiden Castle sitting in the bar parlour of a country public-house of to-day might not be able to play a game of the well-established fives and threes but he might well be able to show how they used to play in his time.

Some ornamented bone counters marked with various num-bers of circles or dots were undoubtedly used in playing a game, and one square, marked along one edge with seven dots with eight on the opposite edge, could have been part of a set running up to double-nines. The only thing that seems to be missing is some kind of pegboard to record the scoring, and that may turn up some day. So it seems likely that the playing of "table" games goes back a lot further than the tables them-selves as there could have been no table in an Iron Age pit; these dominoes had to be shuffled around on the bare floor.

4

THE presence of a respectable bread wheat at least four thousand years ago may surprise those who still think of Neo-lithic man as existing on what he could pick up, and also those who believe all real agriculture is the development of recent years. Of course in such a damp climate no actual wheat grain has survived, but when making pottery sometimes an undried pot was put down on seeds lying about and the record has survived with the broken sherd.

In that way the wheat impression can be examined and identified as surely as the grain itself; the impression has no more altered than the fingerprints of the potters, and these would be accepted by any police force of to-day. They also had more than one kind of wheat, which suggests that their agriculture was something more than rule-of-thumb, and had already started on developing the different and presumably better breeds of wheat. Nor was wheat their only grain, as barley was also picked up in the soft clay of their pots.

By the time of the Iron Age the people were unintentionally

much more considerate towards future inquirers, and that may be simply because they had developed their cooking methods to the pitch where they could sometimes have more heat than they wanted. In that way they had accidents and burnt a loaf of bread until it was carbonized, so that with luck it has survived to be properly examined. Some bread was entirely of wheat except for an occasional grain of barley, such as might get in any sample, but the millers were not particular about a few grass and weed seeds going into the mill, and it is also likely that those who ate the bread did not mind such things.

There is no way of even suggesting whether wheat or barley bread was the more popular item, as barley bread, with the odd intrusive grains of wheat, was found as well as a mixture of both in almost equal proportions. It would be interesting to know if they were the same as modern people and preferred to eat up their stock of wheat first, only eking it out with barley as it ran short, to finish up the season with barley alone. The grains of rye-grass seeds may not be entirely accidental, but a sign that the stocks were getting low before the new harvest.

The meal produced in the primitive hand-mills was not very finely ground, as there was very little weight in such small upper millstones, many of which were also made out of stone that is not suitable for grinding. But considering the quality of the tools with which the stone was dressed it is remarkable that anyone ever went to the length of milling corn rather than pounding it into a coarse meal. To make the mill a man had first to find a stone about fifteen inches across and somehow make it round; then from the centre he bevelled the milling surface on a slope towards the outer edges, while leaving the centre as high as possible to act as the axle of the upper stone. That was straightforward work, though it must have been tedious with tools that would not stand up to being forced against hard stone, but the upper stone had to be shaped into a kind of hollow cap to fit compactly over the lower stone; until the two stones were made to fit they would not mill at all, as the grains of corn would just roll around in the space. Yet even then the job would not be ready for use until a hole had been punched right through the upper stone to feed the grain into it, and also two holes put into the sides to hold some kind of handles. It is safe to assume that many millstones came to grief when having the feed-hole put through as, unless the tools cut well, stone absorbs the shock of the blow and small pieces such as these millstones are very liable to break apart.

And after a man had made his mill he still had to get it home, as he would shape it up on the site where he found the stone if only to have as light an object as possible to carry, and when he had got it safely into his pit or hut there was still the great effort needed to grind even a handful of corn. To turn the best of those hand-mills was hard two-handed work, as until the two stones were well worn the upper would be inclined to slip off and there could be no such thing as a continuous rotary motion; at each half-turn it was necessary to change hands. At the same time the miller had to bear down as much as possible, as the upper stone was seldom heavy enough in itself to apply the weight needed for grinding.

Even when in working order some of those mills must have been almost useless for grinding meal, as many of the stones were of the kind which would wear into a polished surface. It is not surprising that those made of calcareous grit or sandstone were often very much worn and some of the limestone ones show little use. The part of the town which possessed a good mill probably considered itself lucky and perhaps queued up to use it; in any case milling must have been a long, laborious job, and many people would stay content with parched corn as long as they had teeth. The loss of the bread which somehow became carbonized and so survived must have been rather a domestic tragedy to those concerned after all the effort put in to produce it.

It was possible to bake a respectable loaf in an earthenware pot surrounded by a glowing fire, but they also understood the principle of oven baking. There were several clay-built ovens about the town, although they appear to be of the kind that would be too fierce for cooking food and certainly too extravagant with fuel for the small amount of oven space. They were probably used for some kind of smelting process and a small crucible lying near adds to the suggestion. But the knowledge of ovens did exist, and perhaps there were lighter-built ovens for food-cooking which have not survived, while in the home they had a useful girdle or "gridiron" arrangement for cooking on or over the hearth. This was an inch-thick earthenware slab pierced with holes which would have cooked anything that was not too thick and solid.

There was no reason why the townspeople should not have appetizing meals, and during the preparation the whole town must have reeked with the smell of baking and roasting bread and meats, good stews simmering in earthenware pots and boiling joints spitting their overflow into the hot fire. The one thing that might be missing was the aroma of fragrant drinks, but even that may have been there in such things as mint tea and boiled flower petals—they certainly roasted hazel nuts and may have made a kind of coffee drink out of them and other such things.

There is no doubt that they had a considerable amount of primitive comfort in their way of living and a good variety of food, and during normal seasons their fields would supply enough to last through the year. Although the few storage pits carefully lined with stone walls are woefully small for the size of the town's population, each hut or pit could store one or two pots of grain for direct use; but there were no great granaries where grain could be kept in good order. The storage space does not appear to be any more than enough to hold the precious seed corn for another year safe from the vermin which must have overrun the town.

There was no room inside the town walls for the flocks and herds of animals even in times of trouble, which must have meant that when the town did have to call on its walls for defence and retire inside them it was already a defeat, as any enemy who could reach the outermost rampart was in the position to destroy the fields and carry off the stock. This has been unfortunate in that the field tools were seldom brought into the town, and so have not survived to show what they were like and how they were fashioned. There are wheel tracks through the entrances so they did use their animals for draught purposes and therefore would have ploughs in the fields, but a great deal of the field work would be hand-done, first with flint hoes and mattocks and later with the new iron. Yet these tools were left outside and perhaps casually hidden as farm-workers still do; only such things as iron billhooks and sickles and knives were brought home as too valuable to leave out, and they were only used to any great extent during the cutting of the harvest.

The cattle of the Neolithic people were gigantic, wide-horned beasts well suited to make powerful beasts of burden, and perhaps were still primitive enough to gain their whole living in the forest. The horses were the small ponies which all rough conditions produce at any age, but these horses were not very numerous if one can judge from the few bits and harness material found in the town. Such animals would not have anything like as important a place as good oxen in the scheme of things in a purely agricultural civilization; an ox can live well where horses find it hard to subsist and in heavy work the same ox will wear out many horses. Also when dead the horse has nothing like the same value although they ate its flesh too.

The sheep was a valuable source of food, and probably could live as well as anything on the bare chalk hills, but during a hard winter may have found it difficult to hold out in the shelter of the forest. It is likely that their pigs were always semi-wild animals running in the thickest part of the forest and finding their own living at all times, only hunted down and killed when needed without a period of fattening in a sty. This pork would not be prime meat compared with what most people expect pork to be, but the smell of roast pork would be always the same, and must have welcomed many a man as he climbed down into his pit.

They would have known how to deal with the vermin-like rabbit, and certainly would not have allowed it to become the more than tolerated pest to farming which it has become. But fortunately it did not then exist in Britain, so they did not lose much of their early corn to it, nor did that other degraded animal, the goat, seem to have a place in Maiden Castle.

The intensive agricultural work of all the succeeding centuries has altered any definite evidence of how the fields ran outside the walls, but from a military standpoint there would be no kind of cover allowed anywhere near the hill, and every time the forest was driven farther away it not only added to the cleared fields for cultivation and stock but removed the possibility of hidden danger. Nor would there be any need of fenced boundaries between different owners' fields, as their culture had no room for either private ownership of land or, probably, cattle. What boundaries there are still to be seen, and which may have existed from pre-Roman days, were in the form of lynchets or banks, the main purpose of which was to level the sloping lie of the land. What fences were needed to keep animals on the fallow land were too temporary to leave any trace and perhaps never did exist, as the animals would be in the care of herders.

It would be impossible to make even a suggestion as to what area of arable land was needed to support five thousand people entirely. For one thing it is not safe even to say what would be the absolute minimum amount of grain needed nor what area of land would be needed to grow that minimum. Such figures have a way of being capable of great variation even when they have a scientific basis; the personal food needs of a man living at Maiden Castle might have no relation to any modern theories, and the quantity and quality of the food crops grown there could not be worked out with any accuracy now. This could be proved by the different figures that would be offered with such assurance by experts if they gave it their attention.

But even taking in all the available land within easy reach, it is remarkable that so dense a population could live there, as much of the upland space was never very fertile and could not be made so. And there is no evidence that any drainage work was ever done on the watercourses to gain space along the banks, although such evidence would have had little chance of surviving the work of the water itself and all the drainage improvements carried out since. It is likely that all the low-lying land remained swamps, and the only direction in which new space could be found was by clearing the forest between the swamps and the uplands, and at best that is slow work with hand-tools.

Those sloping upland fields needed every bit of manure that the stock and the people could provide, and perhaps that was one of the reasons why so many people could continue living for generations and centuries in such a confined space. If they had developed unpleasant personal habits inside the walls they would have driven themselves out no matter how hardy their stomachs were; all sanitary arrangements must have been out in the fields—where it was a definite asset.

But beyond the arable land there must have been a great area under the control of the town where the animals could find a living, and although all their animals were of the kind that could find a living in wooded country, the space needed grows alarmingly with the density of the trees. Of course the trees of their forest did not include any of the coniferous firs which sour the land, killing all other growth, and may in time starve the world. Almost everything like the oak, hazel, thorn, ash, maple, and willow does provide some amount of feeding to animals that know how to approach them when they are bearing leaves, and even in the dead of winter such animals will chew the twigs and gnaw the bark. Nor do such trees kill the grass growing beneath them. Perhaps only the yew had no food value, and opinion can be very divided about that tree; there are animals which can apparently eat some yew leaves.

A little more than two miles south of the town is an outcrop of Purbeck stone, and it was from there that they obtained most of the stone they used. But it is a hint that their transport was not very developed in that they did not build the town walls of durable limestone. Admittedly it would have needed many thousands of tons, and the haulage would have been more than two miles and uphill, while the chalk was on the site and the trench from which it was dug acted as a defence ditch. But in the long run it would have saved the labour used by every generation in piling up the chalk again as it crumbled and rolled down, and an upright stone wall was a defence in itself and not a mere slope which winded the attackers before they could get to hand-to-hand fighting with the people lining the top.

It was perhaps natural that no generation saw beyond the immediate future, nor was willing to expend a terrific hauling labour on a lasting wall which the coming generations would accept as a gift; and the people who first sited the town could manage the work of digging in the chalk with the deerhorns they used for picks, but it is a different matter to attack a ledge of hard solid stone. So the first man who picked up a piece of stone and decided that he could make a millstone out of it, or

carried home a few thin slabs as hearthstones, did not see the
outcrop as a quarry where later people would dig good stone
to replace the timbers in the walls and form an imperishable
inner spine within the ramparts.

Even in the Iron Age they possessed no heavy bars of iron
to lever the stone out, and only grubbed along the edge of the
outcrop, and when they did get out a large slab it was broken
into pieces rather than cut up. But for all that it would have
been possible to use limestone to a far greater extent than they
did and get permanent results; it was the lack of good tools
as well as transport that held back the development of stone
building.

Farther south beyond where the stone cropped out they
were off the chalk, and perhaps it was an adventure to make a
journey to the sea. And unless they were on friendly terms
with Chalbury Camp, lying on a buttress of the chalk, they
might have felt uneasy having that hill village between them
and home. But most of their sling-stones came from the sea-
shore and represented many journeys there, and if they did
not mind being overlooked by Chalbury they would find unlimited supplies east of the River Wey. Again it was only
another mile or so farther to the Chesil Beach where there
was a world's supply of sling-stones, although there again they
were overlooked by Abbotsbury in the west.

It is surprising to find that the people of the town did not
make more use of the seashore, which is not too far away to
be an easy day's outing; even with the most winding tracks it
would not be more than six miles and that should have left
them with reasonable time to carry out some kind of fishing.
It may again be proof of their very local activities that they had
so few examples of marine shells, because they knew limpets
and mussels and oysters, and the chance of an occasional
change of diet might have tempted them to the shore very
often. People who lived nearer the sea always collected
immense quantities of shells about their living-quarters, and
many men learn to haunt the shore as the tides may provide
any unexpected treasure. If the way to the sea had been
entirely free much more evidence of shore activities must have
found their way up to the town, as in all communities there are
a few persons who take to shore life and bring home all kinds
of odds and ends.

Also, with such a great number of hill towns and villages lying a short distance inland, it is surprising that no coastal town after the style of Hengistbury found a footing on the lee-ward side of Portland. On the west and weather side there was nothing to tempt ships to come near the shore, but in the shelter of the Wey mouth a Continental ship might have found safe anchorage and attempted to open up even the small trade that the country could provide. Again it may be that the Dorset people did not wish to have any further connections with the outside world than they could help, and they had little or nothing to export.

The apparent lack of any trading-place on the Dorset coast was not because there were no suitable sites. Cornwall had its natural harbour of the Fal, but it also had the tin and other metals to attract trade, and new ideas did find their way in with the trade and some eventually reached up as far as Dorset; yet Hengistbury to the east became almost cosmopolitan with nothing behind it except the country of the New Forest, and that has never been very rich in anything.

It is obvious that Maiden Castle did not have any interest in the sea beyond an occasional treat of shore shellfish. And although they did possess a certain amount of Kimmeridge shale which came from the coast of Purbeck some fifteen miles away, this strange material was to be found in many other town sites and may have been the work of a local group living at Kimmeridge. Shale objects were not only known and obtained by people living over a great area of Britain, but held their popularity over a tremendous period of time. Whatever the virtue of this material it was widespread and lasting, and covered many different departments of life. People were buried still wearing it as bracelets; it made spindle-whorls, and platters and vases were turned out later after the introduction of some kind of lathe. In fact, almost anything might be made out of it, and it is by no means a suitable material for many things; it is a light, stone-like and almost black substance that breaks easily, and very soon after exposure to the air it cracks and flakes away. Being easy to work and light in weight it might have suggested itself to some early craftsman, but the finished articles were inferior to the same things made in wood, which in most cases would be more durable, and people who understood the making of pottery could have turned out many of the things in baked clay found under their feet.

Yet for some reason Kimmeridge shale had a great vogue in the south, and must have reached many homes in some form. If it was a local industry based on Kimmeridge it was the nearest approach to industrialism that has shown itself and Kimmeridge was the Brummagem of the day. And that kind of reasoning cannot be applied to the conditions spreading over many centuries during which the shale found its way as far north-east as London and Colchester, and west and north to Glastonbury and Wookey Hole. Later in Roman times it spread as far as Northumberland and into Carnarvonshire, so there must have been some unknown virtue in it beyond being light and easy to work.

Much of the work was completed at Kimmeridge because the extensive work-floors are still there, but there is great reason for thinking that most of the shale was exported in an unworked state and the work done at home by the people who obtained it. If it had been a purely local culture carried out where the shale was found, the objects turned out at any given period would have carried a style or method of working which would serve as a trade-mark, but there is no craft relationship between the things found at Maiden Castle and Glastonbury or any of the other scattered sites which used it. In some places the work was very inferior as well as along other lines of development, and it is begging the question to conclude that the roughly worked objects were manufactured where they were found while the more carefully finished work was brought from the skilled home trade at Kimmeridge.

Each town seemed to have its own way of working out a local style, and that seems to prove that the material was obtained in an unworked state, while the absence of waste shale that could be then expected can be easily explained when it is remembered that such waste was a strong-burning fuel much quicker to light than most timber, and the hilltop towns were sited where fuel was absent and had to be hard-won. No man in such circumstances would waste a handful of shale chippings which would supply more quick heat than many times its bulk of wood.

There is still nothing to suggest why an inferior material

used in unsuitable ways should spread so universally in Neolithic times when there was so little connection between hilltop people living secluded behind their strong walls, and continued to spread in the sophisticated Roman Age when so much new culture was brought into the country and forced on the native people. Such popularity might make any sales manager sit up and take notice, as no sales talk will sell inferior articles over such a long period, and the town of Maiden Castle with so little to spare in exchange had its share of the goods, although in their case the transport cost was not very great.

There is the theory that the age-old magical and medicinal virtues attributed to jet were given to shale as the most likely substitute to be found, but jet was given those properties because of its comparative rarity, and in any case was a very hard substance which would take a high polish and therefore lend itself to ornamentation, whereas even the best of the Kimmeridge shale could and can be obtained from a seam running for a long way along the open cliffs, and is neither hard nor "jet" black, nor will it take a polish under any circumstances, but will shed dirty grey flakes after exposure. Even if the belief in jet had travelled across the world from an Asia Minor river to Britain, it is difficult to see how a seam of grey soft material in a rearing cliff could be mistaken for the same stuff as a bead or stud in a brooch.

5

EVEN the stubborn provincialism of Dorset had gradually to give way to commercial pressure bearing on it from all quarters. From the south-west Cornish cultures based on the tin industry forced new ideas up the country, and behind Cornwall was the steady stream of progress coming across the water from Brittany. Such advancing ideas had flowed westward across the Continent until they reached the Atlantic, and by their very vitality they had to leap the water to turn up then against the backwardness of towns like Maiden Castle.

In the region of the lower Severn commercial vigour had gained strength from the advancing stages of the Iron Age as developed in the rich mineral store of the Forest of Dean. The sheer volume of iron produced there was certain to swamp the small quantities that could be hardly won from the heathlands of Dorset. And as riches of any kind always result in a gathering momentum of circulation, the more artistic metal craft flowed freely down from the north-eastern coast where it had long established itself, and this advanced metalwork brought with it a currency which will always break down any communal system which exists in a hand-to-mouth way.

The lake village of Glastonbury found a widening market for its decorated pottery even if the local potters more often attempted to copy the design at first, and the trade routes which have always trickled from east to west now found it worth while to turn off and visit Maiden Castle. Inside the town bronze began to become common, brooches and rings and other ornaments and swords with bronze fittings; the long-held aloofness of a self-sufficient people was broken down by the sheer weight of new goods and still more powerful new ideas.

Dorset had taken its due place in the new world of commercialism mixed with the security of a flourishing agricultural culture which had well proved its ability to stand alone, and it is likely that the people as a whole experienced a mild form of early and premature Victorian complacency. The most ignorant inhabitant of Maiden Castle was made aware of the distant power behind the new coinage; no longer was labour and town patriotism enough to obtain an ordered life —the small decorated disks of metal were needed because they had somehow undermined all the old traditions. There were not only the strong and the weak with their respective demands and rights, but the rich and the poor had to take each other into consideration.

But no one could have known what had really forced the rapid spread of the new cultures; the hidden pressure which had set people on the move at a greater rate than the natural speed of knowledge was still too far away to be seen in itself. And if word of some irresistible force abroad in the world did trickle along the ridgeway roads it was something that could be ignored as an old wives' tale. The hilltop towns and forts had held out against everything for several thousand years, and with all the new ideas and weapons and better standard of living any whispered hints of danger would be out of place.

But while Maiden Castle basked in the new age of luxury and strove to make headway in the world it had first reluctantly accepted, the power of the Roman Empire was approaching the waters of the English Channel. It is certain that refugees fled across the water before actually feeling the force of that power, but they were likely soon to share the feeling in Britain that such a thing could not surmount the wide water defence ditch in enough strength to do much harm.

The British would not know that although Rome was very far away and had approached them as a land force, at home she was a maritime power on another sea, well able to cross another narrow water, and still not yet satiated while there was another fog-shrouded island not under her rule. So in due course the iron-disciplined legions were marching along the ridgeways, and finding it easy work to demolish each separate hill town, whose people by their very defences proved that they had no idea of unity beyond their walls. Each town that fled within its walls and waited for the assault was playing into the conquerors' hands; if necessary it could be starved out at no cost, although such tactics were not needed by a well-trained army which had learnt the military art of manœuvre. Many of the apparently up-to-date ideas which had arrived before the might of Rome were proved to be outmoded, although the greatest weakness of the country was the provincial outlook of each town and district which had remained indifferent and suspicious of its neighbours.

The Roman invasion of A.D. 43 had reached the Severn valley in three years, and in that time Dorset was overrun by the Second Augustine Legion, which was commanded by Vespasian, who would one day return to Rome and become Emperor. He had already reduced the Isle of Wight and probably Hengistbury over on the Hampshire coast, and as he marched west he and his men must have known they were about to see the biggest town of the south, although they would also know that it was just another earth-wall defence which would not delay them.

They had no need for spies because every town and fort stood up clear on the skyline, and as all roads ran along open

223

ridgeways wherever possible, the chances of being ambushed were very slight, even if the local people had not fled inside their walls. Most of the invasion was easy work to the hardened legions, and although they maintained the discipline of building an earth fort for their night camps, it is likely that many of them privately considered it a waste of effort. Those islanders who remained shut up on the hilltop until the enemy was ready to attack were playing into the hands of any hard compact body which could roam at will.

There came a day when the Roman army came down off the chalk and reached the River Frome, and found an easy crossing where later they would start the town of Dorchester. Two miles away on the hill they could see the multiple ramparts of Maiden Castle, and perhaps halted while they studied the layout. They would be able to march right up to the complicated western entrance and not contact the garrison unless they came within range of the sling-stones, but there is no evidence that they made any attack there.

The town lining its ramparts could merely expend its rage as it watched the apparently indifferent legion march around to the eastern gate, which was somewhat less strong. And these strange soldiers did not behave in any manner which might be expected; they neither answered back with futile gestures nor attempted to storm the walls in one wild rush which would succeed or fall in a matter of minutes. The townspeople had to watch while a regiment of artillery set up its machines beyond sling-stone range, and perhaps they had no idea what to expect from this unknown new weapon of war, but may have been caught unawares on the rampart and mown down when the first barrage of machine arrows was launched.

The town had also weakened its defences in allowing a clutter of huts to be built outside the east gate, and these were soon set alight. Under the cover of the smoke and the machine-arrow barrage the legion was able to rush each rampart and wipe out the slingers' towers; then there would be no need to break down the actual gate, as it was easier to force a way over the last rampart. Once inside the walls the town was helpless against modern weapons they had not dreamed of and disciplined soldiers whose trade it was to use them, but

Dorset horned sheep

the fight must have been obstinate because the legion behaved unusually as if it had lost its temper. Perhaps the town fought on from the high ground of the two mounds after the soldiers had considered the battle as over, but something caused them to start a massacre of men and women of all ages with also small children, and they not only killed but struck many blows at people who must already have been dead from any one of the many cuts they received.

That is and was unusual behaviour for any disciplined army, if only because it is an unnecessary effort, but it did happen at the taking of Maiden Castle. But after the battle the town was soon able to bury its dead, as probably the legion had no more interest in it after destroying the gates and having made sure that the people realized they were no longer an independent township. Also the legion had more work waiting for it farther in the west, where it was to leave other evidence at Seaton in Devon.

During the night after the defeat Maiden Castle must have painfully realized that for the first time in centuries they were out in the wide open world. Their gateways yawned open both east and west, the fighting platforms of the rampart had been thrown down, and above all the Romans had inflicted the terrible lesson that their power was invincible to town-dwellers who sheltered behind earth walls. All that they had held to through the long past had slipped away in one crowded hour, and all they could guess about the future was that it would be a hard way.

No wonder they were afraid to go out into the open country to bury their dead in the usual way, but merely crept outside the broken eastern gate and hurriedly buried them between and over the now useless ramparts. They knew that enclosed towns were no longer a possibility and therefore the line between town and open country no longer counted. It did not matter if the dead did lie under the rampart paths as the guarding patrol would no longer walk there.

The use of new weapons is strongly indicated in that war cemetery outside the eastern gate. The heavy machine-driven arrows were sometimes so deeply embedded in bone that they were not recovered, the Roman swords were strong and keen enough to cut off the back of a man's skull in one clean sweep,

The Swannery, Abbotsbury

although there were cases where a head had been hacked to pieces in a totally unnecessary excess of energy or fury. During a battle it is not necessary to kill your enemy eight or nine times. That the legionaries were aroused or even took steps of revenge is suggested by the way one woman was killed by three blows on the head and buried with her arms bound behind her back. There would have been no point in binding her after striking those three blows.

That the townspeople put up a stiff fight is shown by how often they died with severe wounds on the face, although they were out-armed and none of them were trained fighters as was every man of the legion. The field workers who had wished to live unmolested in rural peace were not cut down as they ran away, and perhaps this was the reason why some of them were maltreated after death.

Despite the hurried and fearful way the survivors had buried the dead in the ashes of the burnt huts right on the threshold of the town, a bowl or mug or a joint of mutton was carefully placed with each one. The hurry is proved by the shallowness of some of the graves and the way the victims were tumbled in to fall face up or down, extended or crouched or even sitting up, and not carefully curled up on the side in the usual way. Nor were they stripped of their ornaments, although some of the things would have been too valuable to throw away without a thought. That they were still afraid is shown by their not daring to venture out in the open country, but doing the best they could outside the town yet still within the ramparts.

Although Rome would not allow a fortified town in the territory it had conquered, it was not ready to set up the new order of things, and the town resumed its way of life for another generation or so. The same entrances were still used, but a new road surface was laid over the wreckage of the gates and the demolished stone towers beside them; no firmer proof is needed that the people were ordered not to or were afraid even to clear up the wreckage. The old way of life was literally trampled into the ground, yet there was no halt in the way town life went on inside the breached walls for about twenty years, and by then Roman law and order had settled the country around. The townspeople were to all intents the

slaves of the new rulers, and had to learn not only how to produce enough substance from the land to support themselves in
comparative comfort, but to export grain to feed the sprawl-
ing empire which still had several more centuries to run.

The first step was the start of a new Roman town on the
banks of the River Frome, and when that was far enough
advanced Maiden Castle was ceremoniously "slighted," and
the inhabitants moved down into their new home. Durnovaria, or Roman Dorchester, has the usual history of such
towns, and long before the empire began to seep away from
the shores of Britain the inhabitants were thoroughly
Romano-British in outlook, and no longer looked up at their
own hilltop with anything like yearning. They probably
believed that they had some kind of contempt for people who
had been content to live up there in squalor and seclusion.
Four hundred years of Roman rule was long enough to forget
even the oldest man who still talked of the old days and hinted
that it was still possible to go back and build bigger and better
walls.

After Dorchester was established the history of Maiden
Castle as a town was at an end. For over three hundred years
the wind and rain did its best to cover the site, and succeeded
to the extent that an undisturbed new surface soil grew in
thickness, and collected just enough odd early Roman coins
and broken sherds to show that occasionally someone climbed
the hill and visited the ruins.

But all such evidence is in and not beneath that new surface
soil. Pagan Rome had no use for the abandoned site, yet suddenly after official Rome had accepted Christianity someone
moved up there again, and a temple was built which was not
to any Christian God nor yet to any particular pagan deity.
Part of a marble Diana was found and a plaque with a figure
of Minerva, also a bronze three-horned bull, as if they wanted
to make sure of everything or, more likely, that inexperienced
priests had thoroughly mixed things up.

This was during the last years of Rome's hold on Britain,
and it might be useful to look at the political development
which was loosening that hold, and made it possible to build a
pagan temple on the site of Maiden Castle at a time when the

official religion had become Christianity. In those four hundred years Britain had not become anything more than a colony, and perhaps even as that had not paid its way. A great effort had been brought into the country, and must have cost the empire much in the way of capital already in its possession, which it had to risk in order to bring about its law and order in a community that for a long while did not know how to help. There was very little to be taken out of the country at first, and even when it got going as a colony the exports were mainly agricultural goods, with little or no internal trading on which privileged classes could thrive and no manufacturing centres to attract wealth.

The Roman who set out for the new country was not likely to find much scope for adventuring in which he could make a quick fortune; he was more likely to end up as just another official holding down a steady job with his eye on a pension as the only reward in the future. Officials on the one hand and workers on the other do not form an exciting society in which things may expand, and during the occupation Britain did not produce a powerful commercial section which might have become more Roman than the Romans, and certainly would have thrown up something able to take charge when the legions were withdrawn.

Whatever the reasons, beyond military greed, which had tempted Rome into the country she was disappointed, and from the empire's point of view the occupation was a failure; while the fact that in four hundred years they were not able to go beyond Northumberland or into Ireland is proof that back in Rome itself they were not putting the full vigour of their power into it. Britain was not looked upon as a very bright gem in the crown.

So it is not so very surprising to find a pagan temple being built in Maiden Castle after the official change in religion; it was either slackness in high quarters of the occupying force, or the Celtic people, who were still merely the workers with no chance to get ahead, were getting out of hand because with native shrewdness they already sensed the weakness in their masters. A Roman priest might have defied the new religion and retired to the old site to set up as a hermit, or a Celt, remembering that the site had once been very important to them, had built the temple with the idea of having some kind of rallying place or organization.

That the new temple was Roman in everything does not affect the idea that the motive was Celtic, as in four hundred years they were thoroughly Romanized and had been trained to work in that style. They would not know how to build otherwise, and had learnt to rely on or at least recognize the gods which were represented in the precincts. And there is good evidence that they had a considerable following and were well supported, as a great number of coins were about the place which were not at all carefully hoarded, as many got mixed up in the materials used in building.

The temple itself was reroofed and refloored several times, and quite a lot of alterations carried out. At times the effect must have been more garish than dignified, and that in itself suggests a strong Celtic influence which knew all about the ideas but did not have much real guidance or creative thought of its own. The whole thing smacks of rusticity, whether the builders were out-of-touch Romans or Celtic copyists.

There is one thing that points to authentic Pagan Rome behind the building of a temple there, as out in the front of it was a crude oval hut built in as primitive a way as was well possible. Such crudeness must have been deliberate in view of the other building methods on the same site and period, and may well have been a representation of the primitive hut often set up in honour of the founder of Rome.

The priests' living-quarters, with many more coins lying around, were behind the temple, and seem to have been placed there to take advantage of such shelter as the larger temple would provide against the prevailing south-west wind. And carefully made paths were constructed to lead down and out of the eastern entrance, where for the first time since the successful Roman assault the gateway was built across once more by a wall, with a small gate to lead into the dedicated grounds. Although there could be no successful attempt to make a garden up there in the bleak wind-swept temple area, it probably had a well-planned effect with its paths and fireplaces set out in the open. And it was still in use after the power of Rome had not only seeped down the hill again but had marched back along the ridgeway roads, and taken ship in an endeavour to save what it could of the wreck of the Empire.

But the temple fell into disuse in time and was no longer repaired. Rome had faded and perhaps there was no longer any need to worship out on the far hilltop, as the Celts could live their own way of life. But that way of life would not return behind the ramparts and ditches, because the town of Dorchester on the river was already ancient enough to be the centre around which they moved. And if the temple had been a gesture of resistance tolerated by a slack authority, all that was a thing of the past and the future of the people was in their own hands for a long time.

Yet Maiden Castle also provides proof that with the withdrawal of their Roman masters another power was to step in and find the Celts still unable to achieve any real unity. Perhaps it is not their fault that they only learnt technical skills from the occupation—that is the fate of conquered people who will stay conquered; but the Saxon invasions during the Dark Ages did little to suggest that the Celts had picked up any more knowledge of organization or military ability than any backward agricultural community might build up for itself.

When the time came Saxons roamed the country and, obviously with an eye on the multiple defence system, some of them visited the old site and must have found it of interest. Perhaps they argued about it as interested fighting men would, or they were rude men who might quarrel and fight at any moment, but one Saxon died there inside the walls and was buried complete with his sword and knife. It would not be out of place to incline to the theory, and even hope, that he died there because some Celt struck one more blow in fighting amongst one of the greatest defence systems in the British Isles.

INDEX

231